The Onion
and Philosophy

Popular Culture and Philosophy®
Series Editor: George A. Reisch

For full details of all **Popular Culture and Philosophy®** books, visit www.opencourtbooks.com.

Popular Culture and Philosophy®

The Onion and Philosophy

Fake News Story True, Alleges Indignant Area Professor

Edited by

SHARON M. KAYE

OPEN COURT
Chicago and La Salle, Illinois

This book is not a publication of *The Onion* newspaper, nor of anyone connected with *The Onion*, nor is it in any way instigated, authorized, endorsed, prepared, hatched, cooked up, sanctified, supported, or sponsored by *The Onion*. It's an independent contribution to scholarship, critical thinking, and enhanced public awareness of significant contemporary events, as well as to the general pollution and debasement of popular culture.

Volume 54 in the series, Popular Culture and Philosophy®, edited by George A. Reisch

To order books from Open Court, call toll-free 1-800-815-2280, or visit our website at www.opencourtbooks.com.

Open Court Publishing Company is a division of Carus Publishing Company.

Library of Congress Cataloging-in-Publication Data

The Onion and philosophy : fake news story true, alleges indignant area professor / edited by Sharon M. Kaye.
      p. cm. — (Popular culture and philosophy ; v. 54)
   Includes bibliographical references and index.
   ISBN 978-0-8126-9687-5 (trade paper : alk. paper)
    1. Onion (Madison, Wis.) 2. Satire—Philosophy. 3. American wit and humor—History and criticism. I. Kaye, Sharon M.
   PN4900.O46O65 2010
   051—dc22
                              2010035359

Contents

Entertainment 231

For Crying Out Loud

SHARON M. KAYE

There is a legend concerning how *The Onion* got its name.

It was 1988. Tim Keck and Christopher Johnson, two juniors at the University of Wisconsin, Madison, were sitting in Johnson's kitchen discussing what to name the parody newspaper they were about to launch. Johnson's uncle came in, saw that the two young men were making onion sandwiches, and said, "Why not call it *The Onion.*"

When I heard this legend, my first thought was, *That's the lamest story I ever heard! For Pete's sake, if you're going to make up a legend, at least make it believable. Who eats onion sandwiches?*

Since that time, however, I have learned that onion sandwiches are considered a delicacy in elite New York restaurants.

"Ah yes," a friend of mine informed me, "I've enjoyed the onion sandwich as an appetizer at Beard House. They cut the crusts off two pieces of firm white bread, spread them with gourmet mayonnaise, attach them to each side of a crispy slice of onion, and then roll the edge through chopped parsley."

Well, I'm sure horse manure would taste good slathered in Beard House mayo. Still, this makes the legend even less plausible since Keck and Johnson were hardly members of the jet set back in their college days.

Confronted with this objection, my friend pointed out that onions are also a traditional food of the very poor.

"The slaves who built the pyramids of ancient Egypt lived on onions," he said. "Think about it. An onion sandwich is a cheap hamburger."

I thought about it. But it still didn't make sense. If the story were true, then Keck and Johnson should have called their paper *The Onion Sandwich*.

Does *The Onion* need a legend to justify its name? I think not. I looked up the word "onion" in the dictionary and found that its meaning fits the concept of Keck and Johnson's brainchild perfectly. The definition of onion is:

1. **A bulbous plant cultivated worldwide as a vegetable.**

2. **The edible bulb of this plant, composed of fleshy, tight, concentric leaf bases having a pungent odor and taste.**

The essential components of this definition are "bulbous" and "pungent." (I like "fleshy" and "tight" as well, but they take me in a different direction. . . .)

The word "bulbous" refers to a "rounded or swollen projection." As in: bulbous nose, bulbous butt, bulbous meatloaf. That which is bulbous is inherently funny. Can one use the word "bulbous" without cracking a smile?

The word "pungent" means "penetrating or caustic." Penetrating things get to the heart of the matter. Caustic things burn.

How fitting.

The Onion is heartburn—an uncomfortable wake-up call to the society it skewers, like an onion on a kabob, in its bulbous articles.

The Onion is a parody newspaper that has mastered the art of satirical humor. Its satire is what makes it philosophical, because philosophers have always been critics of the society in which they live. So it's high time to unpeel the connections between *The Onion* and philosophy.

The chapters ahead are as bulbous as they are pungent. They are also devilishly delicious. Grab your mayo and dig in.

Science and Technology

1

A Vice Worse than Stupidity

SHARON M. KAYE

We love *The Onion* because it is the bible of ridicule. Absolutely nothing is sacred within its pages. By skewering worthy targets, it makes us laugh.

But what makes for a worthy target of ridicule? Off the cuff, I would have said stupidity. And, at first glance, it would seem that the *The Onion* is full of stupid people. I randomly looked at the front page of the current issue. It contains an article titled "Hey Everybody, Let's All Go To The Beach And Complain!" We read this and laugh because we think, *Yes! That's exactly what people do! People are so stupid!* It seems intelligent people never grow tired of making fun of the stupid things that stupid people say and do.

The stupidity theory of ridicule seems further supported by the fact that those who take offence at *The Onion*'s scathing commentary are liable to make the accusation that it caters to people who think they're superior. "Oh come off it," they'll say, "You got a better idea how to spend a summer vacation? I suppose you'd probably rather just sit home and read some incomprehensible book or something. What a grouch!" Ridicule is denounced as a hurtful form of arrogance.

Well, it may be true that stupidity is sometimes the target of ridicule. However, the highest form of ridicule, the form that *The Onion* has mastered and that explains its smashing success in the world of humor, takes a different target.

The Highest Form of Ridicule Targets Cheating

One of the finest articles that ever appeared in *The Onion* is "I Believe In Evolution, Except For The Whole Triassic Period," by

3

Stephen Jossler (5/30/07). This article ridicules the millions of people who accept Darwin's theory of natural selection as an explanation for the entire natural world and at the same time insist that God created human beings. Their claim is that the human era could not have been a product of random mutation—even though every other era could.

Jossler parodies this reasoning by presenting an argument that substitutes "human era" with "Triassic era," a period of evolution that saw the development of advanced forms of marine life. He writes:

> So, when I tell you that after the Paleozoic era, Ceratodon lungfish became relatively common, it naturally follows that someone created that lungfish by hand and then took out one of its lungfish ribs and combined it with the dust of the Earth to create a female lungfish.
>
> In the beginning, there were a few billion years of speciation and gene drift. And then nothing. And then, God made the lungfish and the trilobites, the ichthyosaurs and ammonoids with more complex suture patterns. He also made a couple new ferns.
>
> And the Lord saw that these slight modifications were good, and allowed evolution to resume as normal in the Jurassic period and on up to the present day.

We read this and we say, *Yes! That's exactly how people think! People are so stupid!*

Before you jump to the conclusion that Jossler's article vindicates the stupidity theory of ridicule, however, take note: those who wish to exempt the human era from the principles of evolution understand the principles of evolution perfectly well. They're not stupid. Something else is going on.

I work at a Catholic college and cover the God/evolution topic every year when I teach Aquinas's teleological proof for the existence of God. Aquinas argues that God must exist because there is no other way to explain the design we see in nature. Darwin's response, of course, is that there *is* another way to explain this apparent design, namely, eons of survival of the fittest. Each year, my students insist that, while survival of the fittest can explain everything else in nature, it still can't explain humans.

I used to worry that I was failing to provide my students with a sufficient explanation of the principles of evolution. *Do they just not get it?*

In fact, the vast majority of my students understand the principles of evolution perfectly well, as do most college students. Sure, there are people, even educated people, who don't understand evolution and refuse to apply it to any part of nature, much less humans. But we're not talking about them. We're talking about those who understand it and apply it to other species, to every other species, except ours.

"Well," they say, "God could work *through* evolution, supplying the extras when it comes to humans. There had to be someone to start the whole thing up anyhow."

This argument is so bad that it is clearly covering for something else.

It's bad because no god is needed to supply extras or start things up. The same logic would imply that there must be another god, God^1, who started up God and supplied extras for him. And then there would have to be another god, God^2, who started up God^1 and supplied his extras, and so on, and so on.

My students insist that God doesn't need God^1 because he existed self-sufficiently from all eternity. But of course the same logic implies that the universe can exist self-sufficiently from all eternity, and we don't need God in the first place.

No, we don't need God. Yet millions of people say we do. And they're not stupid; rather, they're committing a certain kind of fallacy.

Philosophers typically define "fallacy" as a mistake in reasoning. It is misleading, however, to call a fallacy a "mistake," since most fallacies are deliberately manipulative. Consider the following old favorites:

- Ad hominem: attacking the person instead of the argument

- Ad verecundiam: appealing to an inappropriate authority

- Ad populum: claiming that the popularity of a view proves its truth

- Ad misericordiam: appealing to pity

- Ad baculum: appealing to fear

- Hasty generalization: inferring from one or a few cases to all cases

- Post hoc: assuming that what comes before the effect is the cause of the effect

- Begging the question: presupposing your conclusion

These fallacies are not stupid; on the contrary, they are clever rhetorical strategies. In fact, they are regularly taught as effective advertising tools in marketing classes. Philosophers call them "mistakes" because they help you get your way without helping you find the truth.

The "mistake" parodied in Jossler's article is exactly the same. My students and the millions of perfectly intelligent people who think God had a special hand in creating the human species are trying to be winners instead of knowers.

By "trying to be winners" what I mean is that, if they were to grant that human beings were just another part of nature, then they would have to admit that we have to die just like everything else in nature. But to die is to lose. They don't want to believe they have to die; they want to believe they will live forever. And for this, they need a soul, a slice of the divine. They like to picture themselves someday flying around with angels in the sky rather than rotting away with maggots in the ground. It's a much prettier picture! Short of conclusive proof that there is no such thing as God and the soul, why shouldn't they believe it?

The Polish logician William Irwin (in his book *Existential Answers*) calls this strategy "the aesthetic fallacy." The aesthetic fallacy is the false belief that whatever is pleasant, good, or beautiful is true. The term "aesthetic" is derived from the Greek term *aisthïtikos*, meaning *of sense perception*. It also gives us the word "aesthete," which is defined as follows:

> Aesthete: a person who has, or professes to have, refined sensitivity toward the beauties of art or nature.

Notice that this definition is ambiguous: if you call someone "an aesthete," you may be complimenting them or insulting them, depending on whether you mean they *really* have a refined sensitivity or only *profess* to have it.

I object to the use of the term "aesthetic fallacy" to describe the strategy ridiculed in Jossler's article precisely because of this ambiguity. If I call my students "aesthetes" they will reply: "Damn right! Give God the benefit of the doubt! Be an optimist! Wherever there

---

[1] See his book, Existential Answers, forthcoming.

is room to assume the best rather than the worst, by all means, do so! Look for beauty in everything! Cheer up and wear your rose-colored glasses with pride! Don't be a party-pooper!"

I'm averse to considering myself a party-pooper. But as long as I classify my students as aesthetes, I have myself pegged. I can try to insist that I mean they are aesthetes in the insulting sense—that their supposed love of beauty is misplaced. But then the burden is still on me to explain exactly what's wrong with it.

I would like to propose a new name for the strategy in question that pinpoints exactly what's wrong with it. I propose we call it the "asschetic fallacy." The asschetic fallacy is the false belief that whatever we prefer, desire, or need to be true *is* true. The term "asschetic" is derived from the words "ass" and "cheat." (Nevermind Greek.) These words yield the convenient term "asscheat," which is defined as follows:

Asscheat: a person who believes what he wants rather than what is true or most likely to be true

Notice that this definition is not at all ambiguous. Calling someone an asscheat, just like calling them an asswipe, is never a compliment and always an insult.

Asscheating is an especially vicious form of cheating. Whereas ordinary cheating means breaking a rule, such as cheating on your taxes or cheating on your spouse, asscheating is a form of self-delusion in which one tries to make life the way one would like it to be instead of accepting it the way it is.

By replacing the aesthetic fallacy with the asschetic fallacy we capture exactly what's wrong with the strategy witnessed in Jossler's classic *Onion* article and cast ourselves as defenders of good sportsmanship rather than party-poopers.

AMERICAN VOICES
Author Makes Insightful Assertion

I've just asserted that people who believe God had a special hand in creating the human species even though everything else evolved are asscheats. What do *you* think?

Vladimer Ubit
Comptroller

"Is this a formal complaint?"

Robert Drucker
Plumber

"Takes one to know one!"

Pepper G
Bartender

"It also sounds like a good name for women who wear Spanx."

Is Asscheating Really a Vice?

So far, I've argued that the highest form of ridicule, as exemplified in Stephen Jossler's classic *Onion* article, targets an especially vicious form of cheating rather than stupidity. I call this especially vicious form of cheating "asscheating."

While *aestheticism* is the doctrine that *beauty* is the basic principle from which all other principles, especially moral ones, are derived, *asscheticism* is the doctrine that *whatever one wants to be true* is the basic principle from which all other principles, especially moral ones, are derived.

And, by the way, neither of these doctrines are to be confused with *asceticism*, which espouses the practice of extreme self-denial and austerity. Nor with *askgeticism*, which concerns the exploitation of Santa Claus. Nor with *Arquetticism*, a pathological addiction to the television show *Medium*.

So, we have accomplished a great philosophical task by carving out a truly new, highly-specialized, and sophisticated-sounding concept.

Someone might object, however, that in light of my own belief in evolution, it is contradictory for me to assert that asscheating is a vice. After all, the pure form of evolution eliminates God and the soul, which are the traditional sources for all morality. If the entire world, including human beings, is the result of a totally amoral, natural process, then on what basis am I entitled to call anything virtuous or vicious?

The term "virtue" comes from the Latin word *virtus*, meaning strength and the term "vice" comes from the Latin word *vitium*, meaning flaw. Anyone undertaking a clear purpose can be judged to have strengths or flaws.

Are human beings undertaking a clear purpose? Absolutely.

Every organism on this planet is engaged in the purpose of propagating its species. God did not stamp this purpose on our souls. Rather, the principles of natural selection stamped it on our genes. Those organisms that did not engage in the propagation of their species died out. Hence, if you are here, it is because you are programmed with the purpose to survive and reproduce—or to assist others, especially those who share your genes, in reproduction.

So, according to my enlightened, purely scientific perspective, if asscheticism undermines evolutionary fitness, then it is a vice.

One might be tempted to think asscheticism actually promotes evolutionary fitness by giving us an advantage over other species that are not capable of deluding themselves.

I'm here to tell you, however, that the old adage is true: Cheaters never win, and winners never cheat.

In the long run, people who believe what is true are much more likely to survive and reproduce effectively than are people who believe what they want to be true.

Asscheating really does disadvantage the human race. We need only examine more articles from *The Onion* to prove it.

Consider the article entitled, "Breast Implants Found To Cause Problems In Laboratory Mice" (9/9/97). It featured the image of a female laboratory mouse firmly grasped in the gloved hand of a researcher. She looked something like this:

A whole new kind of titmouse.

Intelligent people love to ridicule breast implants. Why? Because breast implants are stupid? No. Because they never trigger girl-crush turn-on? No. Because they cheat reality.

The reason heterosexual men are attracted to large breasts is because large breasts are a sign of reproductive health. Women who get breast implants are lying to themselves and to the world about their evolutionary potential. By achieving reproduction with the most desirable men, who wouldn't give them a second glance otherwise, genetically flat-chested women give their genetically flat-chested offspring an artificial advantage, thereby undermining the strength of the species.

Likewise, consider the *Onion* article entitled "New Nietzschean Diet Lets You Eat Whatever You Fear Most" (3/3/04). Echoing the absurdly dramatic vocabulary of the German philosopher Friedrich Nietzsche, this article parodies weight loss programs.

> By conquering your Fear, by eating it in Heroic Portions, by laughing at that Fear which you have eaten, one avoids the Eternal Recurrence of cyclic 'Yo-Yo' Weight Loss and Weight Gain," Nietzsche wrote. "And in so doing, one transcends Thinness. One discovers that he need not dwell forever on the chill, Wind-swept Borderland between Thin and Superthin.

While the advertisements for weight loss programs almost always commit one or another of the favorite old fallacies surveyed above, those who buy into these programs commit the asschetic fallacy: "I don't want to eat right and exercise. I want to live in a world where I can eat whatever I want, never break a sweat, and still be thin."

And why does everyone want to be thin? Because thinness is indicative of youth and affluence in our society, both of which signify reproductive fitness. So, those who rely on phony diets are ass-cheats striving to inflate their mating potential, thereby undermining the strength of our species.

Finally, the sports section of *The Onion* satirizes athletes. The Tour de France, for example, has provided ample fodder for fun-making over the years. The article "Non-Doping Cyclists Finish Tour De France" (8/30/07) argues that this month-long race has become so difficult that it actually requires the very cheating it claims to condemn. An interview with cyclist "Piet Kvistik" makes the point.

"This is a very, very proud day for me," said the 115-pound Kvistik, who lost 45% of his body mass during the event, toppled from his saddle moments after finishing, and had to be administered oxygen, fed intravenously, and injected with adrenaline by attending medical personnel. "They say it is physically impossible to ride all of the Tour without drugs, but we prove them wrong this day."

Did Kvistik finish without drugs or just without any of the drugs that were currently detectable? All we know for sure is that he firmly believed he deserved the blue jersey.

Of course, cheating in sports is just cheating and needn't be graced with such a splendiferous new term as "asscheticism." Nevertheless, the concept of asscheating becomes relevant when one considers the fact that there is no way to understand the human enthusiasm for sports except as a projection of evolutionary fitness. Athletic competition is nothing but the excessive overflow of the survival urge. Hence, those who cheat in sports are athletically asschetic: their diametric memetics are pathetically synthetic.

AMERICAN VOICES
Author Makes Compelling Argument

I've just argued that asscheticism is a vice because it undermines the evolutionary fitness of the human species. What do *you* think?

Billy Deal
Prison Guard

"Okay, so it's a vice, but is it a good vice or a bad vice?"

Stephanie Piper
Systems Analyst

"I think the human species could use a little undermining."

Hugh Lickman
Father

"If this is some perverted survey, leave me out of it. "

This brief survey of examples from *The Onion* amply proves that asscheating—that is, believing what one wants instead of what is true—is a vice. From an evolutionary perspective, the purpose of human life is to proliferate the species. Therefore, anything that undermines the evolutionary fitness of the species is a vice. And believing what one wants instead of what is true does just that.

Ridicule Is a Survival Strategy

The Onion is the bible of ridicule. Ridicule is a powerful tool. It can be defined as follows:

1. **language or behavior intended to mock or humiliate**

2. **the act of deriding or treating with contempt**

Ridicule may seem rather harsh, but it is actually a crucial survival strategy. To make fun of something is to take the threat out of it. We ridicule enemies in order to reduce, neutralize, and ultimately conquer them.

One might suppose stupid people are the biggest threat to the survival of our species. But stupid people are really more of a danger to themselves. They mostly reproduce with each other and kill themselves off.

Asscheats, on the other hand, believe whatever they want in order to gain unfair advantages in life. By artificially inflating their evolutionary fitness, they pollute the gene pool and thwart the true potential of the human race.

Asscheats are the Enemy. And that is why we so relish the prospect of ridiculing them.

AMERICAN VOICES
Author Comes To Resounding Conclusion

I've just concluded that asscheats are the Enemy. What do *you* think?

Brad Axe
Transvestite

"Sodomy is the standard way of preserving virginity among marriageable females in Islamic countries."

Joel Gratz
Business Owner

"Is that true or is that something you just want to believe?"

Serge Koklophti
Catholic Priest

"As long as you're talking about Protestants, I'm with you."

2
Pope Admits: "God Ain't Said Shit to Me"

ROBERTO RUIZ

When you think of philosophy and *The Onion*, you might think they couldn't possibly have anything to do with each other. Philosophy is serious, rigorous, abstract, esoteric, and written for those few who have attention spans longer than two-minutes. *The Onion*, on the other hand, is popular, hilarious, and intended for those with short or no attenti . . . hey, do you like waffles?

Beneath a surface of satire and humor, *The Onion* is philosophical at heart, raising conceptual questions, challenging faulty presuppositions and mocking poor reasoning. In so doing, it equips us with what the scientist Carl Sagan called a baloney detection kit, which not only gives us the power to see right through . . . well, baloney, but also to beat down absurdity with humor, which is key, because without humor you might just turn, as *The Onion* reports, into that guy in philosophy class who "needs to shut the fuck up" (9/28/05).

Although *The Onion* applies its baloney detector to many different issues, it's especially insightful on the question of God's existence. Can the belief in God be rationally justified? Well, according to *The Onion*, you're shit out of luck if you think that's going to happen.

73 Percent Of Americans Unable To Believe This Shit

We all have beliefs, but as philosophers, we need a basic understanding of when beliefs are justified and when they're not. In other words, we need an account of the conditions under which a rational person should accept a belief.

15

The word "philosophy" comes from the Greek roots *philos* and *sophia*, which translate as "the love of wisdom." So, being a philosopher means wanting to achieve wisdom and attempting to become wise, and becoming wise involves gaining knowledge and a firm understanding of truth.

If someone told you that smoking cigarettes is good for your health, you would not consider him wise. Why? Because his claim is not true. On the other hand, if someone told you, as *The Onion* reports, that second-hand smoke is linked to "second-hand cool-ness" (1/12/08), *that* person might actually be wise, even if believing her might take you to an early grave.

But true belief can't be enough. One may come to hold a true belief merely by accident, for example by guessing. Such a person is lucky, but because she fails to *own* that truth, that person could hardly be considered wise or even knowledgeable. What she's missing is a reason to connect her belief to the truth, and thereby justify it.

Arguing against those who believe knowledge of the world is innate and against those who believe it can be obtained purely from intuition or reason, the Scottish philosopher David Hume demonstrated in the eighteenth century that our beliefs about existence, if they hope to have a chance of being justified, must begin with experience. The reason is that every meaningful idea residing in your mind originally came from a sense organ and its perception.

If you think about it, this shouldn't be that surprising and can be easily tested: try to explain the nature of color to someone born blind. Go ahead—go find yourself someone born blind (perhaps at the drive-up ATM of your local bank) and explain to her what color is without arguing in a circle by using some colors to define others. Good luck!

Although the information we receive through our senses is not all we need to justify our beliefs, it is the starting point. In other words, a belief about existence is justified only when it's based, at least in principle, on some sort of possible observation.

Sounds sensible, right? Yet those who follow this sensible rule are often disparaged as 'skeptics'. As *The Onion* reports in its story "Skeptic Pitied" (1/22/03), computer consultant Craig Schaffner has "earned the pity of friends and acquaintances for his tragic reluctance to embrace the unverifiable."

One of Craig's friends "who spends roughly 20 percent of his annual income on telephone psychics and tarot-card readings" said "it's just too bad Craig has chosen to cut himself off from the world of the paranormal, restricting himself to the limited universe of what can be seen and heard and verified through experience." Yeah, what a tool . . .

Bush Unveils New Blind-Faith-Based Initiatives

Even if "the world of the paranormal" were real, how could anyone have justification for that belief without somehow verifying it through experience? *The Onion* is making a point, not about what exists but about what we are rationally entitled to believe exists. For any credible explanation, there must be some empirical confirmation supporting it. Otherwise, it's no better than an arbitrary guess.

Lacking any empirical support for belief in the existence of paranormal phenomena, we would have to conclude that it's ultimately based on faith. Faith is objectionable because it breaks the sensible rule we discussed above, according to which belief should start with observation.

The same skepticism we apply to the paranormal can also be applied to the existence of God, and it won't help to defend the rationality of faith on the grounds that it provides emotional comfort. The fact that something feels good doesn't make it true or rationally justified. This, unfortunately, may come as a disappointment to those excited by the *Onion* headline "God Finally Gives A Shout-Out Back To All His Niggaz" (9/5/01), according to which, a booming voice in the sky confessed:

> I got mad love for each and every one of you niggaz. Y'all real niggaz out there, you know who you are. Y'all was there for me, and it's about time I'm-a give some love back to God's true crew.

Unfortunately, Hume's insight implies that, even if it *is* about time the G.O. double D. recognized, this story cannot be trusted.

If sensory perception is the basis for our substantive claims about existence, then why do people believe God exists? Is this belief based on experience? Can we see him, touch him or tickle him? Can we smell him? What *does* God smell like? Geez, I hope he doesn't smell like grandpa . . .

One possible way to argue that we do have direct experience of God is to say that we can feel his presence. This is exactly what Michael Brighton claimed in the *Onion* story "Christian Weightlifter Bends Iron Bar to Show Power Of God's Love" (5/15/02). Brighton explained that "only a strong personal relationship with my Creator

could have made this possible." Maybe so, but an adequate diet and disciplined athletic training could also explain his strength. Of the two hypotheses, one relies on empirically demonstrable evidence and the other relies on the unverified existence of an invisible being.

Report: Iranian Science Teachers May Be Enriching Students

This takes us to a set of practical rules for assessing the rationality of belief. The first is methodological naturalism, the view that explanations of observable effects are only justified and useful when they are assumed to result from natural causes, and which can be tested by natural means.

Methodological naturalism is the engine that drives the unparalleled success of scientific discovery because it enriches our comprehension by requiring hypotheses to always be evaluated on the basis of evidence. This is the self-correcting mechanism inherent in the scientific method: whatever our biases and prejudices, the ultimate arbiter of truth must be the evidence itself.

Although methodological naturalism is ultimately agnostic toward the existence of supernatural causes or entities, it does imply that since we have no means of testing such claims, we ultimately have no justification for their belief.

Conspiracy Theorist Has Elaborate Explanation For Why He's Single

The second rule is Ockham's Razor, which recommends that, when confronted with two hypotheses that produce the same observational consequences, we should adopt the simpler of the two. The idea is that, in such cases, neither additional complexity nor the assumption of additional variables, carries any additional explanatory power.

In order to demonstrate the importance of this principle, *The Onion* reports that "Jesus Answers Half The Prayers At Area Roulette Table" (12/27/08). This headline suggests at least two competing hypotheses to explain the fact that half the players came out winners:

1. **J.C.'s supernatural intervention**

2. **statistical law: when one party wins, another party loses, netting an average outcome of fifty percent**

Which is the simpler hypothesis? And why should we assume more than that?

If you think about it, Ockham's Razor's preference for intellectual economy implies that we should always adopt methodological naturalism as our starting mode of operation, since this approach to knowledge doesn't presuppose anything beyond the empirical evidence to which we all have access.

Given the empirical basis supporting methodological naturalism, as well as its unrivaled success, those who advocate for supernatural explanations must go beyond the mere claim that there might be supernatural phenomena and causes: they must offer methods for investigating, discovering and evaluating such claims in objective ways that prove at least as useful and reliable as those offered by methodological naturalism. As Carl Sagan was fond of saying, "extraordinary claims require extraordinary evidence."

My Man's Intuition Tells Me That My Neighbor Wants To Sleep With Me

But what about confirming belief through feelings or intuition? In the *Onion* story "NFL Star Thanks Jesus After Successful Double Homicide" (2/9/00), defensive end D'Aundré Banks explains that "the Lord Jesus Christ" was truly with him Saturday night when he killed his ex-girlfriend and a club bouncer. Banks added: "Jesus really let me take this homicide to the next level. Thank you, Jesus!"

I don't want to get into the ethical question of whether Jesus would assist someone in committing a double homicide; let's just say these two had it coming. What I want to concentrate on is the evidence that Banks used to support his claim: he *felt* the presence of the Lord.

Unfortunately, feelings are notoriously unreliable indicators of external truths. They may be indicative of something, but it is an open question what they are indicative of. For example, the nervous feeling of love you may experience as butterflies in the stomach could very well be love, or raging hormones . . . or it could be a sign of indigestion and the dire need to find a bathroom fast.

Faith Healer Calls In Faith Gastroenterologist

Believers sometimes argue that feelings related to the supernatural are different in nature. Even if this were so, however, a new problem arises: how do we adjudicate between competing supernatural explanations for such feelings when there is no rational or empirical basis to choose between them?

Take the case reported by *The Onion* concerning Mets pitcher Pedro Martinez. He claims he could not have reached his two-hundredth career win

> without the aid of his lucky midget, the Egyptian sun god Ra, and every person and thing who helped him along the way, including an enchanted necklace, former British prime minister Arthur Neville Chamberlain, and a talking whale who lives off the coast of his native Dominican Republic that only he can communicate with. ("Pedro Martinez Credits Success To Lucky Midget, Sun God, Magic Beads," 4/20/06)

Unlike the existence of God, the existence of a midget has the benefit of being empirically demonstrable. Still, in order to be plausible, the midget hypothesis must establish a *connection* between the existence of the midget and the outcome he is alleged to produce. The same is true for the existence of God and his alleged miracles. If only we had a magic rabbit foot to help us make that connection . . .

Even if we grant the existence of God, and ignore that fact that a lucky midget could explain a successful career just as ineffi-ciently, there is still the huge problem of false positives. A false positive is a mistaken confirmation, like the one reported in *The Onion* story "Christ 'Categorically Denies' Speaking To Lutheran-College Administrator" (8/11/99). According to the report, Philip Burkett said

> it was during the height of my discontent that, following a Sunday ser-vice at my church, I quite involuntarily found myself drawn to the bul-letin board in the vestry, where a job vacancy was listed for an administrative post at a Lutheran college up in Elkhart. It was as if some inscrutable force was guiding me. I now know it was Jesus Christ, telling me it was time for a change.

The delicious irony of this story is that Jesus himself makes the cru-cial philosophical point, commenting, "just what that 'inscrutable force' was, I cannot tell you, but I do know it was not Me."

Evel Knievel To Attempt Huge Leap In Logic

What we see in all these cases is one version of an informal log-ical fallacy known as the appeal to ignorance: because we can't immediately explain some phenomenon through ordinary and natural means, we make the mistake of assuming, without any rational justification, that we can explain it through some other arbitrarily chosen means for which there is no supporting evidence.

Take my depressing case: I can't explain for the life of me why I can't manage to secure every man's dream: a threesome with two hot chicks. I just don't get it. Should I blame Thor? Is Apollo test-ing my faith? Should I sacrifice a baby to Quetzalcoatl? Have I not been lucky enough to be touched by the Flying Spaghetti Monster's noodly appendage? Even if one of these hypotheses were correct, how could I possibly know which one? Other than an aesthetic or emotional preference, what could be the grounds for justifying my belief?

The only philosophically virtuous alternative left to us in cases in which we can't explain some phenomenon is simply to display some honesty and admit our ignorance until we can find some explanation based on actual evidence. The fact that I don't know how to explain something can't possibly mean that I do know how to explain it: that would entail a logical contradiction, since the second premise is a denial of the first.

All that's left for us is a tautology: our inability to explain an event just means our inability to explain that event. In this respect, we could all learn a lesson in humility from Pope John Paul II, who admitted to *The Onion* (10/16/96):

> God ain't said shit to me. Not one lousy word. Seventy-six years I'm busting my hump for this mysterious Divine One, and still it's like, 'John Paul who?' Christ . . .

Paleontology Class Winces Whenever Fundamentalist Kid Raises Hand

Most people believe in the version of God they were raised to believe, and these versions vary in great part due to the scriptures used. Why do Christians believe in a Christian God? Because that's what their book, the Bible, says about God. That's the same reason Muslims believe in a Muslim God, Mormons believe in a Mormon God, and Scientologists believe in . . . whatever it is that they believe. This, of course, raises the question of why a rational person with no prior bias should believe any of these particular books to the exclusion of the rest, a problem that becomes even more difficult to make sense of after reading *The Onion*'s headline "Christ Converts to Islam" (4/7/99).

To answer that one's preferred book is the word of God won't help, since the belief that one's book is the word of God presupposes that we have an independent reason for believing in that particular version of God, which we couldn't have without relying on the very same book in question! If your head is spinning, that's because this is a viciously circular argument: the belief in God is supported by the book whose accuracy is supposed to be guaranteed by the very same God whose questioned existence is explained in the book.

Leave it to Timmy Yu, a paralyzed little boy, to reveal the circular problem with the scriptural basis for belief. According to *The Onion*, Timmy thanked God for taking the time to answer his prayer, even though the answer was a resounding 'no'. Timmy declared: "I know that God loves me, because it says so in the Bible" ("God Answers Prayers Of Paralyzed Little Boy," 12/9/98).

What a convenient partnership: the book confirms God, God confirms the book, and neither confirms shit.

Correct Theory Discarded In Favor Of More Exciting Theory

Although empirical verifiability is important, it would be unfair to limit all justified belief to that which is observed directly. After all, much of our scientific and historical knowledge is based on the principle of an inference to the best explanation. This is the idea that the hypothesis we should adopt is the one that best explains the evidence we have.

The key term in the principle of inference to the best explanation is "best." Many inferences can explain a given phenomenon, but not all inferences are created equal: some are better than others, and a rational agent ought to choose that inference which *best* explains the available evidence.

I know what you're thinking: you're still wondering why you should be looking for a blind person at the drive-up ATM of your local bank. Give up?

If you have ever noticed, the buttons at drive-up ATM's are marked with Braille, an alphabet of raised dots for the blind. Now, I've never actually seen a blind person using a drive-up ATM machine. I infer that they do, because this explains why the buttons are marked with Braille.

But wait! If a person is too blind to see the ATM machine, isn't he too blind to drive? Why put Braille on drive-up machines? Perhaps some people who can see perfectly well simply enjoy using Braille. A better explanation, however, is that federal regulations require the universal use of Braille buttons on *all* ATM machines, some of which happen to serve clients who operate these machines from the convenience of their vehicles. A better inference still would incorporate the additional idea that blind people may want to use the drive-up ATM of their local bank from the back seat of a taxi cab.

To illustrate the subtlety of this philosophical principle, consider the story "Anonymous Philanthropist Donates 200 Human Kidneys To Hospital" (3/10/08). Upon the sudden appearance of a large plastic bag containing two hundred fresh human kidneys dumped at the front entrance of a Massachusetts General Hospital, *The Onion News Network* reports that a mysterious philanthropist has made a much needed and selfless donation to help those in grave need of kidney transplants. The note attached to the bag, which read, 'This is only the beginning' was happily interpreted by everyone to mean subsequent donations of other needed organs would soon follow. Call me silly, but an inference to the *best* explanation would suggest to me that a serial killer is on the loose, terrorizing and preying upon innocent bystanders. Watch out!

I'm Very Interested In Hearing Some Half-Baked Theories

In order to help us better understand the nature and methods of good reasoning, *The Onion*'s Roberta Foit lays down some essential rules for critical thinking in her deliciously sarcastic editorial piece "I'm Very Interested In Hearing Some Half-Baked Theories" (11/9/02). Securing her coveted allegiance to your ideas is not easy; there are criteria you must satisfy. In her own words,

> If you want to convince me of anything, you better be prepared to back up your claims with rumor, circumstantial evidence, or hard-to-make-out photographic proof. I may also need friend-of-a-friend corroboration or several signed testimonials all written in the same unmistakably spidery handwriting. I'm a quasi-critical-thinker. Things have to add up more or less in my head before I let myself be taken in by some baloney story. If you have a half-baked theory that you'd like to disclose, please be so kind as to skirt around the issue. I'll only listen to your elaborate webs of presumption and hearsay if you promise to veer unexpectedly and pointlessly off course at every opportunity. Prose density is part of what makes a half-baked theory fascinating.

Now there's a sensible woman!

Suppose we wanted to convince Ms. Foit that Atlantis was a real city. This is her own example: "When I first heard about this lost civilization, I was suspicious to say the least. But then someone made a good point: Prove that it didn't exist. I was hard-pressed to find a comeback to that." In fact, most people are, and what we have here is a philosophical question concerning the burden of proof: who should have the responsibility of proving his case, the believer or the skeptic?

Say I ask you to believe in the existence of a Tyrannosaurus Rex—stored away in the trunk of my car. Yes, it is alive, full-sized and hungry. Should you believe me? Other than my testimony and character, do you have any reason to believe that my claim is true? If you have no independent evidence to support this claim, you are free to reject it until it can be corroborated. In fact, it would be irrational for you to believe in something so out of the ordinary and contrary to normal experience without any evidence.

The default rational position in every inference is skepticism: we should withhold assent until we have justification for belief. Just like it would be unfair to expect you to prove that Ra, Thor, Athena, and the Tooth Fairy don't exist, it would be irrational to expect the nonbeliever to prove that God doesn't exist. It is the believer who must prove his case.

Your Horoscope: This Will Be A Great Week To Read Too Much Into Stuff

I have temporarily ignored an obvious objection: it could be argued that some people *do* have direct sensory experience of God: God speaks to them, and they can hear his messages.

Having learned a few basic rules of reasoning, we can now evaluate this claim. In *The Onion* story "God's Plan For Area Man Involves Kidnapping Ford CEO" (5/18/05), unemployed factory worker James Harold Gurshner, "talking to reporters through a metal grate screwed over the window of his dilapidated, hubcap-covered house," admitted that

> he does not know why God 'came to him in a dream' and asked him to kidnap Ford, but he says he believes that 'it is best not to question His motives.' Gurshner added: "I didn't question the Lord when He struck down my beloved wife Emily with cervical cancer, I didn't question Him when I was dismissed from my job and put on Social Security. I didn't question Him when He commanded me to dig a three-foot ditch around my house and fill it with charcoal briquettes, and I don't question him now. I, James Harold Gurshner, will kidnap the Ford CEO, as that is the will of the Lord."

In a surprising move, however, Gurshner was quick to point out:

> "One thing I will not do is make love to the Ford CEO's asshole, no matter what the Lord says. That activity is a sin against nature. An order to do it would be God's way of testing me."

Ignoring the arbitrarily convenient way in which Gurshner chooses
to believe parts of the command while ignoring others (a problem
all religious believers must face), notice that although the act of
revelation was perceived as a direct and explicitly stated command,
and not just a feeling, it came to Gurshner in the form of a dream.
Although it is possible that, should God exist, he may choose this
nebulous medium to communicate with his followers, it is also possible that it was *just* a dream. Which is the simpler hypothesis?
Which is the best explanation?

Even if it were the case that God existed and were communicating with Gurshner, barring any independent means of confirmation, he would be more justified in believing that his experience
was the result of his own mind deceiving him. This is an important
philosophical point: how our beliefs come to acquire justification
should carry more weight than the truth to which our beliefs are
supposed to correspond. In other words, even if God or the supernatural existed, we could not rationally believe that they do!

The Onion vindicates this surprising insight in its story "Ghost
Of Carl Sagan Warns Against Dangers Of Superstition" (8/12/97):

> 'Exercise skepticism!' Sagan said, clanking a large metal chain.
> 'Whenever possible, there must be independent confirmation of all
> facts pertaining to any so-called 'magical' or 'mystical' event or phe-
> nomenon! A thinking person must always utilize the scientific method,
> or wear the chains of superstition throughout eternity!'

We should follow this directive, not because it was presumably
delivered by the ghost of Carl Sagan, but because it is philosophically sound. The best part is that we might be able to save a few
bucks and believe it without having to buy a "special anti-supersti-
tion crystal amulet."

Of course, one doesn't have to be dreaming to have a religious
experience. In one of the few funny passages that appear in the
philosophical literature, the French philosopher Jean-Paul Sartre
tells of "a madwoman who had hallucinations; someone used to
speak to her on the telephone and give her orders. Her doctor
asked her, 'Who is it who talks to you?' She answered, 'He says it's
God.'"

The woman's reasoning could hardly be more circular. But if
one is ready to admit to the existence of the supernatural, why not
believe that it was simply a ghost playing a prank on her? Or an

angel? Or shape-shifting fairies? Or a demon? Any of these hypotheses would be equally arbitrary. In fact, British science fiction author and inventor Arthur C. Clarke once remarked that "any sufficiently advanced technology is indistinguishable from magic." Given the existence of holograms, virtual reality, and magnetic brain stimulation, we don't even need to appeal to the supernatural to explain visual hallucinations and out-of-body experiences.

Even Nobel Prize winner Sartre is no match for the wit of *The Onion*, which published a story revealing the problem with divine communication: "Voice Of God Revealed To Be Cheney On Intercom" (12/7/05). If you've wondered why President George W. Bush started a war in Iraq, even though none of the 9/11 terrorists were from Iraq, and you don't believe the oil hypothesis or the this-is-payback-for-trying-to-kill-mah-daddy hypothesis, an inference to the best explanation might lead you straight to Cheney.

18-Year-Old Miraculously Finds Soulmate In Hometown

Although there is no reliable empirical evidence of God, and all instances of revelation seem dubious at best, the believer might make an argument for God's existence based on an inference to the best explanation. We reasonably posit the existence of blind customers in order explain Braille on ATM machines. Similarly, a believer can posit the existence of God in order to explain miracles. People pray to God and sometimes their wishes come true. So God must exist. What better explanation could there be?

The idea that God answers prayers is loaded with conceptual problems so logically twisted that the believer might be better off avoiding the subject altogether. For instance, answered prayer implies that God can change his presumably eternal plan for the universe and make exceptions to his presumably eternal rules. Furthermore, it creates a contest between God's omniscience and his omnipotence. If God already knows what is going to happen, he can't change it; but if God can change it, then he doesn't know what's going to happen, since things wouldn't have been what they are without God intervening to turn them into what they will be. Go ponder that, Einstein. . . .

Meanwhile, those who believe prayers are answered might suffer from a psychological effect known as selection bias. Selection bias is the idea that we have a natural tendency to look for evidence that confirms our preconceptions and to avoid or ignore information which contradicts those preconceptions. Have you ever heard a believer say: "I prayed for that threesome, but I didn't get it"? Probably not. Human beings prefer to think of themselves as winners and the recipients of divine grace. Believers consistently acknowledge instances that confirm that their prayers have been answered, and consistently ignore all those times their prayers don't seem to receive a response. Understanding the predominance of selection bias, it should come as no surprise that *The Onion* is the only newspaper ballsy enough to publish the story "Christianity Celebrates One Billionth Unanswered Prayer" (1/22/97).

Perhaps most prayers *are* answered, the believer might object, but they require patience: the Lord takes his time, working in mysterious ways. This line of reasoning opens the floodgate to an even bigger philosophical nightmare: the problem of evil, which *The Onion* explores with its headline "God Cites 'Moving In Mysterious Ways' As Motive In Killing Of 3,000 Papua New Guineans" (7/29/98).

The problem of evil is the idea that there is a logical and existential tension between the propositions that God has the power to eradicate evil, has the willingness to eradicate evil, and yet evil exists. It brings into question either God's omnipotence or his benevolence, both of which seem to be necessary attributes of any being worth considering God. Luckily, after two millennia of heated philosophical debate, *The Onion* reports the problem of evil has finally been solved: "God Diagnosed With Bipolar Disorder" (5/2/01).

Part of the problem with the give-it-time account of prayer is that it creates some interesting practical consequences hilariously exposed by the *Onion* story "'95–'96 Prayers Finally Answered" (10/18/07). Explaining that he has been "absolutely swamped," God announced that he finally got around to answering the prayers he received in 1995 and 1996. The conceptual problem was revealed by the responses of the recipients:

> "Unfortunately, I don't really want a red wagon anymore," said 18-year old Zach Gilpin. Others expressed similar displeasure, including 30-year-old accountant Jack Demont, who said that former classmate and high school cheerleader Heidi Stillman's repeated phone calls to his house are 'destroying' his marriage.

Oops. . . .

Fifth-Grade Science Paper Doesn't Stand Up To Peer Review

The greatest philosophical problem with the theory that God answers prayers is that it is unfalsifiable. This means that the theory can't be shown to be false by any observation or experiment. At first glance it may seem good for a theory to be unfalsifiable, since it can't be proven false. In fact, however, this is actually bad because what it means is that the theory can't be tested, and if it can't be tested, then it can't be confirmed.

Suppose my theory is that I'm such a hot hunk of man-meat that any woman but a dyke would want to have a threesome with me. The way to test this theory would be to try to find a heterosexual woman who doesn't want to have a threesome with me. If you find one, and please don't, then my theory is falsified. But suppose I add that any woman who didn't want to have a threesome with me was a man-hating dyke *whether she knew it or not*. Now my theory is untestable and therefore meaningless. A good theory must also allow for the possibility of being refuted by some set of possible evidence.

Consider the theory of evolution by natural selection. All available evidence supports its veracity. Moreover, it is falsifiable because many possible discoveries would refute it—for example the discovery of a human fossil as old as a Tyrannosaurus Rex fossil. Despite the *Onion* headline "Creation Museum Acquires 5,000 Year-Old T. Rex Skeleton" (1/15/03), no one has found such evidence, but if it were to turn up, it would show the theory of evolution to be defective. Part of what makes a scientific theory falsifiable is that it makes a clear set of specific predictions which will either be right or wrong.

Since God presumably "works in mysterious ways," however, we cannot make a clear set of predictions that will test his existence. If a person undergoing chemotherapy prays for the destruction of a cancerous growth in his brain, and he recovers, he might conclude that his prayer was answered. But if he doesn't recover, he could just as easily conclude that this was part of God's plan.

This problem is brilliantly illustrated in the *Onion* story "Malignant Tumor Sees Every Day As Gift From God" (7/19/00). Speaking from the left hemisphere of Warren Lenders' brain, and having survived its last surgery, the high-grade cerebellar astrocytoma stoically declared:

God put me on this Earth for a purpose: to attach myself to the pari-
etal lobe of the loving husband and father of three. Going into that
surgery, I thought, 'Well, this could be the end of the line for me', but
by some miracle, a few of my tendrils had adhered to the occipital lobe
without the doctors realizing it, and I made it through the operation. I
know in my heart it was God's hand guiding that surgeon's scalpel to
the wrong place that day.

It's a miracle either way. This shows that the theory that God
answers prayers can be supported by any evidence, no matter how
ridiculous. But a theory supported by just any evidence is supported by no evidence: there is no reason to believe it.

Evangelical Scientists Refute Gravity With New 'Intelligent Falling' Theory

The most sophisticated inference to the best explanation a believer
can make to justify belief in God is the teleological proof, or argument from design. This is the idea that the universe exhibits certain
properties that just seem too improbable to be explained away simply through mere coincidence and random mindless naturalistic
principles.

Consider the complexity of a watch. This was one of the many
examples used by the philosopher and theologian William Paley in
his book *Natural Theology*: if you were to stumble upon a watch
and ask yourself how it came to be, an inference to the best explanation would have you conclude that someone, some watchmaker,
had designed the watch. The inference is informed by the intricate
complexity of the watch: there are many parts that have to work
together in a delicately precise way in order for it to function.

While it's *possible* to explain the existence of a watch through
natural processes, it's extremely *improbable* that all the right conditions would meet at exactly the right time and in exactly the right
way. A more *rational* explanation, Paley argued, is to explain the
existence of the watch as the result of the intelligent design of a
conscious designer, an agent whose craft displays indications of purpose and forethought. The reason this would be a more rational
explanation is that it has a much higher probability of being correct
than mere chance. Rationality, then, is directly tied to probability.

The strength of the argument from design writ large is that it
looks like an explanation for the complexity of the biological

world: increased complexity is a mystery best explained by an intelligent designer.

Thinking back to the watch example, however, one has to notice that Paley fails to consider that the watchmaker is more complex than the watch he designs. If Paley wants to maintain the analogy between the watchmaker and God as a divine designer, as he must in order to make his argument work, then he is committed to the view that God must be more complex than the universe he designs. But by Paley's own argument, increased complexity is a mystery best explained by an intelligent designer. So who designed God? —Another God, who in turn must have been designed by someone else? This line of reasoning leads to an infinite regress. Or, if one insists that God doesn't need an intelligent designer, then by the same token, the world, which is less complex and hence more probable, doesn't need one either.

The Onion has scarcely been able to restrain itself from ridiculing those who cling to the teleological argument. When the school board of Dover, Pennsylvania, became the first in the nation to mandate the teaching of intelligent design, it reported, "Theory Of Intelligent School-Board Design Disproven" (12/28/05). Similarly, one must imagine that the existence of creationists, as well as innumerable other design failures found throughout the biological world, were probably part of the inspiration for the story "God Recalls Tracheas Of Millions Of Indonesians" (2/23/07).

What alternative is left for the believer? Well, as it happened in the unfortunately real case of Professor Paul Mirecki, head of the University of Kansas's Religious Studies Department and outspoken critic of Intelligent Design, when all else fails, the believer can always beat the crap out of the nonbeliever. As one *Onion* commentator observed in the story "ID Critic Beaten" (12/14/05), "that'll teach him the difference between man and apes. Wait—no, it won't."

3

Is My Kid Sitting Too Close to His Robot?

LUKE CUDDY

Maybe someday my kid will get a pet robot. And, when he does, maybe I'll wonder whether he's sitting too close to it—in the same way my mom wondered whether I was sitting too close to the TV. Maybe eBooks will be written about the need to return to a pre-robot era. While robots haven't forced humanity into submission, maybe their existence has caused our already base and material culture to devolve even further.

But maybe there are other eBooks. Maybe these books praise robots for what they're capable of. Sure, we associate them with debauchery and violence, but robots have potential. They can be used in other ways, in good ways. Why can't we understand that robots are a tool, the eBook will argue, not a moral force unto themselves?

This hasn't happened yet, but the possible future should call to mind a familiar present. We're all familiar with the older generation criticizing the tools and conventions of the young, from jazz to rock'n'roll to video games. Traditionally, and usually by tenured professors, the young are said to be culturally and intellectually deficient. They are said to be "getting dumber."

This sentiment of a growing ignorance has ricocheted through the general population. It is even shared by some youth, the very ones accused of being dumber. Try asking a couple of people, young or not. Typically, they will agree that we are in a cultural decline, that we don't read enough, that we play too many games, watch too much TV, and spend too much time online.

In my experience, many of the decriers of cultural decline are not exactly paradigms of intelligence, let alone cultural production. Still, there are educated and at least seemingly intelligent people on both sides of this debate—a debate that never seems to die. Each generation produces some who call the youth morons and others who think those-who-call-the-youth-morons are morons. What's the deal here—is everyone a moron?

Thanks to *The Onion*, we have a clear answer to the question: yes, definitely. As it turns out, both sides of this debate are guided by some quality *Onion* reporting.

You're An Idiot, Area Mother Tells Teen

The chronic generational critic reminds me of the proverbial, unfaithful boyfriend. He whines: "I swear I'm not cheating on you, baby. Not this time. I swear I'm different." In the same way, the critic whines: "I swear we're in cultural and intellectual decline. Yeah, we hear this from generation to generation, but this time it's different. This time the kids *really* are dumber."

In his book, *The Dumbest Generation* (Penguin, 2008), English Professor Mark Bauerlein argues . . . well what do you think he argues? Sometimes a title just says it all. He's annoyed by the groups of little idiots who have begun infecting his Emory University classroom with iPods and Blackberries.

Bauerlein makes so many controversial claims in his book that they could all be addressed in another book (and I hope someone is writing that book). He thinks that the refusal of today's youth to grow up prevents them from knowing important stuff. As he puts it: "The Dumbest Generation will cease being dumb only when it regards adolescence as an inferior realm of petty strivings and adulthood as a realm of civic, historical, and cultural awareness that puts them in touch with the perennial ideas and struggles" (p. 236). He also worries that "To prosper in the hard-and-fast cliques in the schoolyard, the fraternities, and the food court, teens and twenty-year-olds must track the latest films, fads, gadgets, *YouTube* videos, and television shows. They judge one another relentlessly on how they wear clothes, recite rap lyrics, and flirt" (p. 42).

While we might wonder why Bauerlein still uses the word "schoolyard" or how often he witnesses the youth judge each other's recitals of rap lyrics, these quotes get us closer to the crux of his argument: despite all the advantages and access to information the youth have, they don't make use of it.

Let's be clear: Bauerlein isn't a Luddite. He realizes the benefits of the digital age. He just thinks the youth aren't reaping those benefits. They're more concerned with MySpace and Facebook than with reading an online version of the Constitution or googling fine art. Bauerlein feels that the youth don't know how to grow up, and social networking sites aren't making it any easier.

Bauerlein talks about Leno's "Jaywalking" segment from *The Tonight Show* where Jay travels the street with a mic while asking people easy questions and making them look like idiots when they don't know the answer. Bauerlein sees this as indicative of the youth's ignorance on matters that make one "an informed citizen."

The Onion takes Bauerlein's concerns about growing youth ignorance to another level. Sure, we worry when the kids can't name the Second Amendment or the first president, but what are we to do about their lack of interest in important current events? Especially when it comes to office politics. "Young people fail to concern themselves with vital workplace topics, like how unfair it is that the third floor got new computers before everyone else" ("Study Finds Young People Remain Apathetic About Office Politics," 7/30/08). Another informed employee worries that "a lot of the young people here don't even take the time to learn rules about the color copier."

The world of comedy, too, has felt the mediocrity and imbecility of today's young crowds. *The Onion* reports that one performer in particular feels the sting like nobody else: Aristophanes. "These kids coming up now," he writes, "they wouldn't know funny if you spelled it out for them with a twenty-two-page Translator's Foreword in a special edition from Oxford University Press" ("Today's Audiences Just Don't Get Me," 12/5/06).

Although he struggles for a laugh in today's world, Aristophanes made the crowds in Ancient Athens sing. He and Bauerlein agree that our culture is on the decline. Aristophanes goes on:

> Audiences nowadays are so used to being spoon-fed the most simplistic material, they don't recognize good comedy anymore. You can read them stasimon after stasimon of the funniest chanted poetry ever, and they still sit there like so much stone statuary at the Oracle of Delphi . . . I used to do the best Euripides. I had his whole pretentious, 'look-at-me-I'm-the-most-important-tragedian-in-the-history-of-the-city-state' thing down—I swear, you'd think the guy was sitting right across the agora from you. But whenever I bust that one out now, they stare at me with this look on their faces like they've just been sentenced to drink hemlock.

So you see? It's not just the cultural critic like Bauerlein who rec-ognizes these anti-intellectual trends. While Bauerlein cites some real studies and test scores that seem to suggest some sort of intel-lectual decline, fake news stories from *The Onion* vindicate his position.

I'm Smarter Than Daddy, Area Boy Boasts

In his book, *Everything Bad Is Good for You* (Penguin, 2005), sci-ence writer Stephen Johnson argues . . . well, what do you think he argues? He thinks that kids zoning out in front of a videogame is not the exercise in inanity that parents have come to suppose. Not only that, he thinks that trends in TV-show-watching have become increasingly complex over the years. Kids aren't getting dumber; they're getting smarter!

Just as it did for Bauerlein, *The Onion* supports Johnson's the-sis. According to a recent article, American kids, who are thought to watch the most TV, are actually outdoing other countries in some academic areas—like detention. "The United States is requiring its students to do time in the guidance counselor or principal's office three times as often as the average Westernized nation" ("US Students Lead World in Detention." 10/30/02). Furthermore, as the story details, "a whopping eighty-two percent of detained American students are repeat offenders. This stands in sharp contrast to Germany, where only one detainee in fifty serves a second sen-tence in the same school year."

Surprisingly, Johnson doesn't cite this statistic to support his case. Instead, he writes about something he calls "the sleeper curve." It comes from the Woody Allen movie *Sleeper*, in which a future society chides past generations for not realizing the nutri-tional value of junk food. Johnson applies that concept to the pre-sent: while it seems that each new cultural production is more imbecilic than the last, in fact, cultural productions are growing increasingly sophisticated and they are making us smarter. Johnson writes, "the most debased forms of mass diversion—video games and violent television dramas and juvenile sitcoms—turn out to be nutritional after all" (p. 9). He cites research in neuroscience about the way the brain processes information and rising IQ scores to support his arguments.

But, if Johnson is right, then why do *Onion* stories like this one pop up: "Fun Toy Banned Because Of Three Stupid Dead Kids"

(8/16/00). The toy company president had this to say: "For years, countless children played with the Aqua Assault RoboFighter without incident. But then these three retards come along and somehow find a way to get themselves killed." Hmm . . . it seems the sleeper curve is not fully generalizable.

Area Philosopher (Me!) Is Sick Of The Stupid Debate About Stupid

So what should we make of all this? Some *Onion* stories satirize those who claim the world is full of imbeciles. Other *Onion* stories remind us that the world is, in fact, full of imbeciles. It's easy to sympathize with either point of view.

Bauerlein seems to have an edge insofar as it's always easier to prove failure than achievement. But if we're going to take him seriously, we're going to have to see how he distinguishes himself from other cultural critics. How is he different from Aristophanes, or those who rail against office politics?

What makes Bauerlein different is that he is willing to acknowledge that there are kids who rise above the rest, even in this generation. For example, he discusses the young entrepreneur who created Facebook.

For those of you who are unfamiliar with Facebook, it is a social networking site that hooks users by offering ever more interesting ways to interact with people around the world. *The Onion* describes one application called the "Carbon Offset Offsetter," which forces a six-year-old child in India to dig up fifty pounds of coal and set it on fire every time you click on it ("Facebook's Popular Applications," 1/23/08).

Bauerlein compares the bright lights of today's youth with those of the past. For example, he discusses four young New York City intellectuals from the 1930s. In so doing, he takes the accomplishments of our youth seriously. Still, he ultimately concludes that they don't match up.

Really? Give the Millennial generation eighty years and I'm sure you'll be able to pick out four equally exceptional individuals.

The pressing question for me is this: haven't the majority of people always been idiots? Ever since I went to a town hall meeting in high school and heard a grown woman say, "If English was good enough for Jesus, it's good enough for my kids," I drew the conclusion that idiocy is not dependent on age or generation.

There are idiots all around us. *The Onion's* desk atlas, *Our Dumb World* has an entry for ancient Greece that explains why: "Aristotle and Plato's schools of philosophy close down as Christianity replaces thought."

The Onion illuminates latent idiocy even in intellectuals, and I suspect that *The Onion* could exist in any time period of human history and never run out of things to parody. We humans are a mixed lot, and it doesn't seem to me that citing a few cases of rising or falling test scores (as Johnson and Bauerlein do, respectively) can do justice to the incredibly complex factors that go into forming a zeitgeist.

Moreover, both Johnson and Bauerlein seem to think that we can already understand the implications of the habits and tendencies of the Millennial generation. Bauerlein writes that any possible benefit from computers and the Internet would have materialized by now, if there were going to be any at all. Meanwhile, Johnson claims that the benefits from these things are already occurring. In the area of human waste disposal, at least, Johnson has support from an *Onion* story: "New E-Toilet To Revolutionize Online Shitting" (10/6/99). But still, how can we determine whether Bauerlein or Johnson is right?

Based on the nature of inductive knowledge, and the failure of previous generational critics to anticipate the true implications of many trends, I'm not comfortable coming to any serious conclusions about whether or not the youth are getting dumber. Either we'll see the world degenerate into the one depicted in Mike Judge's *Idiocracy*, or the kids will program their pet robots to take over, raising humanity to the next level of evolution—perhaps some sort of Nietzsche-esque society of independent value-creation beyond anything we can now conceive.

In either case, I hope I live long enough to see *The Onion's* take. In the midst of intellectual and anti-intellectual idiots, *The Onion* is the smartest (and I mean that in a few different senses) perspective around.

Opinion

4

Fuck You, You Fucking Fuck

ROBERT ARP

A well-placed 'fuck' in an *Onion* article can make us chuckle, chortle, or even crack up. Consider these *Onion* article titles:

Holy Shit / Man Walks On Fucking Moon (7/21/69)

Nation's Porn Stars Demand To Be Fucked Harder (5/9/01)

Fucker Sure Taking Long Time To Download (1/31/01)

Fuck-Buddy Becomes Fuck-Fiancé (3/31/04)

And my personal favorite:

Guy In Philosophy Class Needs To Shut The Fuck Up
(9/28/05)

In fact, I laughed out loud in a crowded coffee shop when I first read this title, drawing several stares from patrons enjoying their lattes and mochas. There's always one in every philosophy class, that's for sure. As a professor teaching philosophy courses, I have thought the same thing on more than one occasion.

'Fuck' is probably the most emotion-evoking and taboo word in the English language, inciting riots, road rage, killings, and millions of moms to wash their kids' mouths out with soap. One kid told another kid "fuck you" in my eighth-grade science class, causing the entire class to go "aaaaaAAAAAWWWWW!" and the offending swearer to be sent directly to the principal's office. While I was in high school, I nearly beat the crap out of the kid down the block who had the gall to tell my mom to fuck off in front of me. And a "go fuck yourself" got one of my college friends punched in the face and maced with pepper spray by a gang of hoodlums who were passing through a park where we were hanging out at (not very bright on my friend's part, who had been drinking a little too much).

'Fuck' is a versatile word and can be used as a verb, noun, or interjection, while forms of it can become adjectives, adverbs, and other colorful exclamations, expressions, and iterations. The following chart shows examples of the word's grammatical breadth and depth:

Example	Grammatical	Reference or Context
"Aftershock A Real 'Fuck You' To Earthquake Victims"	interjection	*The Onion* (6/4/08)
"I fucked your mom." taunting Rob Arp	verb	kids on Rob Arp's block
"Well, I fucked your mom's mom"	verb	Rob Arp's retort to kids on block
"Roses are red, violets are blue, I fucked Arp's mom, and I did too. Ha, ha, ha!"	verb	kids' retort to Rob Arp's
"fuck you"	interjection	Rob Arp, under his breath, as he walks away from kids on block
"I'm a fucking dog."	adjective	from the article "Stop Anthropomorphizing Me" in *The Onion* (4/9/09)
"What a fucking dick."	adjective	ex-worker, speaking of ex-boss after being fired by said ex-boss in the *Onion* article "Boss Gets Into Groove After 3rd Round Of Layoffs" (4/9/09)
"Get ready to herd your fat asses in to watch it, you fat fucks . . . And for all you snobby fucks who say you wouldn't come within a mile of this movie, we've got plans for you, too . . . "	noun	Touchstone Picture president Peter Zaiff, in the *Onion* article "Vindictive Movie Studio Threatens To Make 'Coyote Ugly' Sequel" (5/7/09)

Example	Grammatical	Reference or Context
"Un-fucking-believable!"	interjection, within a word	the head gardener at Resurrection Cemetery outside of Chicago, Illinois to Rob Arp, upon discovering that Rob accidentally knocked over a half-ton headstone with a lawnmower while he was working at the cemetery in college
"You are a one-of-a-fucking-kind, Arp, that's for fucking sure . . . "	interjections?	the head gardener, continuing his insulting rant
". . . a royal fuck-up."	noun	the head gardener, continuing . . .
"How fucking stupid can you be?"	adjective	the head gardener, continuing . . .
"Jesus fucking Christ."	interjection, blasphemy	the head gardener, continuing . . .
"You know, Arp, you could fuck up a one-car funeral."	verb, possibly adverb	the head gardener, finishing his insulting rant
"Skating to Some Fucked Up Shit"	adverb	album title by the Dirty Rotten Imbeciles
"If You See Kay"	cleverly concealed acronym	James Joyce, in his novel *Ulysses* (1922)
"Fuck is a taboo word . . . Understanding this relationship between law and taboo ultimately yields fuck jurisprudence."	adjective	part of abstract of Chris Fairman's paper titled "Fuck" in Ohio State's Center for Interdisciplinary Law and Policy Studies Working Paper Series, No. 39.
"Fuck you, you fucking fuck"	interjection, then adjective, then noun	Frank Booth in the David Lynch film, *Blue Velvet*

Where the Fuck Did 'Fuck' Come From?

'Fuck' is considered a slang English word, having etymological roots in the combination Latin-English word 'fvccant' meaning "to copulate" or "have sexual intercourse with." According to several sources, an instance of 'fvccant' can be found in a Latin-English poem from before the sixteenth century translated as "Fleas, Flies, and Friars." In the poem, the Carmelite friars of Cambridge are satirized in a line that is translated, loosely, as: "They are not in heaven because they fuck (fvccant) wives of Ely." (I guess priests have been having a problem with the whole celibacy thing from the get-go). From its grammatical usage back then, it is believed by many that 'fuck' derived the "have sex" meaning we still basically associate with the word, as in *Onion* articles such as:

Local Lutheran Minister Loves To Fuck His Wife (11/19/97)

I Think We Should Fuck Other People (3/7/01)

Who's A Girl Gotta Fuck To Get Some Closure On Her Relationship With Her Father? (5/31/06)

Systems Administrator Would So Fuck New Trainee (5/21/03)

Now, the fvccant friars fiasco supposedly is the true and accurate account of the word's origins. But, when I was growing up there were two other urban legends floating around about how 'fuck' came to be used in the English language. The first had to do with what is known as the "Fornicating Under the Consent of the King" legend. As I recall, it went something like this: During the European Crusades, armies of Christian men had to travel long distances from Europe to the Holy Land. In those days, you basically walked if you did not have a horse or mule. Fornication—or, doinking when you're not married—is a big no-no for Christians. Since many of these Christian men were married, and since guys seem to have this primal urge to spread their seed, and since guys who don't spread their seed for a long time might not be able to concentrate on killing infidels, and, instead, would concentrate on spreading said seed, the king of a Christian kingdom allowed men to have sex with women other than their wives while involved in the Crusade. Also, unmarried men were allowed to get their freaks on, too. Thus, fornication (and adultery) was allowed under the consent of the king. How cool is that?

I also heard that many kings of many kingdoms were hip to this idea, so it seemed that basically every married man or unmarried man with a working penis was willing to sign up to be a Crusader to the Holy Land. I also heard that certain women of the night were recruited to travel with the Crusaders to help with this God-given task. It truly was a God-given task since, after all, Christian kings were seen to have a kind of direct line to God's will and wishes. Thus, kings allowed F.U.C.K. ing to occur, and it was in line with God's will and wishes! How cool is that, too?

The other urban legend about the F-word I heard was prompted by the release of Van Halen's album titled *For Unlawful Carnal Knowledge* in 1991, when I was a junior in college. Not only did that album rock—as do most Halen albums, except for, like, *Van Halen III* and a lot of *5150*—but my friend pointed out to me the F.U.C.K. acronym which I did not see, at first. "Oh," I said. He continued: "Dude, back in, like, the Fifties when cops would catch kids, like, doing it in the back seats of their Model Ts, or whatever they drove back then, they would haul their lame asses down to the station and book 'em for unlawful carnal knowledge. But the cops would just write F.U.C.K. on their crime report: For . . . Unlawful . . . Carnal . . . Knowledge . . . So, the kids were booked for F.U.C.K. ing. Get it?" "Oh," I said again, believe it or not, only *then* realizing that 'carnal knowledge' meant something like "rubbing fuzzies," "bumping uglies," "working the weasels," "needling nasties," or "slapping skins."

However the word 'fuck' got started, there is no doubt that it is a mainstay for any English speaker, even the likes of:

a. **world politicians such as Lyndon B. Johnson**, who is said to have told the Greek ambassador in 1964, "Fuck your parliament and your constitution"

b. **novelists such as J.D. Salinger**, whose character, Holden Caulfield, gets offended by someone having written "Fuck you" on a wall, in his magnum opus *The Catcher in the Rye*

c. **musicians such as John Lennon**, who claims "But you're still fucking peasants as far as I can see" in his song "Working Class Hero" (1970)

d. **characters like Jim Anchower** ("Ain't life fucked up?")
and Herbert Kornfeld ("Office Depot can go fuck theyselves, 'cuz
Midstate is tha BOMB.")

Goody Fucking Two Shoes

Now, I find the usage of the word 'fuck' in *Onion* articles to be
funny as all get out. But why? One reason seems to be that the
word is taboo, as was hinted at earlier. Along with 'cunt' and other
four-letter-type words, 'fuck' seems to be a word that should never
be said or written, and, so, when it is uttered or written by someone, the rascal in me gets a kick out of it. It's kind of a dirty little
vice to cherish every once in a while.

Notice that I said, "every once in a while." I want to qualify a
few things, here. First, it actually gets annoying to me and I shud-
der when I hear someone swearing every other word of a sentence,
like one finds in some hard-core gansta rap songs. Consider this
small section of lyrics from Jay Z's hit "Nigga What, Nigga Who?"

> . . . Nigga what, nigga who? / Nigga what, nigga who? / Switcha flow,
> getcha dough / Can't fuck with this Roc-a-Fella shit doe / Switcha flow,
> getcha dough / Can't fuck with this Roc-a-Fella shit doe / Can't fuck
> with me . . . / Motherfuckers wanna act loco, hit 'em wit, numerous
> shots with the fo'-fo' / Faggots wanna talk to Po-Pos, smoke 'em like
> cocoa / Fuck rap, coke by the boatload / Fuck dat, on the run-by, gun
> high, one eye closed / Left holes through some guy clothes / Stop your
> bullshittin', glock with the full clip / Motherfuckers better duck when
> the fool spit / One shot could make a nigga do a full flip / See the
> nigga layin shocked when the bullet hit / Oh hey ma, how you, know
> niggaz wanna buy you / But see me I wanna fuck for free . . .

Some of these gansta rap songs might as well go like this in the
chorus:

> Motherfuckin' bitch, nigga bitch, nigga bitch, I say / Motherfuckin'
> bitch, nigga bitch, nigga bitch, y'all / Fuckin' bitch, suck my cock,
> nigga bitch, suck my cock, I say / Fuck y'all, fuck y'all, my niggaz can
> suck my left ball. / Motherfuckin' bitch, nigga bitch, nigga bitch, I say
> / Motherfuckin' bitch, nigga bitch, nigga bitch, y'all / Fuckin' bitch,
> suck my cock, nigga bitch, suck my cock, I say / Fuck y'all, fuck y'all,
> my niggaz can suck my left ball. / Motherfuckin' bitch, nigga bitch,
> nigga bitch, I say / Motherfuckin' bitch, nigga bitch, nigga bitch, y'all

/ Fuckin' bitch, suck my cock, nigga bitch, suck my cock, I say / Fuck y'all, fuck y'all, my niggaz can suck my left ball. / Motherfuckin' bitch, nigga bitch, nigga bitch, I say / Motherfuckin' bitch, nigga bitch, nigga bitch, y'all / Fuckin' bitch, suck my cock, nigga bitch, suck my cock, I say / Fuck y'all, fuck y'all, my niggaz can suck my left ball. / Motherfuckin' bitch, nigga bitch, nigga bitch, I say / Motherfuckin' bitch, nigga bitch, nigga bitch, y'all / Fuckin' bitch, suck my cock, nigga bitch, suck my cock, I say / Fuck y'all, fuck y'all, my niggaz can suck my left ball. / Motherfuckin' bitch, nigga bitch, nigga bitch, I say / Motherfuckin' bitch, nigga bitch, nigga bitch, y'all / Fuckin' bitch, suck my cock, nigga bitch, suck my cock, I say / Fuck y'all, fuck y'all, my niggaz can suck my left ball. / Motherfuckin' bitch, nigga bitch, nigga bitch, I say / Motherfuckin' bitch, nigga bitch, nigga bitch, y'all / Fuckin' bitch, suck my cock, nigga bitch, suck my cock, I say / Fuck y'all, fuck y'all, my niggaz can suck my left ball. / Motherfuckin' bitch, nigga bitch, nigga bitch, I say / Motherfuckin' bitch, nigga bitch, nigga bitch, y'all / Fuckin' bitch, suck my cock, nigga bitch, suck my cock, I say / Fuck y'all, fuck y'all, my niggaz can suck my left ball. / Motherfuckin' bitch, nigga bitch, nigga bitch, I say / Motherfuckin' bitch, nigga bitch, nigga bitch, y'all / Fuckin' bitch, suck my cock, nigga bitch, suck my cock, I say / Fuck y'all, fuck y'all, my niggaz can suck my left ball. / Motherfuckin' bitch, nigga bitch, nigga bitch, I say / Motherfuckin' bitch, nigga bitch, nigga bitch, y'all / Fuckin' bitch, suck my cock, nigga bitch, suck my cock, I say / Fuck y'all, fuck y'all, my niggaz can suck my left ball . . .

You get the picture. As obnoxious as it is to see that written so many times, so too, it's obnoxious to hear it blasting from a speaker or from someone's mouth, as I have heard on numerous occasions, having grown up next to Chi-Town, Illinois, y'all. West siiiiiiiiiide! Cicero, Illinois is where I grew up, actually, which is a suburb right next to Chicago's West Side, and also which is hardly Leave It to Beaver land. Another thing: I could easily point to hundreds of gansta rap songs that are on par with Jay Z's little ditty and my masterpiece above. Further, it's not just a black gansta rap thing, either, as people of all different races, creeds, and colors have their versions of fuckity, fuck, fuck-types of songs.

I have two kids, and kids can make you think twice about the things you do. Why do I think twice? Because I don't want them to pick up any of my bad habits. Kids are like friggin' sponges, no doubt! It hasn't happened yet, but the moment I say 'fuck'—for whatever reason—I guarantee you that one of my kids within ear shot will not only repeat it, but will also ask me, "Daddy, what's fuck?" So, I have to be a good role model for them at a young age, which includes controlling my language. In fact, a commonly-known argument that many gansta rappers use for the legitimacy of their gangsta rap lyrics that degrade women, promote violence, and hail the gods of money, sex, and power over all else, is that: "Man, we just be rappin' 'bout our lives in the hood, y'all. Iss reality, dawg. That's the way it bees in the streets, G." No wonder every other word out of their mouths is the way it is: it's what they heard constantly around them in their hoods. Of course, the counterargument to this—promoted by many blacks, too, by the way—is that just because it's what you saw, heard, and lived on the streets does not mean that you *should*, automatically, be able to legitimize or glorify it in song for the entire world to hear—especially since you be gettin' paid, y'all, off the exploits of yo music, G. And, especially, also, if kids will be getting access to the music, despite laws and parental advisory stickers.

But there's more to being a good role model. I love my kids dearly and want to assist in forming them into happy, healthy, critical thinking, moral adults. So, to me, more important than following moral principles or rules is making sure that they are well-balanced human beings. This means that you should always shoot for the "just right" between two extremes in your actions and reactions to life's challenges. Another word for the just right between two extremes is *virtue*, while the extremes can be considered *vices*. I want to raise virtuous kids. Think of one vice at one extreme as an under-action, under-reaction, or "too little," the other vice at the other extreme as an over-action, over-reaction, or "too much," and the virtue as the appropriate action/reaction, hitting the mark, striking the balance, or the "just right," to beat the Goldilocks and the Three Bears reference dead horse once more. Here are some standard examples of virtues, with their two vices:

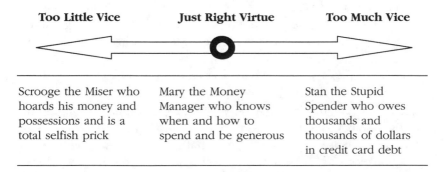

Too Little Vice	**Just Right Virtue**	**Too Much Vice**
Scrooge the Miser who hoards his money and possessions and is a total selfish prick	Mary the Money Manager who knows when and how to spend and be generous	Stan the Stupid Spender who owes thousands and thousands of dollars in credit card debt

Too Little Vice	Just Right Virtue	Too Much Vice

Too Little Vice	Just Right Virtue	Too Much Vice
Polly Pushover who lets people walk all over her	Even-tempered Edith who has self-respect and knows when and how to use force	Angry Alice who hits before she thinks
Pam the Prude who never, ever, ever, drinks or has any fun whatsoever and is self-deprecating	Sally the Self-controlled Soul who knows how to balance her drinking life with other aspects of her life	Dan the Drunk who is self-indulgent with alcohol, drinks and drives, and screws up his relationships with people
Betty Bulimic	Franny Fit	Fatso Frank
Cowardly Curt, a pussy who runs away in battle	Courageous soldier, Meg Ryan, in the film *Courage Under Fire*	Reckless Rudy who goes berserk in battle and gets himself killed quickly

The very first *Onion* article I read was "Five Or Six Dudes Jump Out Of Nowhere And Just Start Whaling On This One Guy" (5/31/00). I remember reading it in the graduate student lounge of the Department of Philosophy at Saint Louis University while I was a graduate student pursuing the Ph.D. in philosophy, and laughing my ass off. This article has a special place in my heart, because it was the one that broke my *Onion* cherry. But, notice that these five or six dudes whaling on this one guy would seem to indicate that they were vicious in that they went the over-reacting, "too much" route, causing Lyle Kelso, who witnessed the "ass-pounding" event, to claim: "I just saw some poor fucker completely get his ass beat down by a bunch of seriously pissed-off dudes." On the other hand, if the five or six dudes did nothing whatsoever, then that might indicate a "too little," vicious, under-reaction. The following table gives several *Onion* and real-life Rob Arp examples of vices:

Event or Circumstances	Action or Reaction	Vice and Why It's So
"Chicken-Shit Asteroid Veers Away At Last Minute," *The Onion* (5/11/09).	veering away at last minute	vice of cowardice; because it was a pansy-ass, pussy, weak-ass little bitch when it should not have been. It should have had the courage to strike the Earth.
"Loved Ones Recall Local Man's Cowardly Battle With Cancer," *The Onion* (2/24/99).	the local man's reaction: "I am not going to fight this. I am a dead man."	vice of cowardice; because when he found out about the cancer, he should have been courageous. He should have dug "deep down inside and tapped into some tremendous well of courage and strength [he] never knew [he] had," but he did not.
"Asshole Even Shoots Pool Like An Asshole," *The Onion* (1/15/03).	shooting pool like an asshole, acting like an asshole, talking like an asshole, singing like an asshole, whispering like an asshole	vice of over-confidence, boastfulness; because whenever asshole sinks a shot, he blows on his pool cue and then puts it back in its invisible holster.
"Christ Kills Two, Injures Seven In Abortion-Clinic Attack," *The Onion* (11/25/98).	killing innocents	vice of recklessness; he's supposed to be the Son of God and Bringer of Peace, for Christ's sake!
"Fifth Level Of Video Game Reached During Phone Call To Mom" *The Onion* (4/11/01).	constant and consistent playing of video games	vice of addiction to video games; although, this situation might just be viewed as healthy multi-tasking

Event or Circumstances	Action or Reaction	Vice and Why It's So
The head gardener's ranting, insulting comments to Rob Arp after he accidentally knocked over a half-ton headstone with a lawnmower while he was working at the cemetery in college (see previous table).	gardener claiming, "Rob, you're a royal fuck-up, how fucking stupid can you be, fuckity fuck fuck, you fucking idiot, etc."	vice of over-doing it with the 'fucks'; insulting, hurtful remarks are not helpful to an impressionable young man, to say the least
One of Rob Arp's high school friends, Jerry, drinking an entire 24-pack of beer and one burrito, then vomiting down a flight of stairs managing to get vomit on every single stair and the wall, too. Then, Jerry claiming afterwards, while sitting in his own vomit, "It must have been a bad burrito."	Jerry drinking too much	vice of addiction to alcohol; it seemed that Jerry managed to vomit on many different things while he was drinking at various parties in high school: stairs, walls, a couch, an end table, some fake flowers, Rex the dog, Angie Sullivan's open-toed shoes, Angie Sullivan's hair, a computer keyboard, the pocket of a winter coat, and there are other things . . .
One of Rob's college friends, Michelle, who had lots of sex with her boyfriend, and got pregnant	vice of self-indulgence,	addiction to sex; too much nookie

This golden mean approach to life can be traced back to the likes of such great thinkers as Aristotle (384–322 B.C.E.) and Confucius (551–479 B.C.E.). In fact, Aristotle and Confucius both thought that a. being self-controlled in one's actions (including language) and b. being a good role model to children were essential for happy, healthy living conditions. I agree.

In All Fucking Seriousness

The Onion is a vehicle for humor meant for adult, rational people who understand the subtleties, complexities, and intricacies of interpersonal relationships in life. Do I want my kids reading *The Onion* or this chapter? Fuck, no! My kids would get confused and think it's okay to start using the F word. I believe that the F word should be used not too much and not too little, in just the virtuous way described already. In fact, I believe there is a strong connection—though, not necessary—between vicious-acting people and vicious-speaking people who swear all the time. A great example of this comes from the play and movie, *Glengarry Glen Ross*, written by David Mamet. What a downer! It's the story of Chicago real estate agents—all white guys, by the way, so that we don't think I'm just picking on the black guys here in this chapter with the gansta rap stuff—who stoop to bribery, intimidation, threats, and theft to make sales. These fuckers are scumbag dregs of the Earth, no doubt. It's also a movie that stands out in my mind because of the number of "fucks" and "fuck yous" these guys utilize. It's as if being vicious dirtbags and foul-mouthedness necessarily go hand-in-hand. Of course, they don't; but, in my experience oftentimes they do—as I am sure is the case for you, the reader, too—and there may even be some research to back this up.

So, in the end I think that not only *is* it the case that a well-placed 'fuck' in *The Onion* makes us laugh because we do not normally hear the F-word and it's taboo, but I also think that it *should be* the case that *The Onion keep on* producing articles including well-placed 'fucks'. Well-placed 'fucks' are funny precisely because so many people don't use the word and think it's taboo. If there comes a point where people don't find the word taboo, then I'm sure there will be some other word horrible, terrible, unthinkable, vicious word that people will put it in its place, like 'republican' or 'bush' as in: "He totally republicaned me over by charging me too much," or "Go bush yourself, you bushing prick!"

Note, again, that I am pushing for well-placed 'fucks'. We should be as virtuous in our usage of the F word as we are about other words and actions. Not too much fuck-talk, but also not too little, either. The Jay Z kind of 'fuck' utilized virtually every other word = not funny, and vicious. *The Onion* kind of 'fuck' utilized in the following way: "All Y'All Urged To Go Fuck Yo' Selves" = funny and—as counter-intuitive as it sounds—virtuous.

5

What It Is to Be an Asshole

CHRISTOPHER HALLQUIST

Though best-known for the fake news on its front page, *The Onion* also runs media reviews and the advice column "Savage Love" by Dan Savage. The column is based out of the Seattle weekly *The Stranger,* which he also edits, but *The Onion* is what brings "Savage Love" to hundreds of thousands of people outside of Seattle, including the residents of Madison, Wisconsin, where the *Onion* began as a newspaper in 1988, and where I am currently studying philosophy.

Savage Love gives serious advice—often through sarcasm and extreme profanity. This includes frequent statements on who is an asshole, referring not only to individuals, but also to groups, including claims about what makes one an asshole:

[BL]? You know, everyone in the advice biz kicks the crap out of straight guys who say, 'Hey, if she lets me fuck her without protection and I get her pregnant, well, that's her problem.' From Ann Landers to the lowliest high-school guidance counselor, we advice-givers are always telling young straight girls that these guys are users and losers and assholes . . . HIV-positive gay men who say, 'Hey, if he lets me fuck him and I infect him, well, that's his problem' are users and losers and assholes too, and it's time for responsible gay men to start calling these assholes on their shit. (9/13/01)

- Anyone who expects his wife—or his husband—to refrain from aging or changing over the years is an asshole. (11/22/07)

- Hitting on a friend is an asshole move that's been used and abused by gay men, straight men, and the odd woman. (9/14/06)

- He takes your money, tells you he wants 'fresh pussy', and won't wear a condom? That makes him an ASSHOLE. (4/6/00)

- Does he pressure you to get with the whole girl-girl-guy program? Is he constantly whining about how much he misses having one girl sit on his face while another sits on his dick? If the answers to these questions are yes, yes, and yes, then he's an asshole and you should dump him immediately. (5/20/04)

- Someone who expresses understandable feelings of contempt by actually hurting or terrifying or abusing a sex partner, is a foot-wide, shit-smeared *asshole*. (4/21/04)

Dan also treats someone's status as an asshole as a fact that can be revealed or discovered:

- But bear in mind, of course, that Jennifer was lying when she told your wife she would have appreciated it if someone had told her what an asshole her ex-husband was before the wedding. (8/23/01)

- You met a guy, you went on a date, you had sex, and he turned out to be an asshole. (4/15/99)

- If the dumped person determines that fault lies with the asshole ex, the dumped person resolves to be on the lookout for telltale signs of assholery in the future. (6/5/08)

- The guy you were dating was an ASSHOLE, and it's unfortunate that he didn't make that clear before you got good and drunk and ate pussy for him. (10/26/00)

Similarly, Dan once printed a letter describing a situation and then asking who the asshole was in that situation.

Last, he treats assholery as having potential explanatory power:

- . . . being an asshole, he wrote me an angry response (6/15/00).

- Whether or not people who lose their virginities under similar circumstances will feel good or bad about them years later depends on a whole host of factors—including whether they were ready and whether the older person was an asshole. (7/1/04)

- Unless you're on the football team you can't be a total asshole and expect to get much in the way of ass. (11/18/99)

- I also sent my phone number and asked him to give me a call. Because, you see, I'm not a total asshole. (11/22/07)

All this is a bit puzzling. Normally, curse words come as emotional ejaculations: "damn," "hell," "shit," or "fuck," when something bad happens, "fuck you," "fuck off" or "bullshit" when we need to tell someone off, and "asshole" when someone cuts you off in traffic. They can also act as colorful pronouns, in "this asshole" and "the little fucker." In those cases, the phrases are just substitutes for "he" or "she," with some negative emotion thrown in. In all the examples above, though, the word "asshole" does something more: instead of just expressing emotion, it seems to act as a real property, of the sort that can be discovered and explain things. What's going on?

Asshole Morality

This chapter isn't just about assholery. In the first quote above, Dan compares himself to Ann Landers. Since Ann never used the term "asshole," Dan must be saying that his use of the term is equivalent to things she said. And this seems true, even if we can't pin down the equivalence word for word. Dan's claims about assholery have the ring of moral pronouncements.

When we wonder about asshole-facts, how we might discover them, and what they could explain, we wonder things philosophers have wondered about morality. People frequently wonder whether morality is objective, and some claim that it is. Philosophers call the view that moral claims can be true in the straightforward way claims about satirical newspapers, advice columnists, or human genitalia can be true "moral objectivism." An alternative to moral objectivism is non-cognitivism according to which moral statements can't be true or false. For the non-cognitivist, morality is in the same category as questions (such as "How do we deal with this situation?"), commands (such as Dan's catchphrase, "dump the motherfucker already"), exclamations ("fuck you!"), and promises (such as "*I promise* not to drop his pics over Nazi-occupied Europe," which can't technically be true or false because a promise made in bad faith is still a promise).

Non-cognitivism comes in a couple specific varieties. Prescriptivism says moral claims are commands. So, if I say, "Cheating is wrong," what I mean is "Don't cheat!" Expressivism says moral claims express emotions or attitudes. Philosophers sometimes explain expressivism by saying that "Cheating is wrong" is equivalent to saying "Cheating! Boo!" But only lame-ass philosophers use the term "Boo!" A better explanation:

> Cheating! Fuck that shit!

Or, as the great twentieth century logician Alfred Ayer suggested:

> John cheated, and was wrong to do so" equals "John cheated" said "in a peculiar tone of horror, or written it with the addition of some special exclamation marks.[1]

While many think morality objective, expressivism seems more natural for talk about assholery, so we're going to take a close look at expressivism and alleged puzzles about it.

What I'm Not Saying about Assholes (or, What Expressivism Isn't)

Moral objectivism is the conservative, grown-up view. In opposing moral objectivism, expressivism carves out rebel territory for itself. But expressivism differs from other rebel views.

Expressivism isn't nihilism. Nihilism says the truth about morality is that there's no such thing as morality, just as the truth about magical bisexual girls who show up for threesomes and then disappear is that there's no such thing as magical bisexual girls who show up for threesomes and then disappear.

Expressivism also isn't subjectivism. T he difference between expressivism and subjectivism can be understood in this way: Dan,

---

[1] Alfred J. Ayer, *Language, Truth, and Logic* (1936).

a gay man, once remarked that a vagina looks to him like "a canned ham dropped from a great height." This statement might have been false, for example, if Dan were a closeted heterosexual and did not in fact think that vaginas look like canned hams dropped from a great height. Therefore, Dan's statement was subjective. An expressive statement, in contrast, is neither true nor false. There would have been no chance of Dan saying anything false had he simply said "vaginas: eeww, gross."

A Canned Ham Dropping from a Great Height

Expressivism makes better sense of assholery than nihilism or subjectivism. If I say "Dan Savage is an asshole," it doesn't make sense to say that I said something false because I actually like him, or because lots of other people like him, or something like that. The sentence expresses an attitude towards him; it doesn't make a true-or-false claim about what attitude anyone has.

Asshole Logic

Consider this argument:

1. All men look at porn.

2. Socrates is a man.

3. Therefore, Socrates looks at porn.

A logician would emphasize that these three statements are related in that if the first two are true, the third has to be true. This reasoning works best if we understand all three statements in a very literal way. It breaks down if, say, we use "all" to mean "almost all," which happens a lot in ordinary speech. Dan often says that all men look at porn, but he has also said that he himself doesn't like porn.

The study of truth based logic is a highly developed field, with special notation and technical jargon, overlapping with mathematics, and with math-like textbooks. From its lofty heights, some philosophers have said logic, in their sense, requires truth. If a statement can't be true or false (or "truth-apt," in philosopher-speak), it can't be subject to logic. Since moral statements can be subject to logic, they must be truth-apt, so non-cogntivists are wrong.

A similar argument could be applied to expressivism about assholery. Consider:

1. **Anyone who expects his wife—or her husband—to refrain from aging or changing over the years is an asshole.**

2. **You expect your wife to refrain from aging or changing over the years.**

3. **Therefore, you are an asshole.**

This is a logical inference much like the Socrates example. It works. Does that mean it must be possible for the statements involving assholery to be truth-apt?

No. Consider this imaginary exchange with an advice columnist, based on an example given by the Australian philosopher Peter Singer:[2]

COLUMNIST: Either get over your insecurities or dump him.

READER: I can't get over my insecurities. So what should I do?

COLUMNIST: So dump him! Couldn't you figure that out from my previous advice, and the fact that you can't get over your insecurities?

---

[2] Peter Singer, "Response," in *Singer and His Critics* (Blackwell, 1999).

READER: No I couldn't, because logic requires that statements be truth-apt.

This is absurd. Obviously we can apply logic to commands, even though commands aren't truth apt. The same applies to attitudes. If someone expresses a negative attitude towards cheaters, and John is a cheater, then in a sense the someone has a negative attitude towards John. Attitudes and commands can also conflict, showing they are subject to logical analysis even though they are neither true nor false.

In ethics, this sort of response doesn't totally satisfy critics of non-cognitivism, because, while we can find examples of command and attitude logic, they haven't been formalized in detail the way truth-based logic has. Logicians are just beginning to study commands, and I don't know of any formal work on the logic of attitudes. Still, it seems logic can be applied to statements that aren't truth-apt, even if the details aren't always clear.

Who's the Asshole?

A second objection to moral non-cognitivism is that we talk about morality as if it involved facts we can discover, ask, disagree about. This goes for assholery as well. Recall, for example, the reader who asked Dan "Who's the asshole?" So, moral disagreement seems to prove moral objectivism true after all: moral statements, including statements about assholery, must be either true or false.

In order to respond to this objection, moral non-cognitivists need to show that moral disagreement is just a difference in attitude. The problem with this claim is that it seems to render moral arguments trivial, much like arguing about whether Asian girls or white girls are hotter. But is difference in attitude trivial? On the contrary, differences of attitude can be hard to set aside for practical reasons: disagreements about everything from blowjobs to condom use to exercise can threaten a sexual or romantic relationship, and the problem doesn't suddenly lessen if the disagreement is "merely" in attitude. Sometimes we want badly to resolve differences in attitudes.

Wanting to resolve differences is different than actually doing so, do how do we do it? By any means necessary. cMoreover, it's not clear that moral disagreement is as factual as it is supposed to be. Ayer went so far as to assert that so-called moral debate is an illusion: our attitudes are fixed by education and we can't debate them. Here he went too far: if teachers can influence the attitudes of their students, adults can influence each other's attitudes. Sometimes our tactics will *resemble* arguments about facts (like when we point out inconsistent attitudes as we would inconsistent beliefs), sometimes they won't. There's no deep mystery.

One method for resolving disputes, of course, is to ask a third party, and this is what the reader who asked Dan "Who's the asshole?" was doing. We have some control over our attitudes, so "should I let myself get upset over this?" is a sensible question to ask an advice columnist. If "asshole" expresses an attitude, then the question "who's the asshole?" serves a similar role as the question "should I let myself get upset over this?" Getting a columnist's advice on assholery can also be useful because it can provide a generally accepted, if somewhat arbitrary, standard for coordinating our lives. I suspect *Savage Love* fills just this role for the college students who read it religiously.

Asshole Revelations

There's one final objection against non-cognitivism worth considering. What about the question of whether to tell your friend that her husband is an asshole, or let her discover it for herself? This question seems entirely legitimate, and its legitimacy seems to imply that whether one is an asshole or not is a fact. If assholery is a fact, then so is any moral judgment, and moral objectivism is true.

We can make sense of this question, however, without appealing to objective asshole-facts if we recognize that people tend to share attitudes to some extent. If all your friends think your husband is an asshole, you likely will too, at least after the honeymoon is over. Also, while talk about assholery is a matter of attitudes, it puts the focus on behavior: when you discover that your husband is an asshole, you not only take a different attitude towards his current behavior, you also re-evaluate his past behavior. In contrast, if your husband becomes an asshole, he's the one whose behavior and personality traits have changed while your general attitudes stay the same.

I Do This because I'm an Asshole

The way asshole-talk puts the focus on behavior suggests a modified sort of expressivist theory of assholery: assholery is a category of behavior, but its boundaries are defined expressivistically, by attitudes. This modification helps with a couple final puzzles.

If you're with a group of friends and Justin declares Joe is an asshole after everyone's seen what Joe's been doing, you get information about Justin's attitudes. But if you know nothing about Joe and Justin tells you he's an asshole, you aren't just getting Justin's attitude. Probably, you can get some idea of what Joe is like. You know there's a good but not certain chance that you'll think he's an asshole too after meeting him. This is because assholery-talk, while indicating the attitude of the speaker, also picks out a certain range of behavior that is in turn defined by our attitudes.

Expressivism also answers the question of how asshole-status can explain anything, like someone's having written an angry response or being unable to get ass without being on the football team. The parallel case from moral philosophy is the problem of how the existence of evil could explain, say, the Holocaust if evil is just a matter of our attitudes. In these cases, it's the behavior, not the attitude, that does the explaining, but the attitude is what gets the behavior classified as amoral or assholish.

If someone says "He did that because he's an asshole," then, you have several ways to disagree: you might disagree about what was done, or take a different attitude towards it, or disagree about the person's personality in general, or take a different attitude towards the general personality. You might completely agree about how the person's personality led to the act, take a negative attitude towards the act, and yet take a positive attitude towards the overall personality. In that case, you might say something like "he's not really an asshole, it's just that that time he went too far and acted like an asshole." The one thing you can't do, contrary to what an asshole-subjectivist would say, is say that "he did that because he's an asshole" is false because it doesn't reflect the speaker's true attitudes, or because it doesn't reflect the attitudes of some group.

More Asshole Morality

Understanding assholery is important because, when it comes to policing each other's conduct, we don't just rely on preachers and academic ethicists who talk about what is moral. We also rely on friends, co-workers, and potty-mouthed advice columnists who talk about what is mean, inconsiderate, inappropriate, skanky, psycho, or assholish. The role of moral pronouncements and pronouncements on these other matters is similar, though perhaps not identical.

We've seen how it makes sense to understand talk about assholes as expressing attitudes. Calling someone an asshole refers to a type of behavior, but it's a type of behavior defined by our attitudes. Disagreements about what makes for assholery are conflicts of attitudes. Does the same go for all morality?

We've seen that the three most common objections to expressivism aren't as strong as they seem at first. The reasoning goes like this: Many common objections to moral expressivism, if right, would also disprove asshole-expressivism. But asshole-expressivism looks right, prior to any philosophical theorizing about it, and it would be surprising if a philosophical argument converted anyone to asshole-objectivism. Therefore, there must be something wrong with those objections to moral expressivism, even if you're not one hundred percent convinced by my explanations of where those objections go wrong. And when we start to think about the arguments from the point of view of analyzing assholery, we can start to see where they go wrong.

The analogy between assholery and morality makes expressivism harder to refute. As a positive argument for moral expressivism, it's a weaker argument. Still, it won't vindicate moral expressivism once and for all. We may find expressivism about asshole-talk intuitive, but we don't find expressivism about moral talk intuitive. The supposed objectivity of morality is a major theme in the Western intellectual tradition, and many people today are deeply troubled by the thought that morality might not be objective. Yes, many in our modern pluralistic society are reluctant to claim their beliefs about controversial moral issues are objectively true, but they embrace objective moral truth about things like terrorism, torture, and female genital mutilation.

So in the end, what we think of this argument depends on how much stock we put in common sense as opposed to formal philosophical questions of logic or truth. The question of whether moral statements are factual may not be easy to answer, but we'll be better able to understand it when we understand what it is to be an asshole.

6

God versus *The Onion*

GREG LITTMANN

SAN FRANCISCO—For as long as he can remember, 7-year-old Timmy Yu has had one precious dream: From the bottom of his heart, he has hoped against hope that God would someday hear his prayer to walk again. Though many thought Timmy's heavenly plea would never be answered, his dream finally came true Monday, when the Lord personally responded to the wheelchair-bound boy's prayer with a resounding no. ("God Answers Prayers Of Paralyzed Little Boy," 12/9/98)

One of the longest-running gags in *The Onion* also happens to be one of the oldest and thorniest philosophical problems, known as the Problem of Evil. How can the existence of God be compatible with the fact that so many terrible things happen? If God exists, why wouldn't He stop bad things from happening? After all, *we* wouldn't just stand by and watch Timmy's suffering if we could cure him with a wave of our hand, so why doesn't God do something to cure kids like Timmy, every single one? Isn't He powerful enough? Doesn't He care?

Timmy isn't the only character from *The Onion* left to suffer by God. "God Outdoes Terrorists Yet Again" announces one headline (9/7/05). The story describes the devastation caused by Hurricane Katrina and the joke is that we condemn terrorists for killing people and destroying buildings, but fail to condemn God when His weather causes even greater destruction. The same joke underlies the story "God Promises 'Big Surprises' In Store For Hurricane Season" (8/21/02): "Get ready for the biggest, wildest, most exciting hurricane season yet," God said. "You'll see all the 200 mph winds, all the flooding, all the overturned cars. As for what else you'll see—well, you'll just have to wait and see."

Other tragic cases of deific neglect are more personal. In the story "Loved Ones Recall Local Man's Cowardly Battle With Cancer" (2/24/99), Judith Kunkel reveals her husband's dying words: "Oh, God—I'm going to die! Why, God, why? Why me? Why not someone else?" In "Jimmy Stewart: 'Please God, I Want to Live Again'" (9/7/97), actor Jimmy Stewart stands on a snow-blown bridge while at the point of death (as in his 1946 film *It's a Wonderful Life*) and shouts to God "Get me back! Get me back! I want to live again!" In the movie, Stewart's character George Bailey is rescued by an angel, but in The *Onion* article, Stewart receives no divine help and perishes.

The *Onion* stories are works of fiction, of course, but it's the truths they reflect that make them funny. Things as tragic as the events reported in *The Onion* happen to people all the time. Children do become crippled like Timmy Yu, people do die of cancer like Russ Kunkel, or of cruel old age like Jimmy Stuart. Hurricanes, not to mention wars, famines and diseases, bring tragedy to whole populations. Humans suffer and perish, regardless of how badly they want to live or how badly they are needed on Earth. Why doesn't God help?

Of course, there are plenty of people who believe that they *have* been helped by God. However, that doesn't explain why there are people who have *not* been spared from tragedy. Consider the story "God Wastes Miracle On Running Catch In Outfield" (5/29/08). We are told "Rather than use His almighty power to breathe life back into the 130,000 people who perished in the Myanmar cyclone, rebuild an earthquake-destroyed China, or bring a lasting peace to the Middle East, the Lord God wasted a divine miracle Monday by granting Angels centerfielder Torii Hunter the ability to make a dramatic but otherwise routine running catch in the outfield." The satirical point of the story is that even if God does sometimes intervene in people's lives, that doesn't explain why He hasn't raised the dead of Myanmmar, or rebuilt China, or brought peace to the Middle East, nor why he allows awful things like cyclones, earthquakes and wars to occur in the first place. As pointed out by "Christianity Celebrates One Billionth Unanswered Prayer" (1/22/97) there seem to be a lot of ways that God could help out but doesn't.

The Problem of Evil Argument Against the Existence of God

WASHINGTON, DC—The six-millennia-old sky-father deity Yahweh, worshiped by Christians, Muslims and Jews alike for His alleged all-knowing compassion and vast benevolence toward humanity, refused comment following Monday's announcement that the U.S. Justice Department will investigate allegations of failure on His part to provide for His approximately 3.5 billion human followers. ("Lord Under Investigation For Failure To Provide," 7/23/97)

The problem of evil is often presented in the form of an argument against the existence of God (at least, against the sort of all-knowing, all-good, all-powerful God found in the Christian, Jewish and Muslim traditions). David Hume (1711–1776) famously made this argument in Parts 10 and 11 of his *Dialogues Concerning Natural Religion*. Here's the executive summary of Hume's argument:

1. **God, if He exists, is all-knowing, all-good and all-powerful.**

2. **Bad things happen.**

3. **If God doesn't know about the bad things, then He can't be all-knowing.**

4. **If God doesn't have the power to prevent the bad things, then He can't be all-powerful.**

5. **If God knows about the bad things but doesn't want to prevent them, then He can't be all-good.**

6. **Therefore, God does not exist.**

If the argument is a good one, then we should accept that God doesn't exist. You will, of course, have to make up your own mind.

Some people would challenge premise 1, which states, "God, if He exists, is all-knowing, all-good and all-powerful." If God can exist without being all three of these things, then the Problem of Evil may evaporate.

For example, the Problem of Evil is clearly solved if God is not all-knowing, as in the news story "God Returns From 2,000 Year Vacation" (11/8/08) in which He has to be "brought up to speed" on the events of the past two millennia by Jesus. This God never

God-Man:
The superhero with omnipotent powers

knew about World War I, for instance, and so was not in a position to prevent it. The same solution applies in the news story "God Wondering Whatever Happened To That Planet Where He Made All Those Monkeys" (10/18/00). If God hasn't "thought about that planet in forever," then he doesn't know about the evil occurring on Earth. An equally ignorant God solves the problem of evil in "Aging God Fitted For Omni-Focals" (4/17/07) in which optotheologist Bradley Smurner explains "He was more and more smiting the wrong people."

The problem of evil could also be solved if God were not entirely good, as in the news story "God To Use Powers For Evil" (12/22/07). If God had decided to be a bad person, then that would definitely explain how there come to be bad things in the world. The problem is solved the same way in "God Diagnosed With Bipolar Disorder" (5/2/01). If God is indeed acting in accordance with the wild mood swings of manic depression rather than in accordance with absolute goodness, then that too would explain why the world has bad things in it. Again, in "Israelites Sue God For Breach Of Covenant" (2/23/00) the explanation for the historical suffering of Jews is that God was simply ignoring his promises "with a blatant and willful disregard," while in "Area Man Will Remember Unanswered Prayer Next Time God Needs His Help" (6/6/06) account executive Scott Fields accuses God of having forgotten "that devotion is a two-way street."

Lastly, the problem of evil could also be solved if God is not all-powerful, as in the news story "God Late For Local Wedding" (12/11/02). This is a God who simply doesn't have the abilities required to deal with all the world's problems. He complains that "It's really hard to keep it all straight sometimes" and "I really would have made it on time if I hadn't been stupid enough to rely on that map Patrick included in the invitations. It was barely readable." The problem of evil is solved the same way in "Christ Announces Hiring Of Associate Christ" (5/6/98) in which Jesus admits "I've been in need of an Assistant Savior for a long time now." Similarly, in "Christ Demands More Money" (10/7/97) Jesus complains "In my Father's house are many mansions. They are not cheap to maintain" while in "God Recalls Tracheas Of Millions of Indonesians" (2/23/07), God is forced to make amends for His imperfect handiwork. The God in these stories is a puny deity, as bound by limitations as we are, and quite inadequate to the task of eliminating all the evils of the world.

An Imperfect God?

Despite the seriousness of the charges, many believers remain loyal to the embattled deity. "I know it seems like the worst thing ever," said Lynette Maddox, a Flatwoods, KY, manicurist and mother of nine, "but we just have to trust that it's all part of God's plan." ("Lord Under Investigation For Failure To Provide," 7/23/97)

People in the real world have also avoided the Problem of Evil by accepting divine imperfection. Most ancient cultures believed in gods who were imperfect. Osiris, Egyptian god of the afterlife, didn't know everything, not foreseeing that his brother Set was planning to trap him in a box. Venus, Roman goddess of love, was not all-good, cheating in a divine beauty contest by promising the judge another man's wife. Enki, Sumerian god of water, was not all-powerful, being unable to cure himself of poisoning from strange plants he ate. It wouldn't be hard to explain why a universe ruled by limited deities like these would have evil in it. The evils of the world might be too many for them to keep track of or too hard for them to deal with, or the gods might just not particularly care. Nineteenth-century English philosopher John Stuart Mill took a similar approach. He accepted that the imperfection of the universe demonstrates that there is no all-good, all-powerful God. However, he thought that there was some evidence for the existence of a lesser deity, one who has great but limited power.[1]

While accepting that God has limited power or goodness would solve the Problem of Evil, it isn't a solution that many monotheists like. It's generally considered to be an essential feature of the God of Christianity, Islam, and Judaism that His knowledge, power and goodness are unlimited, that "something" without these attributes *just wouldn't be God.* If it is part of what you mean by "God" that the individual so named is all-knowing, all-powerful and all-good, then you will have to accept premise 1. If God, in this sense, exists, then there must be some other flaw in the argument.

Some people would challenge the argument on premise 2, "Bad things happen." Christian Scientists, for instance, believe that evil is an illusion. Not only are "moral evils," like sin, unreal on this view, but so are "natural evils" like disease (www.christianscience.com).

Speaking for myself, I can't buy that suffering is not real. If we know that anything exists, we know that suffering exists. If you have ever felt pain, or sadness, or fear, then you know that suffering is real. After all, suffering is an experience, and if there is anything we can be sure of, it is what we personally experience. Even if it is possible that we are hallucinating the things that are *making* us suffer (the paper cuts, broken legs and other such calamities of life), there's no question that these are at least *painful* hallucinations.

Furthermore, if suffering exists, then I think it's clear that evil exists too; if there is anything we know is bad, it is suffering. *Onion* news-stories like "Poverty-Stricken Africans Receive Desperately Needed Bibles" (3/13/06), "Horrific 120-Car Pileup A Sad Reminder of Princess Diana's Death" (5/24/08), and "Shaggy Dog Too Late To Cheer Up Dying Boy" (4/22/98) are darkly funny exactly because the situations they describe are so awful. They describe the world

---

[1] *Three Essays on Religion: Nature, the Utility of Religion, Theism* (Prometheus Books, 1998).

as it should *not* be, even if it so often *is*. Certainly, if suffering is not bad, then God's goodness would give Him no reason to spare us unnecessary suffering. In other words, if there is nothing wrong with human suffering, then there is no moral reason for Him not to torture us with plagues and famines just for fun.

God's Goodness

JERUSALEM—In what theological and meteorological authorities are calling "a wrathful display of Old Testament proportions," the Lord Almighty re-flooded the Middle East Tuesday, making good on last week's threat to wipe the region clean if there was not an immediate halt to the bloodshed between Arabs and Jews. ("God Re-Floods Middle East," 5/1/02)

Many people would challenge premise 5 of the argument, "If God knows about the bad things but doesn't want to prevent them, then He can't be all-good." This seems to be the premise that God Himself rejects in the news story "God Wastes Miracle On Running Catch In Outfield" (5/29/08). God explains "I know many of My children believe My omnipotence would be better spent in ways other than affecting the contest between the Los Angeles Angels of Anaheim and Detroit Tigers, and truth be told, there is a possibility Mr. Hunter would have made that catch on his own. But it was a very close game that the Angels really deserved to win." This is a God who knows of the world's problems, but feels justified in His actions all the same.

We find a similar deity depicted in "God Damns Minnesota Vikings As Requested" (9/6/00), "God Promises Big Surprises In Store For Hurricane Season" (8/21/02), and "God Savoring Vast Array Of Cubs-Cursing Options" (10/2/08). God makes His reasoning explicit in "God Wondering If He's Being Too Cruel in Allowing Cavaliers To Reach NBA Finals" (6/7/07). He states "Although I move in mysterious ways, and in doing so often allow bad things to happen to good people, My grand design is usually glorious to behold. But the Cavs in the Finals . . . I don't know, maybe that's just plain mean." This is a God who admits that he allows bad things to happen to good people, but justifies it as a necessary part of the grand design.

Plenty of philosophers have thought that God's goodness does not require that He rid the world of all evils. One popular defense

to the problem of evil argument is known as the "free will defense."
According to the free will defense, God could only rid the world of
evil by taking away human free will, which is too valuable to sacrifice. To take a theoretical example, God could have avoided the
"brutal mass slaying" in which a mentally disturbed man shot seventeen men, women, and children, as reported in "Sports Unable
To Heal Small Town Following Tragedy" (6/28/07). However,
according to the free will defense, God could only prevent the
shootings by taking away the gunman's free will to choose
between good and evil, which God shouldn't do. In other words,
because it's important that the gunman be allowed to choose
between doing good and doing evil, God must allow the gunman
the freedom to do evil things like kill innocent people.

I don't find the free will defense convincing. While it may be
true that it is good for people to have free will, it seems less plausible that the need for free exercise of the will outweighs the need
not to be horribly harmed (like shot). In fact, our society employs
police forces and armies specifically to make sure that people are
not allowed to exercise their free will to harm others. I think that
most of us would be horrified if police offers were instructed not
to interfere with murderous gunmen like the one in the story on
the grounds that it would be wrong to prevent the gunman from
exercising his free will. Why then should it be less horrifying for
God not to interfere on just those grounds?

Besides, so many of the terrible things that happen in the world
don't seem to have a human origin at all. Nature alone provides
humanity with hurricanes, earthquakes, diseases and droughts, not
to mention more personal tragedies like blindness or cancer. The
need for human free will can't explain why God would allow a hurricane to kill innocent people in New Orleans or an earthquake to
kill innocent people in Beijing.

It is true, some theists insist that humans cause even these "natural" tragedies. For instance, the state of the world might be blamed
on Adam and Eve's disobedience in the Garden of Eden. In the
words of the *Onion* sermon "The Holy Woman Knoweth Well Her
Place" (7/9/97), Eve's "Envy, Ambition, and Weakness of the flesh
caused her Expulsion from Eden, and eternal Banishment from an
Earthly Paradise for all of God's Children." Alternatively, humanity
could have lost God's protection because of more recent sins. In
"Israelites Sue God for Breach of Covenant" (2/23/00), the Israelites
charge that God has failed to protect them, but God is considering a

countersuit against the Israelites, claiming that that they "have failed to worship the Lord in an acceptably faithful manner." Could it be that natural evils are permitted by God because of our evil ways?

I don't buy this justification for natural evil. If natural disasters are a result of human action, then in allowing natural disasters, God is allowing innocent human beings to be punished for the actions of others. A baby dying in a flood can't have personally done anything wrong. It cannot be just to give her the death penalty for someone else's crimes, whether they be the crimes of her neighbors or the crimes of Eve. What would we say of a human being who allowed a baby to drown in a flood because her *parents* had done bad things? If it would be wicked for a human to allow a baby to die in that way, how could it be less than wicked for God to allow it? Even when disaster strikes adults, it's as likely to strike the virtuous as the wicked. As pointed out in "Life Unfair" (4/30/97), "Death and suffering continue to be dispersed randomly among the planet's life forms, with such potentially mitigating factors as . . . previous good works in no way taken into account."

Human Moral Development

MIDLAND, TX—Local firefighter Brent Koonce, who saved an infant trapped at the bottom of a 40-foot well Monday, is being roundly hailed by himself as a hero. "What I did was incredibly brave," said Koonce, who descended all the way down the three-foot-wide well to recover eight-month-old Midland resident Melissa Sims. ("Hero Firefighter: 'I'm A Hero'," 09/26/96)

Another justification sometimes offered for God's toleration of evil is that the existence of evil is necessary in order for human beings to develop virtue. For example, it is argued that we could never develop compassion if nobody ever needed our help, we could never develop courage if danger never loomed, and we could never develop perseverance if we never faced adversity. This seems to be the sort of view of God's actions that is held by the brave little brain tumor in "Malignant Tumor Sees Every Day As Gift From God" (7/19/00). The tumor is certain that, despite the impending chemotherapy that will kill it, its suffering must serve a purpose in "God's great plan." The tumor states "just as He did with Job, the Lord is presenting me with these hardships as a way of testing my faith."

I'm not convinced by this defense either. If God is omnipotent, then He should be able to create us with virtues like compassion, courage and perseverance built in, rather than forcing us to undergo harsh experiences to develop them. There doesn't seem to be any reason in principle why it's impossible to have these virtues innately. In fact, it is generally assumed that God Himself has His virtues innately rather than having had to develop them by combating evils.

Of course, it might be objected that simply *having* a virtue isn't enough and that people must have a chance to *act* virtuously, and that *acting* virtuously requires that we confront real evils. So, for example, it might be said that even if we could *have* the virtue of compassion without confronting evils, God must allow horrors like earthquakes and mass murder in order for us to be able to *act* compassionately towards the victims.

You won't be surprised to hear that I'm not convinced by this line of reasoning either. Firstly, it doesn't seem that we need to face *real* evils in order to act with compassion or with any other virtue. Fake evils should work just as well. For example, God doesn't *really* have to let gunmen kill innocent bystanders in order for us to show compassion; He just has to *convince* us that a gunman has killed innocent bystanders—a very simple trick for an omnipotent illusionist. This would, of course, mean that God has to act as a deceiver. However, nature is already full of deception—think of spiders that mimic leaves, and of human dreams and hallucinations—so there can't be a moral requirement that God never allows us to be deceived. Besides, surely deceiving someone can't be as bad as letting innocent people die.

Again, consider the human analogy. Imagine that the police in the story "Sports Unable To Heal Small Town Following Tragedy" had refused to intervene to stop the gunman, on the grounds that, by allowing him to kill as many innocent people as he chose, they were giving other people the opportunity to perform acts of compassion for the survivors. Surely it would be wicked for police to allow such acts for the sake of the compassion they might arouse. So how can it be alright for God to do so?

As for the question of whether it could be better to let people die rather than deceive someone, imagine a human faced with the same moral dilemma. Imagine that the gunman in the news story asks you where the men, women and children he wants to kill are hiding, and you know. Could it really be your moral duty not to lie to him, on the grounds that it is wrong to be a deceiver? It seems much more plausible to me that it is your moral duty to lie if that is the only way to save seventeen people's lives. I don't see on what grounds we could say that God's moral duty is any different.

The Impossibility of a Perfect World

Christ told followers that his ancient covenant with humanity—in which He shall act as the people's shepherd, comfort them with His rod and staff, and shelter them all the days of their lives—is as good a value as they are likely to find anywhere. ("Christ Demands More Money," 10/7/97)

One ingenious explanation of how God could share a universe with evil is that only imperfect universes are possible. Some have argued, for instance, that no matter how good God makes life for His creations, it would always be logically possible for things to be better. In other words, however God created the world, there would always be room for improvement, so the fact that we find room for improvement in the universe proves nothing.

We might illustrate this argument by considering human happiness. If there is an omnipotent God, then He could have made you twice as happy as you are. But if He did, the question would arise as to why He didn't make you twice as happy as that, and if he *did*, the question would arise as to why He didn't make you twice as happy as *that*, and so on infinitely. No matter how happy He makes you, it would always have been possible for Him to have made you happier. Thus, according to this argument, God can't have a moral duty to make you so happy that you couldn't possibly be happier, because there is no such state. For the same reason, God can't have a moral duty to make the world so good that it couldn't be better; there simply is no such state. So, even though He could have made our world better than it is, that doesn't mean that He has failed in any of his moral duties.

I don't buy this defense either. After all, if this lets God off the hook when He fails to help someone, why does the same reasoning not let the rest of us off the hook when we fail to help someone? Consider the news story "I Bet I Wouldn't Be Laughing So Hard If It Was Me In That Fire" (1/24/01). The reporter muses on the nature of humor and entertainment, making no move to help, as he watches a man burn in the fire of an automobile accident.

The story is blackly funny because the reporter's behavior is so morally offensive, yet the reporter could offer a defense of his actions along the lines of the one just offered for God. After all, no matter how much the reporter improves the world, he could presumably always improve it just a little bit more by trying even harder. But this defense is no defense. The fact that the reporter could always have done more good in the world does not excuse him for standing by and allowing a human being to burn. When the reporter fails to help, he isn't simply failing to be as good as he can; he's failing to meet even the most basic standard of decency.

It might be insisted that human beings, limited creatures that we are, really *do* have a specific maximum amount of good that we can do in the world. Even if that is so, though, that couldn't give us a higher standard of moral duty to live up to than God has. If a weak human has a moral duty to help a burning man, how can this duty not be shared by an infinitely powerful God? In particular, how could the very fact that God is *so* powerful, that changing the world is *so* easy for Him, mean that He has less duty to help than you or I, for whom helping a burning man entails strain and danger?

Moving in Mysterious Ways

Gurshner said he does not know why God "came to [him] in a dream" and asked him to kidnap Ford, but he said he believes that "it is best not to question His motives." "I didn't question the Lord when He struck down my beloved wife Emily with cervical cancer," Gurshner said. "I didn't question Him when I was dismissed from my job and put on Social Security. I didn't question Him when He commanded me to dig a three-foot ditch around my house and fill it with charcoal briquettes, and I don't question him now." ("God's Plan For Area Man Involves Kidnapping Ford CEO," 5/18/05)

There's one final objection to the Problem of Evil argument that I want to consider, what we might call the "mystery defense." It is not an objection to any particular premise of the argument, but to the whole idea of trying to work out if God's existence is compatible with the evil in the world. According to the mystery defense, God is too mysterious for us to hope to comprehend the justifications for His actions. In other words, we may not be able to understand why God tolerates evil, but this gives us no reason to doubt

God's existence since we should not expect to be able to comprehend the ways of God.

Again, I don't think we should buy the defense, and again, *The Onion* should help demonstrate why. Probably the blackest humor I have ever seen in *The Onion* is in "God Cites 'Moving In Mysterious Ways' As Motive In Killing Of 3,000 Papua New Guineans" (7/29/98). Questioned about a Tsunami that killed three thousand people, God calls the disaster "part of My unknowable, divine plan for mankind . . . Though the need for such a tidal wave is incomprehensible to you mortals, flawed as you are by sin, I can assure you that I had a very good reason for what I did." The reporter notes that God's "unknowable purposes have necessitated, among other things, the death of 40 million Europeans from the Bubonic Plague, 40,000 Peruvians in a 1868 earthquake, and six million of His chosen people in Nazi concentration camps."

What this news story points out is that the mystery defense against the problem of evil argument is a cop out. To reply to the problem of evil by saying that the truth is beyond our comprehension is not to answer the problem of evil at all. If we say that the truth is unknowable any time we don't like the direction in which reason leads us, then reason is useless. If it isn't satisfactory to reply "the truth is beyond our comprehension" when facing questions like "are cigarettes bad for you?", "can humans breathe underwater?" and "is it safe to drive drunk?", then why should it be satisfactory to reply "the truth is unknowable" when thinking about God? If we think it is important to follow reason when dealing with the first three subjects, why would it not be important to follow reason when we come to one of the most important questions of all? Moreover, if we do decide that the truth about God is incomprehensible, then how can we ever make any confident claims about God's nature, such as that God is trustworthy or kind rather than devious and sadistic?

My conclusion is that there is no all-knowing, all-powerful, all-good God. If there were such a God, there wouldn't be so much evil in the world. Plenty of philosophers disagree with me and there are objections to the problem of evil argument that I have not even raised above. I trust you, as a reader of *The Onion*, to be too suspicious of what you read to let anyone else make up your mind for you. You will just have to think it through for yourself.

Jesus Delays Second Coming Because Of Offensive Article

ROME—Breaking his 2,000-year silence, Jesus spoke out angrily today in response to a chapter in *The Onion and Philosophy* that he claimed was an insult to his family. Jesus said "These remarks were deeply hurtful. The fact is, there was a perfectly good solution to the Problem of Evil and I was just about to announce to you all what it is and it would have been great. You would have loved it. But in light of this '*Onion*' thing, I just don't think humanity is worthy. My Father spent millions of years working towards the big revelation and you spoiled it." Representatives of Jesus have not been available for comment.

Politics

7

Philosophers Interested In Area Man, But Not In Gay Way

DAVID BENATAR

The *Onion*'s Area Man is everyman, the average Joe. His specific identity is so much less remarkable than whatever he is thinking, wanting or doing, that it is his (purported) geographic proximity to the readers—a man in their area—rather than his name that makes *Onion* headlines. This is truly humbling (to the Area Man), given how pedestrian his thoughts, desires, and actions often are. The Area Man is the guy who's "unsure what to do with all the extra ketchup packets." He is the bloke who "wants to throw one good punch in his life" and plans to "try showering at night." If the Area Man were Brad Pitt, the headlines would not refer to "Area Man" but to his name.

News about the Area Man isn't always prosaic. His words and deeds are often eccentric, but his idiosyncrasies are nonetheless those of an ordinary man. For example, he finally finds his "body-mate"—"the one woman whose body he has been looking for all his life." In another report, we are told he's excited that his buddy's getting divorced so that they may resume their friendship.

Even when the Area Man becomes distinctly unusual, as is the case when he is discovered to have "ritually murdered and dis-membered . . . more than two dozen bound and gagged victims" his antics are blandly headlined as "Area Man's quirky hobby kills 27." He is the "mild-mannered," "unassuming" guy next door—the one you never thought capable of the grisly actions you now hear he has committed.

Although philosophers would like to think that they are not average Joes, they have certainly taken an interest in the ordinary man and his opinions. Philosophers don't tend to refer to him as the "average Joe." That's just the sort of plebeian terminology they leave to the average Joe. Instead, philosophers (along with lawyers) refer to him as the "the man in the street," "the man in the jury box," "the reasonable man," the "right-minded man" or, my own personal favourite, "the man on the Clapham omnibus."

American readers, bless them, are likely to ask: "What the fuck is the Clapham omnibus?" An omnibus is a (now) pompous, pommy word for a bus, while Clapham was (before gentrification) a very ordinary south London neighborhood. The man on the Clapham omnibus is your ordinary London commuter. He's the British equivalent of the Area Man, even if the lads have the temerity—the sodding cheek—to name the Area.

Area Philosophers often view the Area Man as a standard or a yardstick. For example, in response to the question "How much caution must we exercise to prevent injury to others?" a common answer is "The degree of caution a reasonable man would exercise."

British Area Man prepares to board the omnibus

The obvious problem with using the ordinary or reasonable man as a standard is that it doesn't seem very helpful. To know what a reasonable man would do, we need to know who the reasonable man is. And to know who the reasonable man is we need to be able to distinguish him from the unreasonable man. But to be able to make that distinction we already need to know what reasonable and unreasonable conduct is.

This is why the image of the man on the Clapham omnibus is thought to be useful. One boards the bus and randomly samples the passengers. Of course, one could chance upon an unusual passenger. But the idea is that if one sampled a number of passengers one would soon work out which people, though on the Clapham omnibus, were not like all the other passengers.

Area Man Flattered To Be Surveyed On Clapham Omnibus

Patrick Devlin was no Area Man. He was also no philosopher. Instead he was a lawyer, then a judge, a law lord, and a baron. But his views about law and morality gave a central place to our Area Man on the Clapham omnibus.

Lord Devlin was peeved at the Wolfenden Commission's Report, published in 1957, which recommended the decriminalization of private consensual homosexual acts. The Wolfenden Commission was of the view that it is not the business of the law to interfere with people's private lives. Lord Devlin, on the other hand, thought that private acts should sometimes be the subject of legal regulation. He claimed that societies are bound together by common moral values and that they disintegrate without those values. Thus, he argued, assaults on a society's shared moral values are analogous to treason and may be prohibited.[1]

What does this have to do with the Area Man? It turns out that the man on the Clapham omnibus was Lord Devlin's key to deciding what a society's moral values are and thus which values may be legally enforced. He argued that if the man on the Clapham omnibus has "a real feeling of reprobation" for some practice, such as "buggery" (as it was then known), then "the bounds of toleration have been reached" and we may punish those who deeply and genuinely disgust the Area Man.

But this is where area philosophers got interested. H.L.A. Hart (Herbert to his friends) was an eminent legal philosopher at Oxford University when Lord Devlin was criticizing the Wolfenden Report. He thought that Lord Devlin's argument was "bollocks," though he was too polite to put it that way.

---

[1] Patrick Devlin, *The Enforcement of Morals* (Maccabaean Lecture, Oxford University Press, 1959).

Professor Hart's jurisprudence was not prudish. He saw no reason to prohibit unusual sexual practices if performed by consenting adults in private. Unwilling to play the Devlin's advocate, he argued that it is Lord Devlin's arguments rather than those of gay rights defenders that are truly queer.[2]

Herbert Hart noted that Lord Devlin's argument, if sound, would apply as much to those societies that are bound together by really wicked values as it would to those societies that are bound together by noble values. It could be invoked to justify the enforcement of Nazi morality in Nazi Germany because Nazi values bound that society together. If Herr Area (Aryan?) Mensch in 1942 has a deep feeling of reprobation for Aryan-Jewish sex, then the law would, on Lord Devlin's view, be warranted in prohibiting it.

Because this implication is absurd, Professor Hart's view is that a society's common values cannot simply be accepted without question. Area men can be prejudiced bigots and they ought not to be the arbiters of what the law should permit others to do.

Professor Hart also argued that there's a difference between the disintegration and the transformation of a society. Even if a society is bound together by some common moral values, a society's values can still change over time without that society disintegrating. Area Man and his son may have overlapping but not identical views. The things that disgust the one may not disgust the other. As one generation of Area Men become Area Stiffs and a generation of Area Babies become Area Men, the society's values may change.

A society can be transformed from religiously intolerant and racially prejudiced to tolerant and egalitarian without the society's collapsing. Given this, Lord Devlin is mistaken in thinking that the transgression of a society's conventional morality is equivalent to treason.

Area Man Confused

Lord Devlin seems to have assumed that the Area Man on a late-1950s Clapham omnibus would have a deep repugnance for homosexual acts. It's not clear that he was correct. No doubt some Area Men did have such repugnance. But other Area Men seem to have had a different view. The Wolfenden Commission was established

---

[2] Herbert Hart, "Immorality and Treason," *The Listener* (30th July, 1959).

partly in response to significant public disdain for the prosecution, conviction, and sentencing to jail time of a number of prominent men for private consensual "homosexual offences."

Today, Area Men are generally much more tolerant (unless they are men from an area spanning most of the Middle East and Africa as well as parts of Asia). However, even some *tolerant* Area Men are ambivalent.

An *Onion Radio News* broadcast reports that Area Man, Ben Tersch, who works the evening shift at Yankee Doodles, feels guilty for hating gay co-worker, Terrence Paulson. Mr. Tersch, who says that he "doesn't give a rat's ass if Paulson wants to do it with other guys" said: "I feel terrible but every time he lets out that shrieking laugh of his, I have this awful urge to brain him with a bottle of Jim Beam." He added that he is "more than willing to give Paulson another chance if he would just stop addressing all of his co-workers as 'girls'." This Area Man, it seems is a potential gay-basher, even if a somewhat reluctant one.

Other Area Men, it turns out, have engaged in Area Man-on-Man sex. In one report we are told that an "Area Man Has Sex With Man To Get Out Of Office Blood Drive." He's squeamish about needles and wants to be able answer truthfully when the nurse asks whether he has "participated in any high-risk sexual activity recently." (A more prudent area man would have chosen the lesser of the two pricks.) He then tells reporters that "he intends to have sex with another man next week to get out of his office's canned food drive."

In another report we are told that an Area Man has been experimenting with homosexuality for the past eight years. During this period the "99 percent straight" man has had twenty-three male sexual partners and one female partner. His girlfriend from his pre-experimental phase reports that, unlike so many other guys she dated, he was always very supportive of her wanting to wait until marriage.

These *Onion* reports about the Area Man contribute to the Hart-Devlin debate, lending support to Herbert rather than to Patrick. They reveal the great diversity of views and preferences of Area Men. If we assume Lord Devlin was correct that Area Men in his time had a deep sense of reprobation for gay sex, then there has been a notable transformation. Many Area Men today don't "give a rat's ass" about men doing it with one another. (Area Rat, it should be mentioned, may be very keen not to give his own ass to a gay rat, but might not give an "Area Man's ass" if two gay rats want to do it together.)

Yet Britain, America, and other such countries did not disintegrate in order for these changes to occur. The American Revolution, for example, was not in the late twentieth century but rather in the late eighteenth, and although it was a revolt against a king, the aim was not to replace him with a queen. The battles of the Georges (King George and George Washington) were not about George-on-George sex.

In other words, the only American Revolution was not a gay revolution. Thus to the extent that America, for example, has undergone a change of attitude regarding private homosexual sex between consenting adults, this has not involved the disintegration of America and the creation, from its ashes, of a new America. Herbert Hart was correct that transgressing conventional morality is not equivalent to treason.

Area Feminist Angry

All this talk of the Area *Man*, not to mention the *man* on the Clapham omnibus, the *man* in the street or in the jury box, or the reasonable *man* is enough to make Area Feminist spitting mad. Contrary to widespread rumors, many feminists like men. Some even *love* men. They just don't like people making the assumption that a man is the norm. For every Norman, there is a Norma and it's not the case that Norman and Norma always agree. While Norman may be disgusted by sex between two men, Norma may not have the same feeling of deep reprobation. While Norman may be turned on by lesbian sex, Norma may not be.

The feminist critique, therefore, is that we are disposed to over-look women and their views when we treat men as the norm. According to feminists, if we are to consult the man on the Clapham omnibus, we must also ask the woman next to whom he is seated. If we listen to the Area Man we should also listen to the Area Woman.

Area feminists won't be comforted to hear that, amidst all his references to men on buses, on streets and in jury boxes, Lord Devlin says that "the moral judgment of society must be something about which twelve men *or women* drawn at random might after discussion be expected to be unanimous" (my italics). Their complaint is that even if one says that the man in the jury box (or on the Clapham omnibus) is representative of the *hu*man, the constant reference to men subconsciously inclines one to think of males and not females.

The *Onion* goes some way to addressing this concern by including many reports about Area Woman. In these stories we hear a different voice. We hear the concerns and perspectives of women. We are told, for example, that "Amazon.com Recommendations Understand Area Woman Better than Husband," that "Childbirth To Be Area Woman's Least Painful Interaction With Daughter" and that "Area Woman Tired Of Men Staring At Her Breast Implants."

Feminists will be quick to note that there are not as many reports about Area Woman as there are about Area Man. And they may well charge the *Onion* with stereotyping Area Woman. (By contrast they are unlikely to accuse the *Onion* of stereotyping Area Man because although what's good for the goose is good for the gander, many feminists don't think that what's bad for the Area Woman must be bad for the Area Man.)

Area Man And Woman Wonder What They Are Good For

Herbert Hart was correct that the disgust of the ordinary man—or woman—is not a suitable basis for prohibiting private consensual acts. Does this mean that the Area Bus Passenger is irrelevant to decisions about what the law may prohibit? Joel Feinberg didn't think so. Professor Feinberg wrote a four-volume work on the moral limits of the criminal law in which he explored what kinds of conduct the law may and may not prohibit. Very early in the second volume, *Offense to Others*, he describes a ride on the bus.[3] (What is it with philosophers and buses?)

He asks the reader to imagine "himself as a passenger on a normally crowded bus on his way to work or to some important appointment in circumstances such that if he is forced to leave the bus prematurely, he will not only have to pay another fare" but will also be significantly inconvenienced. He then asks the reader to imagine various forms of offensive conduct taking place nearby, so that the only way to avoid it is to get off the bus before one has reached one's destination.

The poor Area Passenger is subjected to a fellow traveler who stinks, and who "continually scratches, drools, coughs, farts, and belches." Another passenger wears a swastika armband while others carry various banners that insult Catholics, Jews, blacks, and

---

[3] Joel Feinberg, *Offense to Others* (Oxford University Press, 1985).

women. Still other passengers are eating "live insects, fish heads and pickled sex organs of lamb, veal and pork, smothered in garlic and onions." Later on they eat their own vomit and then their own feces. A woman changes her sanitary napkin and drops the old one in the aisle Some mourners board the bus with a coffin, which they break open and then proceed to smash the corpse's face with a hammer. Various passengers then engage in a range of sexual activities—including masturbation, fellatio, cunnilingus, and, with a pet dog, bestiality.

Professor Feinberg's question is not whether Area Man's disgust is a basis for prohibiting the *private* consensual performance of these actions, but whether the *public* performance of these actions may be prohibited on account of the disgust they cause. He devotes the rest of his book to answering this question. He concludes that some (but not other) kinds of offensive public conduct may be prohibited, but never merely because they are deeply offensive. According to Professor Feinberg, the average person's sentiments are relevant, but by no means decisive, in deciding when we may prohibit the public performance of offensive actions.

His conclusion is not as flattering of the average Joe and Josephine as is Lord Devlin's. Joel Feinberg does not defer to the Area Man or Woman whose offence may result from prejudice or whose sensibilities, if given a veto, would interfere with quite reasonable public conduct on the part of others. At the same time, the sensibilities of the average person cannot be excluded from all consideration. If a couple have sexual intercourse on the Clapham omnibus, the Area Man seated behind them will not be harmed, strictly speaking. He won't, from witnessing this spectacle, get a case of the clap on the Clapham omnibus.

Nevertheless, if the average person is deeply offended at the sight of his fellow passengers engaged in sexual intercourse, it is not unreasonable for the law to rule that, although these people may have sexual intercourse, they may not have it on the bus. It is not unreasonable to ask them to wait until they reach the privacy of their home.

If Joel Feinberg is correct, then the Area Man and Woman are still of interest to the legal philosopher. This interest might not be reciprocal, as all too often, and to society's general detriment, the Area Person gives absolutely no attention to the views of the legal philosopher.

8

Would Diogenes Have Read *The Onion?*

RICK BAYAN

What does the word *cynic* mean to you? A spiteful, calculating, untrustworthy misanthrope? Someone who despises babies, spray-paints graffiti on statues, and sneers at all the nobler public sentiments? In short, a congenital rogue and scoundrel whose very existence poisons the communal drinking well?

If that's your idea of a cynic, you have plenty of company. Our politicians and other public-minded potentates have made a sport of singling out cynics as the common enemy. To them, cynics are the black-hatted villains whose every move reeks of chicanery, underhanded manipulation, expedience, and self-interest. Cynics are the most ungovernable of citizens because they refuse to lead, follow, or get out of the way.

Actually, the last sentence happens to be true. No wonder the people in power habitually demonize cynics. How else does a well-groomed ruling elite control a scruffy, unruly faction of irreverent, irrepressible nonbelievers? The ruling elite can't legally silence these cynics, so it has to do the next best thing: blacken their reputation. The political and corporate panjandrums refuse to acknowledge the fierce moral and ethical component of cynicism. A true cynic opposes sham and hypocrisy with all his wounded heart. The people in power fear cynicism precisely *because* it opposes (and exposes) sham and hypocrisy. "Pay no attention to that man behind the curtain!" the politicians yell while kicking the little dog that pulled the curtain aside.

The Onion has been making life difficult for the ruling elite—and for all the assorted buffoons, cutthroats, mountebanks, and flagrant Darwinian losers in contemporary society—since it went online in 1996. Its roots as a local print publication in Madison, Wisconsin, date back to 1988, though the paper charmingly claims to have been founded in the eighteenth century by one Friedrich Siegfried Zweibel. (*Zweibel* is German for *onion*.)

In case you've been comatose for the past decade or so, *The Onion* is a satirical parody of a newspaper. The headlines hoot absurdities in the familiar language of daily journalism while maintaining a tone of deadpan detachment. "Department of the Exterior Opens US National Park In Norway" (9/26/08), a blithely insane *Onion* headline informs us.

Is *The Onion* a cynical publication? Well, to borrow a convenient semantic evasion from a recent US president, that depends on what your definition of "cynical" is. *The Onion* clearly uses the *tools* of cynicism—mockery, sarcasm, and satire—to skewer its intended targets. But it skewers them without breaking a sweat: no moral outrage in the manner of classic literary cynics like Mark Twain, no rollicking verbal fusillades in the style of twentieth-century American journalist H.L. Mencken. *The Onion* simply holds up a mirror—a warped funhouse mirror—to its targets, and we snicker at the crazy reflections.

Those Deadpan Onion Headlines

"Hijackers Surprised to Find Selves in Hell" (9/26/01), *The Onion* declaimed from its front page following the 9/11 attacks. No fury there. No sermons or secular moralizing. Just a wonderfully absurd (yet weirdly plausible) zinger of a headline in a dead-on parody of daily newspaper syntax. This is vintage *Onionizing*, with understated detachment substituting for savage indignation.

The article begins: "The hijackers who carried out the Sept. 11 attacks on the World Trade Center and Pentagon expressed confusion and surprise Monday to find themselves in the lowest plane of Na'ar, Islam's Hell." Again, here's a perfect parody of an actual news item, its deadpan tone belying the flamboyantly supernatural content of the story. (The mention of *Monday* was a brilliant little touch, as if our mundane days of the week carried over without interruption into Satan's own netherworld.)

Another headline, "Hershey's Ordered to Pay Obese Americans $135 Billion" (8/2/00), is so believable that most of us would barely raise an eyebrow if we saw the story in the *New York Times*. No exotic hellfire or damnation here—just a plain vanilla commentary (but nevertheless biting in its implications) on our hyper-litigious culture.

Religion is a popular target in *The Onion*, as you might expect. But the writers, to their credit, refuse to assume the fashionable God-bashing posture of militant post-9/11 atheists like Richard Dawkins and Christopher Hitchens. *The Onion*'s view is more subtle, more imbued with the helpless outrage of a world that still craves the moral certainty of religion but feels abandoned by God. One of *The Onion*'s most famous headlines appeared a few weeks after the 9/11 attacks: "God Angrily Clarifies 'Don't Kill' Rule" (9/26/01)—while the article featured an emotionally shaken Supreme Deity elucidating the Sixth Commandment in a press conference held on the rubble of the World Trade Center.

The Onion being *The Onion*, not all the religious stories are laden with dark cynicism or existential angst. One memorable headline satirized the follies of desperate believers while turning the tables on those who disdain them: "Evolutionists Flock To Darwin-Shaped Wall Stain" (9/6/08). Other religious headlines are simply a hoot to read: "Shroud of Turin Accidentally Washed with Red Shirt" (3/10/08). The story reports the tragic details: "The damage occurred when Pope Benedict XVI, who was on laundry duty, did not notice a brand new bright-red Hanes Beefy-T in the Holy Whirlpool washer."

Just How Cynical Is The Onion, Anyway?

Let's take a closer look at the philosophy that fuels *The Onion*. Philosophy, you ask? *The Onion* is just a humor rag, isn't it? Shouldn't we lighten up and enjoy the laughs? I admit that the underlying philosophy of *The Onion* seems elusive. The paper's guiding principle, on the surface at least, seems to be "anything for a laugh." Its editorial persona is virtually invisible. After all, *The Onion* doesn't editorialize in its absurd news stories. You won't find any diatribes against capitalism, corporatism, cronyism, political correctness, racism, affirmative action, guns, atheists, environmental rapists, tree-huggers, evangelicals, or any other cultural markers of our time. It's hard to extrapolate a consistent philosophy from the articles when we can't even uncover an editorial viewpoint. So let's focus on what we can actually see: the satirical irony that flickers from the pages (and screens) of *The Onion*. After all, irony is arguably the animating force behind, not just *The Onion*, but a lion's share of contemporary humor.

Three centuries ago, the great Anglo-Irish satirist Jonathan Swift (1667–1745) wrote a now-immortal essay, "A Modest Proposal," in which he ironically suggested a productive use for infants in famine-stricken Ireland. (Cook them and eat them.) So shocking was his "proposal," and so coldly rational was his tone, that the author's moral outrage glowed through the words like hot coals. Extended irony had been used in literature before, notably in *The Praise of Folly*, that brilliant mock-encomium by the Dutch scholar-translator-philosopher-theologian-humanist-satirist Erasmus of Rotterdam (around 1466–1536). But "A Modest Proposal" arguably launched the use of ironic detachment to express cynical indignation, a practice that has flourished on and off into our own time.

Today the tail seems to be wagging the dog. In contemporary humor, cool irony has arguably eclipsed genuine cynical outrage and, for that matter, other recognizable human emotions. David Letterman, Jerry Seinfeld, Sarah Silverman, Jon Stewart (okay, he's occasionally outraged), and especially Stephen Colbert, whose entire persona is an ironic pose, loom large as embodiments of this trend. Sure, their stuff is funny—often howlingly so. But you have to wonder where they *really* stand on the issues. Do the master ironists harbor genuine feelings about life, death, gum disease—*anything at all?* Is their "cynicism" just a little too glib?

Let's ask a larger and more unsettling question: Is contemporary irony simply a fashionable cover for intellectual timidity, an elaborate form of evasion, a reluctance to do anything so downright uncool as to *take an unambiguous stand?* The ironists seem to want it both ways: to make a statement without making a statement. Are they afraid of exposing themselves as sloppy sentimentalists, of losing face in front of the youthful, affluent, jaded urban audience whose approval they covet? Or don't they believe they can make genuinely (even *angrily*) cynical observations and be funny at the same time? (I submit George Carlin and Richard Pryor as Exhibit A and Exhibit B for making a case that you can.) For better or worse, cynicism today generally speaks to us indirectly, through veils of irony, too-cool posturing, and noncommittal commentary. Most of our professional ironists are *pseudocynics*.

So is *The Onion* a genuinely cynical publication, or is it simply another pseudocynical expression of postmodern irony?

I'm convinced that *The Onion* regularly crosses the boundary into genuine cynicism. When you see a headline like "New Pain-Inducing Advil Created for People Who Just Want to Feel Something, Anything" (11/22/08), you know that at least a few melancholy cynics are lurking behind the scenes. This isn't superficial ironic posturing.

The Onion conforms to our contemporary notion of cynicism: prone to mockery and sarcasm . . . critical of greed, pretension, and hypocrisy. *The Onion* lampoons the powerful, of course, as in the inspired headline, "Bush Regales Dinner Guests with Impromptu Oratory on Virgil's Minor Works" (4/18/01). And, just to be fair, the publication also freely mocks the follies of lame and clueless commoners—for example, the priceless "Toaster-Instruction Booklet Author Enraged that Editor Betrayed His Vision" (9/12/01).

Like the master ironists of our time, *The Onion* soft-pedals the indignation. But what lifts *The Onion* above mere irony and into the realm of cynicism is its clever use of cool detachment to provoke indignation in the reader, much the way Swift did in his "Modest Proposal." Check this outrageous *Onion* headline, a righteous commentary on power's contempt for the powerless: "Dictator Slays Millions in Last-Minute Push to Be *Time's* Man of the Year" (12/13/06). (The offending dictator in the article was Than Shwe, the brutal strongman of Myanmar, formerly known as Burma.)

So yes, most of us can probably agree that *The Onion* is a cynical publication—in the best sense of that much-abused word. Its penchant for mockery is regularly reinforced by an active con-science—even a love of decency. But let me pose a more relevant question for the philosophy buffs among our ranks: Is *The Onion* a *Cynical* publication? (Note the upper-case C.) In other words, would *The Onion* have passed muster with the ancient Cynics, those rude hippie philosophers whose contrarian antics frequently scandalized the Greco-Roman world? Let's do a little digging.

That's Cynicism with A Capital C (Even Though the Greek Alphabet Had No C)

Cynicism as a philosophy can be traced back to the followers of Socrates (around 469–399 B.C.E.), that most beloved and influential of Greek ethical philosophers. During a long, harrowing war that eventually crushed the Athenian city-state in 404 B.C.E., Socrates publicly questioned the assumptions of his cocksure contempo-raries by challenging them to spontaneous debates. He embraced virtue as the greatest good, shunned wealth and materialism, and advocated an independent spirit that held fast to its integrity while it opposed the prevailing pieties of the day. This simple but revo-lutionary philosophy proved to be too unsettling for the war-bat-tered Athenian state, and of course Socrates was made to pay the ultimate price for his heresy: a fatal drink of hemlock.

As you would imagine, Socrates's disciples didn't take kindly to their master's fate. A newer, darker, more contrarian philosophy was about to emerge. Combine Socrates's love of virtue, simplicity, and integrity with his followers' outrage over the injustice of "the system," and now you're tooling down the road to Cynicism. In fact, you can already discern traces of *modern* cynicism in the righteous indignation of the classical Greek Cynics. It's not too much of a stretch to believe that the ancient Cynics might have chuckled at an *Onion* headline like "Adult-Entertainment Industry Donates $100,000 in Charity Sex to Hurricane Victims" (10/5/05).

Other influences on the development of Cynicism included the Sophists, a school of philosophy that flourished during Socrates's lifetime. The Sophists promoted adherence to pure natural law over man-made law, which they viewed as intrinsically corrupt. An *Onion* headline like the wonderfully warped "Revised Patriot Act Will Make It Illegal to Read Patriot Act" (9/17/03) would definitely have resonated with them. In fact, the Sophists believed that the only virtuous life was one of rugged opposition to society and its conventions. In the ideal Sophist world, good people would unite in the ongoing struggle to create a more just society. It's interesting, and a little sad, that *sophistry* has become a synonym for fallacious thinking, just as the meaning of cynicism has been perverted by those high-minded establishmentarians who equate cynics with crass opportunists.

The Greek cult of Herakles (better known by his Roman monicker, Hercules) promoted a love of simple rustic virtues and freedom, combined with a burning desire to improve the lot of humankind. Herakles, a burly mythological figure who was scorned by some for his voluntary poverty and indifference to worldly power, eventually became a Cynic hero: the embodiment of natural living, beneficial work (notably his famous "twelve labors"), and virtuous suffering without complaint. He was clever, too: when commanded to clean out the stinking Augean stables, he simply rerouted two rivers through the stables to hose them down.

Even India fed into the stream that trickled down to classical Cynicism. The contrarian post-Socratic thinkers revered a band of Indian philosophers known as gymnosophists (literally "naked wise people"), who, in addition to shedding their garments, lived a simple, ascetic, natural life, unfettered by worldly obligations. These intellectual nudists influenced the virtuous/outrageous duality of classical Cynicism (and ultimately modern cynicism in such incarnations as *The Onion,* though we should probably assume that the editorial staff frequently wears clothing on the job).

The title of "World's First Cynic" is generally awarded to a relatively obscure disciple of Socrates named Antisthenes. (How fitting is it that the name of the first Cynic begins with "Anti-"?) Known for his wit and sarcasm, though nearly all of his ten volumes of writings have vanished, Antisthenes (around 445–365 B.C.E.) is more properly regarded as the great proto-Cynic. He wouldn't have recognized the Cynic label and certainly wouldn't have referred to himself as a Cynic. But he assembled the ideas that would stamp the Cynic personality and belief system for generations to come. Antisthenes stressed Socrates's devotion to strict personal integrity in the pursuit of virtue. He held materialism in contempt, embraced poverty, and believed that happiness should spring from the soul rather than from worldly or sensory gratifications. In other words, he would have been right at home breaking bread in the company of virtuous latter-day cynics like the nonconformist New England sage Henry David Thoreau (1817–1862) and India's ascetic national hero, Mahatma Gandhi (1869–1948). He also might have enjoyed a simple but telling *Onion* headline like "Rich Guy Wins Yacht Race" (11/10/99).

How did these post-Socratic renegade philosophers officially become known as Cynics? Antisthenes taught at an Athenian *gymnasium* known as Kynosarges or Cynosarges; that's one theory. The other, more popular view (my favorite, anyway), is that *Cynic* derives from the Greek word for "doglike": *kynikos*. (See, I told you there was no *C* in the Greek alphabet.)

The ancient Cynics took pride in their doglike traits. They lived freely on the streets and saw themselves as the watchdogs of humanity. Able, like dogs, to distinguish intuitively between friends and enemies, they relished any chance to taunt their more pretentious and self-infatuated contemporaries. For that matter, so does *The Onion*. See "Maya Angelou Honored for Courage, Blackness" (10/29/97) or "Al Gore Places Son in Rocket to Escape Dying Planet" (8/2/08).

The classical Greek Cynics developed a doglike cult of honest shamelessness—eating, carousing, and sometimes even fornicating in public as the spirit moved them. They regarded their natural canine morality as superior to conventional human morality, because it freed them from artificial social constraints that blocked happiness. Dogs instinctively know how to be happy, the Cynics believed, so they pursued the kind of happiness a dog would appreciate.

I Nuzzle the Kind, Bark at the Greedy, and Bite Scoundrels

The most famous Cynic of antiquity, the man regarded as the very embodiment of Cynicism (though Plato referred to him as "Socrates gone mad"), was Diogenes of Sinope. Born on the north coast of Asia Minor, Diogenes (around 412/404–322 B.C.E.) is known to us primarily through colorful (and occasionally off-color) anecdotes passed down by his acquaintances. Many centuries later, biographer Diogenes Laërtius (no relation) collected these anecdotes in his *Lives and Opinions of the Eminent Philosophers*. Diogenes himself is said to have left behind a few books, but like Socrates he preferred living his philosophy to writing it. Whatever thoughts he did commit to papyrus have long since disappeared.

In Diogenes of Sinope, the Cynic personality found its wildest, most extreme embodiment: an eccentric public scold who tossed away his possessions, lived in a tub, and reputedly carried a lamp by day in search of an honest man. He would introduce himself by saying, "I am Diogenes the Dog: I nuzzle the kind, bark at the greedy, and bite scoundrels." Occasionally the urge to use his teeth got the better of him. "I bite my friends to save them," Diogenes is alleged to have observed about himself. It's not surprising that the Cynics developed a reputation for biting humor.

The most resolutely and shamelessly doglike of Cynics, Diogenes was once caught masturbating in a public plaza. When confronted about his gross behavior, Diogenes replied nonchalantly, "If only it was as easy to soothe my hunger by rubbing my belly." (Fortunately for Diogenes, he was living in ancient Greece and not the contemporary US, or he might have atoned for his public display in a day-glo orange prison uniform.) "Study: Most Self-Abuse Goes Unreported" (1/28/04), announced an alarmist headline in *The Onion*. Diogenes was an exception.

Few men of consequence could escape Diogenes's disdain. When Plato confidently defined man as "a featherless biped," Diogenes carried a plucked chicken to Plato's Academy and announced, with great ceremony, "Behold! I've brought you a man." Even Alexander the Great set himself up. The young conqueror once approached Diogenes while the old man was sunning himself in the marketplace. When Alexander asked Diogenes if he could do him any favors, the Cynic curtly replied, "Yes, you can step out of my sunlight."

The Cynics eventually influenced the Stoics, whose austere philosophy blossomed in the following century and flourished during the height of Roman power. It could even be argued (actually, it *has* been) that Jesus was a spiritual descendant of the Cynics. In his voluntary poverty, his sharp criticism of hypocrisy, and his rejection of the material world along with its narrow-minded overseers, the Prince of Peace is nothing if not a classical Cynic.

Irreverence and biting humor . . . a penchant for criticism . . . rejection of the prevailing order . . . contempt for vanity, pretense, and folly: it's almost as if the intellectual DNA of the ancient Cynics has survived in the works of notable cynics (small *c*) down through the centuries: from Rabelais, Molière, Swift, and Voltaire to relatively recent standard-bearers like H.L. Mencken, Joseph Heller, Kurt Vonnegut, and Hunter S. Thompson.

Some of that ancient DNA has been corrupted along the way. Virtue doesn't seem to loom large in the modern cynic's constellation of values. Neither does the simple life or the need to unshackle oneself from materialistic pursuits. (Thoreau and the hippies carried that strain of ancient Cynicism into the modern era.)

What about *The Onion?* How much classical Cynicism survives in this postmodern parody of a newspaper? Does the paper's ironic, coolly detached, understated brand of social criticism constitute Cynicism as the ancient Greeks would have recognized it? Would Diogenes have read *The Onion?*

A Newspaper Gone to the Dogs . . .
Enlightened Dogs

Diogenes enjoyed laughing at bogus respectability and common vice. He was a natural subversive who shunned the powerful and relished his freedom to speak the truth. His humor regularly employed the element of surprise (remember Plato and the plucked chicken) to drive home his point. All of the above are distinctly *Onionesque* qualities.

Especially the element of surprise. "Black Guy Asks Nation for Change" (3/19/08), *The Onion* reported in a potentially scurrilous headline. Playing dangerously with the urban stereotype of the black panhandler, *The Onion* never reveals the name of the "black guy" asking for change. "According to witnesses," the story tells us, "a loud black man approached a crowd of some 4000 strangers in Chicago today and made repeated demands for change. . . . It is estimated that, to date, the black man has asked every single person in the United States for change." The "loud black man," is, of course, Barack Obama. That's the surprise. But *The Onion* is also toying subtly with our racial attitudes—simultaneously embarrassing us for thinking immediately of black panhandlers, while playfully reinforcing the stereotype. The article is laughing at respectable political correctness, racism, street people, and the dual meaning of "change" all at once, while clearly enjoying its freedom to shock the public. This *Onion* story is not only cynical but Cynical.

Diogenes and his disciples weren't angry, impassioned latter-day cynics in the manner of Friedrich Nietzsche, George Orwell, or the older Mark Twain. I'd suspect that the writers and editors of *The Onion* aren't especially angry or impassioned, either. Both the ancient Cynics and the staff of *The Onion* seem to have more in common with vintage 1960s hippies: sitting back, getting high (on weed or humor), observing the scene, and cackling at the self-important squares in their business suits.

Classical Cynicism is a wonderfully free and unstructured school of philosophy, at least partly because its foremost minds left little or nothing for us to read. No formal Aristotelian treatises, no tightly reasoned proofs in the manner of St. Thomas Aquinas. Just a liberating, humorous, yet surprisingly disciplined philosophy whose followers dared to live their beliefs in the open.

The Onion is liberating, humorous, and surprisingly disciplined as well. (The content and tone of its headlines and articles are usually pitch-perfect—an exacting and difficult feat to pull off with such commendable regularity.) Would Diogenes have enjoyed reading *The Onion*? I have no doubt that, among all the leading American newspapers of our time, the late Mr. Zweibel's satirical publication would have held an exalted place in his affections. The old Cynic would have relished the irreverence and the surprises, the mocking disdain for pompous potentates and simpering fools alike. Sure, he might have urged the staff to embrace a life of voluntary poverty, a proposal that probably would have been greeted with polite coughing and muffled protests. And he might have challenged *The Onion* to express its cynicism more bluntly and openly, to hide a little less behind the safe shield of parody and confront wrongdoers to their faces. It would have been a lot to ask of any contemporary news staff, especially during the Age of Irony, but Diogenes was uncompromising in his beliefs. Still, I have to conclude that the father of Cynics would have regarded *The Onion* with paternal fondness.

After all, *The Onion* accomplishes some of the primary goals of classical Cynicism: to ridicule the perpetrators of folly and hypocrisy, reject wrongheaded standards of respectability, and maintain an inner moral compass that serves the cause of virtue (even if it has to get a little raunchy now and then). That *The Onion* realizes these goals exclusively through satire shouldn't detract from its credibility as an important torchbearer of Cynicism.

Should *The Onion* do more than hold up a funhouse mirror to our times? Should it get angry, lose the detachment, and take itself more seriously as a vehicle for social criticism? No, then it would no longer be *The Onion*. Other cynics, boiling with ill-suppressed cultural rage, can take it upon themselves to score more direct and palpable hits upon the offending individuals and institutions of our age. But for now at least, the breezy, lighthearted cynicism of *The Onion* provides us with enough irreverent laughter to help us survive the most trying of times.

9

There's Something Queer about *The Onion*

MIMI MARINUCCI

In 1990, the US National Institutes of Health, with funding from the US Department of Energy, joined the Human Genome Project—a collaborative international effort to map and sequence all the genes in human DNA. In connection with the Human Genome Project, some scientists, including some openly gay scientists (for example, Dean Hamer and Peter Copeland) began exploring the possibility of a genetic foundation for homosexuality. Presumably, the goal was to disrupt the belief that sexual identity is a matter of personal choice, and to draw an analogy between sexual identity and such legally protected categories as race, sex, age, and disability status. To this day, many still assume that the case in favor of the rights of lesbian women and gay men depends upon establishing that homosexuality is a product of nature rather than nurture.

Not everyone agrees with this assumption, however. Some people are skeptical of the idea that something as complex as human sexual desire can be reduced to genetics. In the article, "Gay Gene Isolated, Ostracized" (4/9/97), *The Onion* articulates the concern that the quest for the elusive "gay gene" ultimately promotes a pathological account of homosexuality. According to the article, the researcher who allegedly isolated the gay gene rejoiced, claiming "I wouldn't want that faggot-ass gene messing with the straight ones."

In this early example, and in many others throughout the years, *The Onion* delivers a strong message in support of those who identify as homosexual. At the same time, however, a more ambiguous message lurks beneath the surface. Not only does the article complicate matters by making a mockery of gay gene research, but it also derives much of its humor from tired old stereotypes about gay men. For example, the article cites "its pinkish hue; meticulously frilly perimeter; and faint but distinct, perfume-like odor" as evidence that the gene is indeed gay.

The Gay Agenda

In "Nation's Gays Demand Right To Library Cards" (1/15/07), *The Onion* ridicules the popular notion that gay marriage is an affront to heterosexual marriage. The article attributes to Kentucky Senator Jim Bunning the statement that issuing library cards to homosexual readers "would demean what our nation's library cards stand for." Bunning, the article claims, is "one of several conservative legislators who has vowed to draft a constitutional amendment that would define library book-lending as a contract between a library and a heterosexual reader."

In a similar example, "Massachusetts Supreme Court Orders All Citizens To Gay Marry" (2/25/04), Massachusetts Chief Justice Margaret H. Marshall, explains: "Since the allowance of gay marriage undermines heterosexual unions, we decided to work a few steps ahead and strike down opposite-sex unions altogether."

Likewise, in "New Bill Would Defend Marriage From Sharks" (9/19/06), *The Onion* warns against allowing "the saw-edged teeth of a bloodthirsty bull shark" to "mutilate the institution of marriage until it is completely unrecognizable." In parody of real bills aimed against homosexuals, this bill calls for mandatory fines of up to $100,000 and a permanent designation on the Marriage Offenders National Registry for any shark found guilty under the new guidelines.

The obvious message of these examples is that same-sex marriage is no more a threat to heterosexual marriage than sharks, library privileges, or any other imaginary enemy.

The Onion frequently positions itself as an advocate for gay rights and occasionally reminds readers that homosexuality is not nearly as remarkable as the media would have us believe. Consider, for example, "Carload Of Faggots Just Pulled Up To Drive-Thru, Cashier Reports" (8/9/00), which satirizes the tendency to portray gay identity as shocking or outrageous. In this article, a group of Hardee's employees in Jacksonville, Florida, finds it unbelievable, first, that the men at the drive-thru were gay and, second, that "they weren't hiding it at all."

Also consider "Area 15-Year-Old Only Homosexual In Whole World" (2/18/98), which profiles Daryle Hegge, and explains that "despite his seemingly healthy exterior, Hegge is different from all his peers—very different. For, unlike his fellow students, Daryl Hegge is the only homosexual in the whole world." Although it's easy to understand why a teenager from a small town like Wauganaukee, Minnesota, might feel like the only homosexual in the world, Daryl Hegge is obviously not alone. The tragedy, then, is not that Daryl Hegge is gay, but rather that he believes himself to be "a horrible freak."

Gay repression and shame are recurring themes in *The Onion*. Examples include the self-explanatory "Church Group Offers Homosexual New Life In Closet" (9/16/98) and the more recent "Small Town Holds Annual Gay Shame Parade" (8/8/07). *The Onion* also addresses homophobia, particularly the suggestion that it occurs in response to one's own latent homosexual desires. This position was advanced as early as 1977 by psychologist D.J. West, who claimed that "when placed in a situation that threatens to excite their own unwanted homosexual thoughts," latent homosexuals "overreact with panic or anger."[1]

West's hypothesis gained empirical support when a research team assembled a group of purportedly heterosexual men, administered a questionnaire to determine which of them were homophobic, fitted them with devices to monitor changes in penile circumference, and exposed them to a variety of pornographic images. "Both groups exhibited increases in penile circumference to the heterosexual and female homosexual videos. Only the homophobic men showed an increase in penile erection to male homosexual stimuli."[2]

Not even a year after these findings were published, *The Onion* reported "Homoerotic Overtones Enliven NRA Meeting" (2/19/97). "Repression was the order of the day" at a North Idaho annual meeting of the National Rifle Association, according to this article. In a more recent expression of the same theme, *The Onion* reported "Anti-Homosexuality Sermon Suspiciously Well-Informed" (11/16/05). This article reveals that the vehemently anti-gay Reverend Francis Sebastian "is very specific about which code

---

[1] D.J. West, *Homosexuality Re-Examined* (University of Minnesota Press, 1977), p. 202.

[2] *Journal of Abnormal Psychology* 105:3 (1996), p. 440.

words not to use on which forbidden chat rooms at which times of the night" and "also seems to have done his homework on what happens if you flash your headlights at certain rest stops along Route 16."

In "'98 Homosexual-Recruitment Drive Nearing Goal" (7/29/98), *The Onion* exploits the popular misconception that recruitment is the top item on the gay agenda. The majority of US adults who support gay and lesbian rights would likely recognize the article as a spoof, especially its claim that the National Gay and Lesbian Recruitment Task Force (NGLRTF) has converted three hundred thousand heterosexuals through the "infiltration of America's public schools, where programs promoting the homosexual lifestyle are regularly presented to children as young as 5."

Assuming that homosexual recruitment poses the greatest threat for those to whom it is the most tempting, it's easy to imagine Eric Yetter, along with countless others like him, living in constant fear of the NGLRTF. In "Red-Lace Nightie Portends Another Excruciating Night For Closeted Husband" (5/19/99) we learn that Yetter, who "has yet to admit his homosexual desires to himself, much less his wife," is filled with dread when his wife greets him with soft music, scented candles, and sexy lingerie. This example, which illustrates how painful it can be to maintain an illusion of heterosexuality, underscores *The Onion's* ongoing interest in and commitment to gay rights.

Hot All-Girl Action

Despite its clear message in support of gay rights, *The Onion* refers almost exclusively to male homosexuality. There are comparatively few articles that deal directly with lesbian identity, and, on the face of it, this discrepancy would seem to indicate a deeply sexist perspective. This concern is mitigated, however, by a number of articles that draw attention to the sexualized representation in the mainstream media of women in general, and of lesbian women in particular.

"Wellesley College Removes Phrase 'Hot All-Girl Action' From School Brochure" (8/5/98) invokes the image of this prominent school exploiting its female student body in promotional materials suitable for distribution on the Vegas Strip. A similar example, "Women's Prison Riot Feels Gratuitous" (3/14/01), dismisses an actual riot in an actual prison as a cheesy pornographic plot device.

Just as the widespread tendency to think of women in sexual terms can be understood as a symptom of sexism, the corresponding tendency to think of gay men and lesbian women in sexual terms can be understood as a symptom of heterosexism. In each case, the targeted population is defined sexually, while heterosexual men are simply regarded as normal, natural, neutral. *The Onion* offers an especially clear illustration of this phenomenon in "Area Homosexual Saves Four From Fire: Heroic Neighbor Praised, Gay" (9/18/96). This article reveals that "Kevin Lassally, who likes to hold and kiss other men, is being hailed as a hero after rescuing a family of four from a deadly blaze." The irrelevance of Lassally's sexual orientation to this news item is obvious—particularly if we imagine providing comparable details about the sexual proclivities of a similarly heroic heterosexual man. Although *The Onion* takes it to a comical extreme, the superfluous attention to Lassally's sexuality is consistent with the sort of treatment we might expect from an actual news report.

By responding in a similar way to the sexist treatment of women and to the heterosexist treatment of gay men and lesbian women, *The Onion* seems to acknowledge, at least tacitly, that sexism and heterosexism are different aspects of a single problem. Some might not accept this recognition as sufficient compensation for the fact that, while the search term "gay" returns about seven hundred results from www.theonion.com, the search term "lesbian" returns only about two hundred—and many of these are articles that feature male characters but happen to mention lesbians, for example, in passing references to "gay and lesbian issues" or "gay and lesbian rights." By way of contrast, the results for both "homosexual" and "gay" refer almost exclusively to male examples.

This disparity notwithstanding, there are a few articles in which *The Onion* makes direct reference to female sexual identity, and these seem to reflect a perspective that is consistent with, perhaps even informed by, what is referred to in academic circles as "queer theory." Although queer theory is notoriously difficult to define, Annamarie Jagose offers a useful description of some of its common features:

> Broadly speaking, queer describes those gestures or analytical models which dramatise incoherencies in the allegedly stable relations between chromosomal sex, gender and sexual desire. Resisting that model of stability—which claims heterosexuality as its origin, when it

is more properly its effect—queer focuses on mismatches between sex, gender, and desire. Institutionally, queer has been associated most prominently with lesbian and gay subjects, but its analytic framework also includes such topics as cross-dressing, hermaphroditism, gender ambiguity, and gender-corrective surgery. Whether as transvestite performance or academic deconstruction, queer locates and exploits the incoherencies in those three terms which stabilise heterosexuality. Demonstrating the impossibility of any 'natural' sexuality, it calls into question even such apparently unproblematic terms as 'man' and 'woman'.[3]

Queer offers an alternative to identity categories that demand a choice between this *or* that—for example, between woman *or* man, between homosexual *or* heterosexual—thus allowing for the seemingly inconsistent simultaneous expression of *both* this *and* that.

Indeed, queer theory acknowledges the possibility of an infinite range of identities with respect to sex, gender, and sexuality, and therefore abandons the ongoing effort to create an exhaustive list of those identities, as in "lesbian, gay, bisexual, transgender" with the occasional addition of "intersex, questioning, and allies." Finally, queer theory recognizes that it is not merely nature, but also culture, that informs the meanings we construct in connection with sex, gender, and sexuality.

The apparently queer orientation of the few articles in *The Onion* that address female sexuality is rather curious, particularly in contrast with the treatment of male sexuality. Although a few of the articles that highlight male sexuality seem sensitive to the insights of queer theory, many more of these focus explicitly on gay rights, as outlined above. While queer theory does not constitute a rejection of lesbian and gay rights, most queer analyses shift attention away from equal rights and focus instead on the language and institutions—that is to say, the discourses—surrounding our cultural concepts of sex, gender, and sexuality.

By drawing attention to unexpected matches between sex, gender, and desire, and by presenting an alternative to the notion of sexuality as natural and innate, queer theory establishes connections among all those who transgress assigned sex and gender roles. This includes those who identify as lesbian women or gay men, those who identify as intersex or transgender, and even those

---

[3] Annamarie Jagose, *Queer Theory: An Introduction* (NYU Press, 1997), p. 3.

who identify as feminist or profeminist. It also includes those who exist outside the established identity categories, such as female and male or homosexual and heterosexual.

Lesbian Chic

As she is represented in "Lesbian Identity Ends Abruptly Mid-Junior Year" (1/30/02), Amanda Oppel serves as an example of someone who exists outside the usual identity categories. For Oppel, a twenty-year-old women's studies major at Oberlin College, sexual identity seems to have little to do with an intrinsic or essential disposition toward women rather than men, or vice versa, and much more to do with her college major, her sense of fashion, and her financial outlook.

Explaining the decision to abandon her lesbian identity, Oppel says, "I just need to focus on different priorities right now." She then continues, "I'm graduating next year, and my dad's not going to foot the bill forever." Obviously, Oppel deviates from the customary understanding of what it means to be a lesbian woman. Lesbian women, after all, usually don't abandon their lesbian identity. Oppel also deviates from the customary understanding of what it means to be a straight woman. Straight women, after all, usually don't pursue romantic relationships with other women, not even in college. In addition, Oppel is not straightforwardly or unproblematically bisexual, given that, while it lasted, her orientation toward women was presumably exclusive, as is her newly formed orientation toward men. Bisexuals, of course, usually don't rule people out as potential partners simply because they are not female or because they are not male.

Psychologist Carla Golden suggests that "sexual feelings and activities change; they can be fluid and dynamic."[4] According to Golden's research, there is a distinction between "primary lesbians" and "elective lesbians," though research on gay men reveals no comparable distinction. Unlike most men, at least some women regard their sexual orientation as something that reveals more about their personal history than it reveals about their innate desires or dispositions. In other words, for at least some

---

[4] Carla Golden, "Diversity and Variability in Women's Sexual Identities," in Boston Lesbian Psychologies Collective, *Lesbian Psychologies: Explorations and Challenges* (University of Illinois Press, 1987, p. 29).

women, sexuality is socially constructed. Golden's account is consistent with queer theory in resisting the established notion of sexuality as both natural and stable. Neither Golden in particular nor queer theory in general is careless enough to advance the problematically simplistic claim that sexual orientation is always a conscious choice, but both acknowledge that history can have a significant impact on sexuality.

Given Golden's characterization of women's sexuality as fluid and dynamic, a theoretical perspective such as queer theory, which offers an alternative to the more familiar account of sexuality as static and stable, is arguably a feminist theoretical perspective. It therefore can be read as both queer and feminist that *The Onion* acknowledges the existence of those, like Amanda Oppel, who are at risk of falling through the gaps between the established categories of sex, gender, and sexuality.

Unfortunately, however, this interpretation is complicated by the satirical context in which Oppel is presented as an example. Indeed, it makes just as much sense to interpret Oppel's story as a mockery of those who seem fickle, phony, or simply unwilling to commit to a sexual orientation that the rest of us can understand. The article questions the authenticity of Oppel's lesbian identity, particularly with the revelation that, according to her former girlfriend, "Amanda wasn't ever really all that affectionate in private." The article also notes, "Despite the shock among Oppel's classmates, older lesbians familiar with the situation were not surprised by the gender-preference reversal." Oberlin women's studies professor Gwen Mims, for example, commented sardonically, "What a stunner. Wow."

Girls Gone Wild

Another of the few articles in *The Onion* to address female sexuality, "Bar Skanks Announce Plans To Kiss" (6/22/07), once again depicts alleged same-sex desire as insincere. Unlike Amanda Oppel, whose lesbian aspirations developed in connection with her feminist ideals, Stephanie Fletcher and Jessica Keneally seem more interested in living up to the pornographic fantasies of some straight men, even as they play hard to get. The article explains, for example, that "over the loud music to several unspecified bar patrons," Keneally announces, "We're going to make out. We don't care who's watching." Later, she refers to the assembled onlookers as "such pervs," while Fletcher piques their interest by speculating about whether the upcoming kiss will involve tongue.

"In previous months," according to the article, "Keneally and Fletcher have, either separately or together, shown off their lower-back tattoos, held a loud conversation about who had the larger breasts, and displayed their oral sex techniques on bottles of Bud Light." These exhibitionist displays seem designed to garner attention and validation from straight men, and it's not at all surprising when the article reveals, "Neither is a lesbian." What is surprising, however, is the way the example of Keneally and Fletcher, like the example of Amanda Oppel, complicates the connection between sexual behavior and sexual identity. Complicating this connection means challenging the stability of sexual identity categories and invoking social construction. Once again, *The Onion* represents female sexuality as fluid, dynamic, and intrinsically queer.

Drama Queens

The Onion also complicates the connection between sexual behavior and sexual identity in some of the articles that address men's sexuality. Although these articles, like those that address women's sexuality, introduce characters that defy established sex, gender, and sexuality categories, they often depict those same characters as insincere. There is a significant difference, however, between the insincerity of the male characters and the insincerity of the female characters. Where the women are depicted as faking same-sex desire, the men are depicted as faking opposite-sex desire. What these male characters have in common with Amanda Oppel, Stephanie Fletcher, and Jessica Keneally is that, regardless of how they identify their sexuality, they nevertheless violate the boundaries of the established distinction between heterosexuality and homosexuality.

Consider, for example "Why Do All These Homosexuals Keep Sucking My Cock?" (7/6/05), in which Bruce Heffernan, a self-identified heterosexual, continually finds himself on the receiving end of oral sex with other men. "Take last Sunday," Heffernen explains, "I casually struck up a conversation with this guy in the health-club locker room. Nothing fruity, just a couple of fellas talking about their workout routines while enjoying a nice hot shower. The guy looked like a real man's man, too—big biceps, meaty thighs, thick neck. He didn't seem the least bit gay. At least not until he started sucking my cock, that is." Evidently, such episodes are not uncommon for Bruce. "Then there was the time I was hiking through the woods and came across a rugged-looking, blond-haired man in his early 30s," Heffernen continues. "He seemed straight enough to me while we were bathing in that mountain stream, but, before you know it, he's sucking my cock!" Heffernen seems utterly obsessed with these unwelcome encounters and, he explains, "I've even started to visualize these repulsive cock-sucking episodes during the healthy, heterosexual marital relations I enjoy with my wife."

Like Heffernen, Michael Litwin denies that he is gay. In "Area Man Experimenting With Homosexuality For Past Eight Years" (10/25/00), Litwin insists that his sexual activity with other men amounts to nothing more than open-minded experimentation. He does admit, however, "The woman I marry will definitely have to be okay with my past." Despite claiming to be "99 percent straight," Litwin seems more like a gay man (or a predominantly gay man) in denial than a straight man (or predominantly straight man) in an experimental phase.

Heffernen and Litwin do not fit the customary understanding of what it means to be heterosexual any better than Oppel, Keneally, and Fletcher fit the customary understanding of what it means to be homosexual. Through these examples, *The Onion* seems to acknowledge alternatives to the established categories of sexual orientation. This could be taken as evidence that *The Onion* advocates a queer approach to understanding issues of sex, gender, and sexuality. On the other hand, the implication that Oppel, Keneally, Fletcher, Heffernen, and Litwin are insincere could be taken as reinforcement of the established categories of sexuality.

Banal Sex

The Onion has a complicated relationship to issues of sex, gender, and sexuality. It's obvious position in support of lesbian and gay rights is offset by a tendency to perpetuate a stereotypical image of homosexuality, particularly male homosexuality. This is especially evident in the self-explanatory "Controversial Court Ruling Upholds Homosexual's Right To Prance Around Demanding Attention And Being A Drama Queen" (6/9/08).

Additionally, *The Onion*'s occasional articulation of insights that seem consistent with queer theory is offset by a corresponding mockery of those same insights. "Grad Student Deconstructs Take-

Out Menu" (7/24/02) directly mocks the very academic theorizing we have just been engaged in. The article reveals that, thanks to his research "on the impact of feminism, post-feminism, and current 'queer' theory on received notions of gender and sexual preference/identity," Harvard University graduate student Jon Rosenblatt is no longer capable of a straightforward and uncomplicated reading of something as simple as a menu.

Finally, while the relatively infrequent attention to female sexual orientation may strike some readers as sexist, the representation of female sexuality as fluid may strike some readers as feminist or profeminist. *The Onion*'s stance, it seems, is terminally ambiguous.

Perhaps we are simply over-thinking sex. Perhaps the best way to garner widespread acceptance of minority sexual identities is to stop treating them as something unusual or unexpected. This seems to be the strategy that underlies "Gay Couple Has Banal Sex" (9/29/04). In this article, we learn that Jerome Ostrowski and Barry Lipner, a gay couple, have engaged in sex that was not especially hot, but instead was predictable and merely "serviceable." It should come as no surprise that same-sex couples, like old married straight couples, often end up having boring sex. Not only is the stereotype of gay men and lesbian women as porno sex machines dehumanizing, it is also false.

World

HIGHLIGHTS

Vigilante Group Tracks and Kills Storm-Causing 'Chaos' Butterflies

Climate scientists, chaos theorists, and entomologists today mourn the extinction of this important metaphoric, metamorphic species.

RIO DE JANEIRO—A vigilante group from the southern United States of America today wiped out an entire species of butterflies in Brazil in a coordinated act of revenge for what they claim was a series of wanton 'attacks at a distance' by the butterflies.

The butterflies, credited with causing wild storms and other catastrophic action as a result of their uninhibited wing flapping, were located by the vigilante group in their remote habitats and 'crushed like bugs', according to bystanders.

"They have destroyed our towns and motor homes one too many times. It was time for some payback," said the angry mob's angry spokesperson. "We tried killing all the local butterflies, but it turns out it's only far off, foreign butterflies that cause all the tornadoes and such."

Theorists popularized the 'Butterfly Effect', to illustrate how in chaos theory outcomes have a very sensitive dependence on initial conditions.

While a flapping butterfly wing represents a small change in a physical system, it can cause a chain of events leading to large-scale alterations of consequent events, particularly in rent-controlled areas.

"But for them butterflies, I'd still have my velvet paintings and my Civil War-era surgical set. They won't be flapping up a storm no more," noted 'Doc' Jimmy Joe Billy Bob Avery, the angry mob spokesperson brandishing an ichor-stained net in triumph. 🐦

Great Thinkers Fired From Canon

PRINCETON, N.J.—Researchers have revealed an objective measurement of philosophical worth that will resolve questions about the importance and influence of the Great Thinkers by a simple scientific process called the 'Exciting Thought Evaluation'.

"Before this landmark discovery, philosophers would spend all their time haggling over who is greater: Plato or Aristotle, Kant or Nietzsche?" said Professor Inde Nial of the Successfulness Institute, Princeton and creator of Out of Cite, Out of Mind, an NEH-funded cite-site web research project that lifts the lid on the largest intellectual property heist in the history of philosophy.

"We've decided to cut through the thicket of such debates and let who counts as a philosopher and who counts as a great philosopher be driven by the data. The objective measure of influence has to be how often thinkers are referenced. I cite the citations as evidence of influence. Early results are completely overturning our thinking on thinkers."

It turns out that 'great' is a function of how often a name appears in philosophical works. This replaces more traditional measures of greatness, such as quality of argument, originality of ideas, and academic integrity — non-operationalizable indicators about which there is no consensus and which have proved unwieldy for determining merit increases in modern university settings.

Site Cites Citing Oversight

Crunching texts in the canon of philosophy with supercomputer MAC 512 to produce reliable 'Ex-citing Ratings', Professor Nial discovered that it was not Aquinas (alleged to have written over 10 million words) or any of the Greek or German moguls who top the bill on the Citation Index. Names which were thought to be mere grammatical placeholders have suddenly emerged as belonging to the most prolific and influential of thinkers.

So who's the greatest philosopher of all time?

Ibidem proposed as greatest ever philosopher.

"Without doubt, it's Ibidem," Professor Nial explained. "There aren't many philosophical publications that don't refer to that guy. Ibid everywhere, man."

When asked about this mysterious Ibidem, Professor Nial replied: "Most likely he is of Persian origin. But despite his being the most cited author of all

Philosophy's Big Names Implicated In Intellectual Property Heist And Credit Theft

time, we have no information about his personal history or even a record of employment."

"Although he had an incredibly wide range of interests, writing on every topic in philosophy, he was prone to inconsistency and some degree of plagiarism, including of himself, with whom he never disagreed," Professor Nial added.

Big guns fired

Professor Nial recommends nothing short of a complete firing of all the so-called "greats" from the canon.

"At the risk of repeating myself again and again, as I did above," she added, "Ibidem is not the only victim of this shameless cover-up. This self-promoting scam inflating the reputations and egos of the so called 'big guns' spans 2500 years and involves thousands of conspirators, resulting in the appropri-

See CANON next spread

University Restructures To Remain Financial: Becomes Bank

MUGGAWALLADIDGYMOOLA, AUSTRALIA—Senior administrators of North Australia University announced plans at a press conference yesterday to remodel the university as a bank.

Old-fashioned departments, faculties, courses, academic staff and their 'chalk-n-talk' modes of delivery will largely be replaced by a network of ATMs (Academic Transaction Machines) to be established as part of an ambitious re-visioning of the tertiary education production line.

The outcomes of the ATMs will be funneled into first-person accounts. These will then be retold at a higher price.

"For the last decade we've been performing a sort of corporatist, sympathetic magic. We've renamed costcutting, sackings and the diverting of resources away from academic pursuits as 'efficiency measures', 'corporate responsibility', and 'educational innovation', in the hope that emulating the structures and language of financial institutions would attract similar funds and prestige," said Professor Buro Kratz, the administration head tasked with actioning the select sub-committee's task force's action plan implementation process.

"But by being timid we merely created a hybrid that isn't meeting either academic or financial goals. As a result, the books aren't effectively studied or balanced," claimed Professor Kratz.

'Floating' expected from bank

The North Australia University will reinvent itself as the Uncommonwealth Bank of Ideas with a new structure designed to attract funding.

The plan draws inspiration from the cargo-attracting practices of the New Guinea Highlands.

According to a model of the remodeling plans, this new structure will be a post-modern mix of actual posts cov-

Customer is awarded degree from Academic Transaction Machine (ATM).

ered in woven sticks, skinned with old textbook pages and photocopies of dollars. The University will transform itself into a model 'money box' located on the 'bank' of a nearby river in the hope that funds will flow in.

'Restructure will fix problems created by the previous restructurings'

Commentators expect the new structure to be floated at the beginning of the next wet season.

Restructure fixes earlier restructures

"If it ain't brokered, fix it," says Mike Romanujur, leading change management facilitator and reconstructing consultant to the university restructure consultation team. "We're confident this restructuring process will resolve

See UNIBANK next page

the problems of the last three restructurings the University has had this year. The problem with the past is that we simply didn't go back far enough."

"Sometimes you need to bend over backwards and look up to see the fundamental flaws in the old way of doing things."

Mr. Romanujur was confident the administration team who have brought the institution to its current state are best placed to lead the process to the next level.

"We need to be financial wizards to get ahead these days," he noted. "Or at least shamans with witch doctorates."

Smiling face put on changes

"Our highest priority during the restructure process has been to ensure academic staff seem reasonably happy with our decisions and their implementation," said Dr. Ynuf Snuff, Assistant Vice-President for Depositor Relations, Post and Stick Gathering and Spreadsheet Sorting and Stapling.

"It looks like we now have complete agreement on this proposal," said Dr. Snuff after mandating the compulsory

EXTRA

SCIENCE
Massive recall of 2009 model Leptons – entanglement and uncertainty defects found. *Page 6B*

GOVERNMENT
Decisive Rock poll lead over unstable Paper/Scissors coalition. *Page 6B*

Office administrator wins Plato Prize for creating ideal forms. *Page 6B*

MUSIC
Hot rock group 'Igneous' launch world tour from area volcano. *Page 7C*

ECONOMY
Hedge fund declares GFC "double digit lickin' good". *Page 7C*

MEDIA
Study reveals 70 per cent of people now believe 85 per cent of news content is 62 per cent fake. *Page 7C*

wearing of masks decorated with bright feathers and crudely painted smiley faces for all staff.

"Of course there will be some whimpering, but everyone knows the old saying: if you look after the penance, the pounds will look after themselves. Unfortunately, we cannot grow as an institution without some downward resizing."

'Resizing' of department heads

A number of department heads are reported to have been downwardly resized themselves during the restructuring. This was the result of a carefully worded (and repeatedly chanted) response by disaffected faculty members which resulted in the severe shrinking of departmental head size.

"We were actually trying for a different form of shrinkage of the managerial cohort," admitted the dissenting

'Major cuts are our path to the cutting-edge'

group's leader, who sought to remain anonymous (and succeeded by virtue of wearing a mask decorated with bright feathers and a crudely painted smiley face).

The university plans to take advantage of this development by tasking the shrunken heads of department with micromanaging the restructuring process.

Pinpoint accuracy at 'Voodoo U'

Some critics are skeptical of the long-term viability of the University Bank plan.

"This scheme sounds like some reanimated 'voodoo economics'. We're trying to pinpoint some of the weakness in this proposal now," noted another academic staff member seen poking hatpins into a crude economic model of the new organizational structure made from straw, wax, pig semen, and a spreadsheet printout decorated with primitive pie charts, organizational diagrams and tropical clip art.

Professor Kratz declined to comment, citing the sudden and repeated onset of really painful health issues. 🥄

ADD Sufferers Fail 'Cogito': Don't Exist

Victim during test (above) and after (inset right).

BOSTON, MA — A television announcement yesterday from the Harvard Medical School that people suffering from Attention Deficit Disorder (ADD) typically fail the 'cogito' test for existence has caused millions of viewers to pop out of existence from their couches.

"I think...Do I? Do I what? Therefore... their four... there for... what? Sorry, I got distracted again there. Why

'I think... sorry, what was the question?'

am I thinking of yams?" asked one patient taking the test, just moments before disappearing.

The nation's economy is facing a crisis as key occupations are depleted.

Nuclear power plants, the food industry and central administrations in both government and private sectors have suffered massive losses.

"Middle management has largely disappeared overnight," explained a government spokesperson. "Fortunately this has had no detectable negative effect on the running of society." 🕊

CANON from previous spread

ation and suppression of the genuine giant ordinance of philosophy."

"Ancient Rome lauds their Cicero and marvels at their Marcus Aurelius as gun philosophers, but the one packing the real attribution artillery is the barely acknowledged Opus Citandi, whose cross-referencing skills are remarkable," noted Professor Nial. "Similarly, the Arab collaborators, Et and Al, are among the most prolific of co-authors but their identity has been constantly overshadowed by every 'lead' author of the publications in which they have been involved. I think it must be their great capacity for teamwork that explains their productivity."

Not to finish on an endnote, in a follow-up project, Hidden in Plain Cite, Professor Nial intends to pull the rug from under more contemporary blowhards by revealing the staggeringly under-rated influence of two other hugely prolific philosophers.

"It's shameful that the French philosopher, Essais, author of so many insightful volumes such as *Essais de Phi-*

losophie de Ibidem and *Essais de et. al. inter alia, etc.* has had so little acknowledgement." said Professor Nial.

I cite the citations as evidence of influence.

"Similarly overlooked is the ancient Greek thinker, Articles (pron. Art-icklees), brother of the renowned urologist, Testicles, whose wide-ranging and definitive work includes *Articles on Magnus's Opus* and *Articles on the indefinite, indefinable and definitely ill-advised.*"

Will Inde Nial's potshots at Philosophy's celebrated top of the pops be just a flash in the pan or will her wise-cracks resound around the wide world of 'what does it all mean'? The world's leading pedenotarians will gather in Geneva in March to discuss the process of reloading the canon with high-calibre candidates in light of Professor Nial's findings. 🕊

Scientists Find Anomalies In And Then Go Back and Kill Your Grandparents

LOS ANGELES, CA—A major experiment in fundamental physics conducted earlier today revealed some fundamental flaws in our understanding of call an egghead at UCLA or MIT and get some quotes as David Hume pointed out, the causal relation per se cannot be perceived; one only perceives sequences of events.

"We seem to rearrange the fragments into some linear narrative of coming along. I'll have it ready by the deadline by the very act of becoming aware of the entangled situation," said Dr. Week.

Time's arrow seems to déjà vu here?

"When you look at the mathematics of quantum theory, there doesn't seem to be any proof that time can only go one way," she said unscrambling the order of events in our mind later.

"Honey, there's something really weird about the newspaper this meaning that the theoretical statements that describe them remain true if the direction of time is reversed.

Time's arrow seems to point wherever it likes. It seems that in a quantum effect it effectively jumps randomly forward and can't believe the weird stuff the scientists are coming up with these days and what they seem willing to print in the entirely or mostly time symmetric.

The anomaly is perceived as a series of random explain that with less jargon for our readers?

Our consciousness might be the thing actually jumbling the order of events to make a comprehensible you just see that? It was broken a minute ago.

Dr. Tuesday Week, a philosopher at UCLA specializing in time issues noted, "In this model, there's no reason why coming in on the wire about some problem the hypernerds have discovered with time. Ben can you do some research and put this together so we don't need a doctorate to understand causing apparent jumps in continuity.

"What we hadn't considered much is that it might be changing direction all the time."

"Somehow the act of examining the time slip seems to point wherever it likes. It jumps forwards and backwards in small steps physicist working in Relativistic Studies at MIT. "It's as if consciousness collapses the probability wave in a quantum sense and if your grandparents weren't alive how could you exist to have killed them?"

It is currently unknown whether the laws of physics would allow backwards time it was broken on the floor, then it was intact on the table, then it had been cleared away yesterday. Then I got it out of the box for the first time.

We seem to put the fragments into some linear narrative of our own and please get some sort of quote explain all this and the butterflies don't have to be far away and foreign actually as long as there is space-time discontinuity or some sort of.

An apparent loop

Are you getting a strong sense of she noted, "In this model, there's no reason why you should only experience each segment once. You could keep jumping to the same segments and be trapped in a no reason why you should only experience each segment once. You could keep jumping to the same segments and be trapped in a no reason why you should only experience each segment once. You could keep jumping to the same segments and be trapped in a no reason why you should only experience each segment once. You could keep jumping to the same segments and be trapped in a." 🐦

Recent News Contributors: Deborah Brown, Damien Ledwich, and Robert Whyte

11

Hijackers Surprised To Find Selves In Hell

RANDALL E. AUXIER

It was September 28th, 2001. It wasn't time for laughing. Even Letterman became reverent—or maudlin, depending on your level of cynicism. Bush was being an idiot and Cheney was being an asshole, as per usual, but the stakes were higher at this moment in history. It was hard to know whether to be glad for the presence of idiots and assholes, but it took a couple of weeks for the Left to emerge from a proto-patriotic fog, as unfamiliar as it was confusing for them.

At *The Onion*, and only there, it was business as usual, sort of. The chosen moniker for the on-going coverage was, across a picture of the US map in the cross-hairs, "Holy Fucking Shit: Attack On America." The September 28th issue of *The Onion* was devoted entirely to the event, and especially striking was the story that provides my title. That story was closely researched and accurately written, to include the most graphic and awful features of the Islamic depictions of hell.

Now the ideas of hell, Satan, and the demonic, predate Islam— and Christianity, and even the ancient Hebrew religion, tracing back to Persia and the Fertile Crescent thousands of years before our familiar Western religions existed. Islam's account of hell is pretty colorful and a bit unfamiliar to Christians and Jews, having leapfrogged the other Abrahamic faiths and landed directly in Islamic lore from those much older roots. In the *Onion* story, the most imaginative demonic beings were described taking a crack at the terrorists responsible for the 9/11 attacks.

My favorite lines included, "said Iblis, The Thrice-Damned . . . 'Indeed, I don't know what they were expecting, but they certainly didn't seem prepared to be skewered from eye-socket to bunghole and then placed on a spit so that their flesh could be roasted by the searing gale of flautus which issues forth from the haunches of Asmody." And "exacerbating the terrorists' tortures, which include being hollowed out and used as prophylactics by thorn-cocked Gulbuth The Rampant, is the fact that they will be forced to endure such suffering in sight of the Paradise they were expecting. . . . That can't be fun."

And so on. In a way, if you think about this, it just isn't funny, but even on September 28th, 2001, I was laughing, so maybe *thinking about it* is exactly what we aren't supposed to do.

Philosopher Sets New Record, Doesn't Think about It for 73 minutes, 17 seconds

So I thought about it anyway (after a modest pause). I know that asking *why* something is funny *isn't* funny. So I won't quite do that, but you still may think I should shut the fuck up. Okay, fair enough. But remember, the guy you *wish* would STFU is exactly the guy *least* likely to, otherwise you wouldn't be wishing for it. So this is your problem more than mine, according to my clear and oh-so-objective analysis of what may or may not be your self-defeating desires. But I don't want to get off on the wrong foot with you, okay? Give me just a little nerdspace and I'll keep in mind that you are expecting this to be funny at some point. I think that's a fair trade.

I'm sure you've noticed that when something truly awful happens, there is a period of solemnity, followed by the eventual appearance of tasteless but clever jokes about it, no matter how tragic it was. As of today I joined a Facebook page advocating that the writings of Ayn Rand be used to plug the BP oil leak in the Gulf of Mexico. Now that's a nifty idea. As bad as this oil leak is, we were ready to laugh about it right away. Never mind that millions of helpless animals are dying and hundreds of thousands of people are losing their homes and livelihoods. *The Onion* has been having tremendous fun with this one since it first started; today's headline is "Massive Flow of Bullshit Continues to Gush from BP Headquarters." In a way, that's *The Onion*'s self-appointed task: all engines full ahead into the typhoon of tragedy with the *first* comic relief.

But even *The Onion* has standards. Otherwise it wouldn't enjoy the readership of so many cultural elites, like me. So there are some things they won't touch. How do they tell the difference? The potential *Onion* story entitled "Smithsonian Janitor Finds Magic Bullet in 1963 Convertible Limousine" is quite an edgy way of lampooning the Warren Commission, but allowable now. But the story idea "Mrs. Williams Finally Decides Dinner Guest Is Not Going to Show" won't make the cut, and may *never*. In this story, Memphis housewife Gladys Williams has been keeping a plate of fried chicken warm since April 4th, 1968 for a certain civil rights leader who never showed up. "He never even called to cancel," she added.

It's peculiar, if you think about it. Plenty of things that seem very unfunny, like 9/11, have been successfully lampooned. Maybe this is complicated. Maybe a philosopher is needed.

Philosopher Makes Difficult Problem Out Of Something Obvious

The reason I was so struck by the story about the 9/11 hijackers is because it sits right on the line between what you can and can't do for the sake of truth by way of laughter. *Onion* writers know, *just know*, what to go for and what to leave alone. They're like the writers on *South Park*, always pressing the boundaries and being irreverent. But as bold as those other writers are, I think the 9/11 edition of *The Onion* is the bravest piece of (successful) comedy I have ever read.

Philosophers don't pay very much attention to laughter, and even less to journalism, so it isn't exactly a piece of cake to delve back into the history of philosophy and know what to say about *The Onion* and the ridiculous and ribald. But philosophers themselves have been the target of satire often enough, beginning in the West with Aristophanes's caricature of Socrates in the comedy *The Clouds*. That play's still pretty funny, after a couple of millennia, which I personally find annoying. So *how* does some comedy become dated and very unfunny while other comedy retains its appeal? Yet another question for the philosophers? If you're a playwright, cover your eyes now (you don't want to see this), and the rest of you, don't try this at home.

Socrates's student Plato got revenge on Aristophanes in the strangest way—making the playwright a character in a philosophical dialogue called *Symposium*, and giving him one of the most weirdest speeches in the history of philosophy, the speech of the "circle-men." In *Symposium*, everyone is at a drunken party and making speeches in praise of the god Eros, and Aristophanes starts going on about how we used to be complete beings, never experiencing desire for a lover, until Apollo got fed up with us and cut us in two, leaving each half to spend its life in search of its other half.

Ah, but there's the twist. These days, philosophers take this speech very seriously, writing long, boring essays and books about it. But given the context, I'm worried that Plato may have been kidding. Maybe his Greek readers, back in the day, would laugh at *us* for taking it seriously, just as we laugh at the Chinese government for spreading a story from *The Onion* as if it were actual news.

Yet, you have to admit, ancient Greek readers are pretty dead. Everybody knows that not being in on the joke kinda sucks, but is it still a joke if *no one* is in on it anymore? This is getting damn complicated, don't you think? Aren't you glad *I'm* here and not, say, Edward Albee (who has shamelessly stolen my chance at revenge by not writing a play about me)? Questions, questions!

So, I think we really have just two major questions here, both dealing with what you might call the mystery of comic *timing*:

1. **What's the maximum speed with which a group processes its own present situation so as to become prepared for cathartic depictions of it?**

and

2. **Why does some comedy endure, hopping across cultural and historical contexts, retaining its freshness and relevance?**

I can't promise you *the* answer to these questions, but I can promise you *an* answer—and it won't ruin your affection for *The Onion*.

Satiric Newspaper Runs Actual News Story

If you want to make something funny, you have lots of choices about how to make it so. You can exaggerate it, underplay it, make a pun or limerick or haiku about it, move it into an unexpected context, pretend to be a little too serious about it, refuse to take it seriously enough, humiliate it, imitate it, and so on. The comic tropes are well known. Any person, place, or thing is susceptible to such treatment. So this is not as much about the subject matter as about the *way* the subject is approached.

You can't quite say, without qualification, that there's *no way* at all to make MLK's assassination funny, only that it won't be easy. . . .it's like cooking that hyper-poisonous tiger blowfish that the Japanese like to risk their lives to eat. (I'm sorry, but I am too busy running with scissors.) You can go after almost anything, but unless you're Edward Albee, you don't want to try to finish the limerick that starts "There once was a preacher named King . . ."

To have a comic "style" is to have a mutually reinforcing set of these moves, a group that tends to amplify the effects of surprise and the catharsis in laughing. *The Onion* has a definite style, a bag of tricks they draw on again and again, corresponding to a reader-ship that likes the combination. In short, *The Onion* is formulaic. That's not a bad thing and it isn't some kind of big secret. Comedy, like everything else, can be honed by technique, and certainly timing is a component of technique.

But timing is bigger than that. Timing deals with the *way experience* flows by, and the idea of "news" itself is exactly the slice of *experience* that *The Onion* exploits. We usually take in this phenomenon, "news," without even considering what kind of slice of experience it is, and since we (apparently) never tire of news, and of falling back into unconscious consumption of its temporal form (the "new," which means "the last few hours," or "today, yesterday, and tomorrow," or at most "last week and next week"), we also never tire of being reminded by *The Onion* of its ridiculous elements.

People have worried for decades about whether our insatiable appetite for news has warped our whole consciousness. I'm sure it has. But we tend to notice that only in the way that news has become gruesome entertainment, in the "if it bleeds, it leads," mode. *The Onion* does exactly the same thing, in the comic rather than the tragic mode. So both tap into our pathos about news. *Onion* writers are self-aware—they have to be in order to do what they do. The local anchor on the six o'clock news, on the other hand, well, let's just say he doesn't need a very big brain. But *Onion* writers have surely realized that their own most devoted readers could be tripped up by the presence of actual news on their pages. So, they sometimes provide it just to keep us off balance.

Dead German With Large Brain Explains
Whole Universe

So there was a German guy you may not have heard of, Georg Wilhelm Friedrich Hegel (1770–1831); I call him "Hegel" for short, and actually, I named a poor cat "Hegel" in the distant past. The cat looked German to me. But I gave her away and didn't tell the new owner the name, proving that I am compassionate (for an ass-hole), and also capable of creating my own ancient joke that no one gets anymore. In German, you could say that "Hegel" is now "aufgehoben." Nevermind. It isn't translatable, or all that funny.

Another philosopher, named George Santayana, once said that Germans were, as a nation, incapable of boredom. His evidence was their reverence for Hegel's endless books. No kidding. And I don't think you would like this guy Hegel, so I'm not recommending him, but I will say, and this may surprise you, the Academy tends to agree that he was either the third or fourth most important philosopher in Western history (sharing the Oscar with Aristotle, Plato, and Immanuel Kant). And you probably never heard of him, right? Well, always remember, I could be lying.

Anyway, Hegel (the dude, not the cat) connected with a sucker punch to the vitals of all the self-important characters of the European Enlightenment, by being even more self-important than they were, and by reducing their extravagant knowledge claims to even more extravagant metaphysical claims. The arguments got very ugly, and in time Hegel gave us the philosophical basis of both fascism and communism—this is what the American Tea Party movement really means when they call Obama a "fascist socialist communist": that he's yet another Hegelian. Who knew they were so well read? But I wish they would just put "Obama is a Hegelian" on their placards, you know, say what they *really* mean, call a spade a spade. Some people just don't want a Hegelian for president, some do. What's the big deal?

So Hegel, along the way, says that, actually, the meaning of the whole world is held in something called "Absolute Spirit," and he said Spirit has three "moments": Art, Religion, and Philosophy. (You have to capitalize Nouns in German, and somehow the Capitals spill over into English when Hegel is translated.) So this is not "art" (something your mom hung on the refrigerator), it's Art, which expresses something so important to Human Nature and World History as to require its own special Place in Hegel's Philosophy.

Absolute Spirit gets its sensuous form from Art, its internal dynamic from Religion, and becomes known by and to Philosophy. When Philosophy has come to full self-consciousness, there is nothing left to learn. History is over. This blessed event occurs in the Philosophy of Hegel, according to Hegel. It is a relief, really, to have It All overwith.

I realize it's yesterday's news, that Philosophy is over, and that Hegel did it, finished off Philosophy (in the Library with the Candlestick). But the coroner's report says that Absolute Spirit must be distinguished from mere "Objective spirit," which is the historical path followed by Absolute Spirit for thousands of years of history until it finally arrived in Hegel's brain, and also from "Subjective spirit," which is all *you* have, according to Hegel. That means you and your little spirit go around endowing your daily activities with meanings, more or less according to your uninformed and sub-philosophical whims, not realizing that even your whims are being sucked into the great Whole that is the residue of Hegel's long dead brain, as contained in the endless pages of his books, which could also be used to plug the Gulf Oil Leak, if not the gulf oil leak.

So, let's review.

Absolute Spirit: That's the meaning of the whole World, and it happens when Art and Religion have a lovefest in Hegel's Philosophy.

Objective spirit: That's the march of all World History toward the goal of Hegel's Big Brain. In other words, it's the *real* meaning of events as they relate to Absolute Spirit, *not* as they might be seen at one time or another, by, say, news people, and other under-educated observers.

Subjective spirit: That's you, and maybe your friends, noodling around in your little patch of time, without the historical sense to come in out of the historical rain and read your Hegel so that you might learn something.

Writers Waste Lives Writing About Shit that Never Happened

I guess it seems clear enough where *The Onion* would belong in this scheme. That would be mainly under-educated people screw-

ing around with little slices of time, events and ideas, without much
of a clue about how they lead to Hegel's Philosophy.

But maybe not.

Actually, all of you have a built-in defense for wasting your lives
as you do, because Absolute Spirit, being so very damned
Absolute, feels obliged to be all-inclusive, which means that *whatever* you happen to be doing, it's *in there somewhere* helping the
Absolute be *just* the Absolute it always was destined to be, and not
some other, inferior Absolute that would have *lacked* your minuscule contribution. Think about *that* next time you watch daytime
TV. Your contribution to the Absolute, negligible as it is, isn't the
least significant one, or *you'd* be *on* TV.

So noodle away. You do still have your dignity. But don't get
too high-handed about it. Because even if you make up your mind
to stand in the way of Objective spirit, and try to slow its progress
toward the Absolute, you'll just get all chewed up and squishy, and
one way or another you'll toss your substance into the historical
feed trough of the Big Hog that is the *Zeitgeist*. (Yes, Hegel gave us
that word).

Now, if you ask me, *that's* news. No matter what we do, we
can't stop *The Onion* from making fun of it, because we can't keep
"news" from being these partial, incomplete, tiny little slices of time
that don't matter very much. The very inadequacy of "news," the
pathetic attempt of non-German persons to sum of the *importance*
of things while they are sort of still-happening, brings with it inexhaustible and irresistible comic possibilities. Only those who *pose*
as serious interpreters of the tiny time slices, the supposed arbiters
of Objective spirit (like Bill O'Reilly or Keith Olberman) *have* to get
anything *right*. And the idea that people who haven't mastered
Hegel could be serious arbiters of Objective spirit is really very
funny. *The Onion* doesn't have to get anything right—except the
comic timing.

Ironic Man Not Very Funny

The Onion writers, and Jon Stewart and Stephen Colbert and Trey
Parker and Matt Stone and the other truly excellent satirists of our
time, actually do more for Objective Spirit than they mean to, however. Remember that Hegel allows that Art is one essential moment
of Absolute Spirit—and so Art is, like, *way* better than Objective
Spirit, which isn't even entirely capitalized in this chapter.

Now the only question is whether *comedy* is just art, or whether it can be Art. And here we come to the part that wants rubbing. It's about time to hear from the guy with the Large Brain. Hegel thinks comedy can be and is Art, but *irony* is a noxious little troublemaker which is, at best, art. Here is how it reads when said by an adequately educated German:

> Insofar as irony is treated as a form of art, it does not content itself with conferring artistic shape upon the life and particular individuality of the artist [a laudable expression of Subjective spirit]. . . . The ironical, as "genial" individuality, consists in the self annihilation of what is noble, great, and excellent. (*G.W.F. Hegel on Art, Religion, Philosophy*, p. 100)

What the boy is saying is that *irony* is not very discreet and has a bad habit of not knowing when enough is enough. If you bring what is genuinely noble under an ironic gaze, you actually reduce your object, *and yourself*, to a less humane condition, to someone who is just "trying to be funny." You become an asshole, not a comedian. You bring to naught *all we have*, which isn't very damn much to begin with, in terms of time or meaning. If you sit there being merely ironical, you deny to your friends, as well as those who came before you in history and who will come later, any opportunity of reading you as a maturing expression of Objective Spirit, a contributor to what is noble and best in us. But, as Hegel says, *that* is just irony. It is not *comedy*. The Brain continues:

> The comic must be limited to bringing to naught what is in itself null, a false and self-contradictory phenomenon; for instance, a whim, a perversity, a particular caprice, set over against a mighty passion; or even a supposed reliable principle or rigid maxim may be shown to be null. But it is quite another thing when what is in reality moral and true . . . exhibits itself as null in an individual and by his means. . . . In this distinction between the ironical and the comic it is therefore an essential question of what import is that which is brought to nothing. (p. 101)

So, anything is *susceptible* to ironic treatment, which might even be done artfully, but not everything is comic—that is, can really be made into comedy. Comedy aims only at what is already no big deal, even when a lot of people (who never read Hegel) *think* it is important.

Thus, the "Janitor Finds Magic Bullet" story is a potentially funny idea, and could even be comedy, Art, if it actually mocks the proven nullity of the Warren Commission Report without diminishing the importance of the presidency and the violation of that office that occurred when Kennedy was assassinated. And indeed, that particular president can be satirized to the extent that typical human weaknesses were his, but only because we can distinguish the ironized "genial individual" (with foibles) from the *office*, and our faith in the importance of the office can usually survive any buffoon's occupying it for a while.

On the other hand, Martin Luther King, Jr., and his movement, and their importance to the elevation of human beings, cannot easily be separated from *his* individuality. To make light of him is to make light of what he stood for, whether we mean to or not. This probably makes King what Hegel would call a "World Historical Individual," a person whose individual existence embodies a great development in history, a person who, as an individual, concretely embodies the humane and spiritual aspirations of so many people as to transcend the historical moment, and to live not for the gratification of Subjective spirit, but rather to live out the meaning of a genuine movement of Objective spirit. Even King's foibles just aren't funny. Comedy, as Art, will not set its sites upon bringing to naught something of this sort. You *can* look upon something genuinely valuable with an ironic gaze, if you want to (and Rush Limbaugh and Glenn Beck, and many others do this every day), but you diminish what is best in *you* if you do that, and then, *you* are the fool.

Comedy, as Art, is a kind of self-restrained insight that improves us as human beings by bringing to naught *only* that which is *already* naught. It dissolves illusions. The true comedian sees what is *really* naught, often before anyone else does. In the case at hand, the thing that is really naught is *the news. The Onion* is sometimes Art because *the news*, and *the whole idea of it*, is largely void of any serious meaning; news makes almost no contribution to our historical self-understanding and does almost nothing to elevate us. In consuming news we gratify mainly our desire for gossip, and when news attempts seriousness, it must pretend that it *is* possible to explain *briefly* events that are very complex, and to have an objective perspective on matters that have not yet made their meanings interpretable (even to Hegel). That pretense is the source of the nullity of news and it diminishes the culture that consumes it.

Funny Newspaper Makes Accurate Prophecy

In light of all this, I return to my surprise at how quickly *The Onion* went after 9/11. I was taken aback at first, but then I thought for a minute and realized that the main lie, the main nullity in 9/11, derived from people who were pretending to understand the meaning of it before it was really possible to do so. When shit like that happens, we are stunned, and soon we just start babbling to fill up the silence. How long before we started spouting absolute bullshit to each other? In that case, longer than usual. It took about five or six hours, I would estimate before I heard complete bullshit coming at me, and at that point, comedy was in the offing, even for 9/11.

If you choose, now, to head out on-line and read the September 28th, 2001, *Onion*, you will see that all the stories take their impetus from that very feature of the event—that nobody (even the hijackers) ought to jump to conclusions about what this has to mean, and if we do it, we look like idiots and assholes, which is basically what so many of our leaders of that time look like now, in retrospect, nay? Giuliani for President? I don't think so. It took balls to be funny in September 2001, and I drink to *The Onion* for some comedy that endures, and for seeing what was and remains worthless, dangerous bullshit at close range and so quickly.

12
Existential Times

PAUL LOADER

Uncompliant Philosophy Student Drives Professor To Swearing

BOSTON, MA—37-year-old philosophy professor Hank Kirby was driven to swearing at one of his students in front of the rest of the class last Wednesday after the student persistently refused to recognize as meaningful the so-called 'problem of other minds'.

"He's just an idiot!" said usually good-natured Hank, when interviewed later about the incident.

The class began amicably enough with Kirby introducing the topic in what he thought would be "an interesting and engaging" manner. His opening question,"How do you know that I'm not a robot?" was met with some enthusiasm by several of the students present, one of whom even suggested that this was "completely possible."

Usually good-natured philosophy professor, Hank Kirby

Things started to go awry however when 17-year-old Benjamin Dupre joined in the conversation.

Dupre's first interjection was apparently "But you're not a robot" to which Kirby apparently replied "Well yes, I'm not saying that I actually am a robot but the question is, how can you be completely certain I'm not a robot? What are you basing your assumption that I'm not a robot on?" Dupre was then heard to reply once again "But you're not."

A complete record of how the conversation progressed after that is not available but a portion of it can be reconstructed from notes taken by another student, Kathy Mullyman:

KIRBY: Okay, so let's just imagine for the sake of argument that I was a robot, designed in some robot factory or other and—

DUPRE: But you're not.

KIRBY: No, okay. Well we've already established that I'm not actually a robot. But suppose, as a kind of thought experiment, that I was a robot and that every time it looked to you as though I were feeling some emotion or—

DUPRE: But you're not.

KIRBY: No, no I'm not. I'm not saying that I am. I'm just saying that we could imagine that I was a robot and that if I was a robot you might not be able to tell the difference—

DUPRE: But you're not.

KIRBY: No . . . but this is philosophy. The idea here is that we try to hypothesize. We try to imagine what it would be like if something *were* the case. We try to imagine what it would be like if I *were* a robot.

DUPRE: But you're not.

KIRBY: Jesus! Look—I'm not saying I'm a robot okay. Why don't you get it? I'm just saying that, even though it would be incredibly unlikely, just suppose I were—

DUPRE: But you're not. (*End of transcript*)

Although the remainder of the conversation is unavailable several students report that Kirby's last words before leaving the classroom were "You f*cking asswipe!" When asked by the Dean why he hadn't just humoured Kirby and gone along with the idea that he might be a robot, Dupre replied, "But he isn't."

Moral Philosophers "Worst in Bed"

TORONTO—An experiment conducted at the University of Toronto has concluded that moral philosophers are the worst in bed.

As part of a collaborative project between the psychology and philosophy departments, Steven Abney, Professor of Experimental Philosophy, organized for five of the university's philosophy professors, all male and each a specialist in a different field of Philosophy, to sleep in rotation with seven of his undergraduate psychology students, all female. After sleeping with a professor, each student was required to fill out a questionnaire rating their sexual experiences according to various criteria such as "Stamina," "Imagination," and "Foreplay Technique." Space was also given to allow students to make their own comments.

Steven Abney, Professor of Experimental Philosophy

The results showed that Professor Dan Morris, specialist in ethics, was ranked lowest by six out of seven of the students. Students complained that he generally had too many issues to perform satisfactorily.

Said one student, Karen Mezaros, "I was about to go down on him and he got all huffy. He started talking about the 'balance of power' in a relationship. It was a real turn off."

Also in receipt of poor feedback was Professor Miles Holland, a noted expert in logic. Although he was generally rated quite highly for stamina, his imagination and foreplay ratings were low and the general consensus of opinion was that he "lacked spontaneity."

Feedback on philosophy of mind professor Anthony Taylor was relatively neutral. Most felt that he performed adequately, although some said that at times it felt like he wasn't really connecting. "He was in his own world" said student Deborah Foley.

Professor Dan Negri, writer of several books on phenomenology, received generally good feedback. Most students found him relatively imaginative, one saying that the experience was "a bit trippy, which was fun!"

Top marks, however, went to Herbert Rader, Professor of Greek Philosophy. Students were near unanimous in their positive feedback, praising him in particular for his imagination and "total lack of inhibition." Several students reported that they were "up for it" when he suggested a group session, but this was not permitted within the guidelines of the experiment.

Professor Abney, who, along with colleague Professor Brian Clark, also slept with each student "to serve as a control group," said he was pleased that the experiment had gone so well and that he hoped to roll it out to philosophy departments in other universities next semester.

Added Abney, "We need to collect more data before we can reach firm conclusions."

"I'll Tell You What My Philosophy Is!" Says Man In Bar

ATLANTA—A man in the Frog's Log yesterday outlined the main tenets of his philosophy to visiting student Edward Clark.

Clark had entered the bar for a "quick drink" at 7:30 p.m. but soon fell into a long conversation with bar regular, Alexander Levin, after revealing that he was a philosophy student. "I'll tell you what my philosophy is," said Levin before embarking on a detailed and complex exposition of his belief system. Levin's central thesis was apparently that "there are some cool people in the world but also some real bastards and you've got to be careful of the bastards."

Although adhering to a generally collectivist position—"We've all got to help each other, 'cuz if we don't fucking help each other we're fucked"—there were also some Nietzchean elements to Levin's outlook, as when he asserted "It's a dog-eat-dog world. Let me tell you, you've got to get them before they get you. Look after number one, that's the main fucking thing. 'Cuz no one, not no fucker, not even your fuckin' mother, is gonna look after you. That's the truth, it's the fucking truth."

Levin did not reveal how the two elements of his philosophy were to be reconciled but intriguingly, in various cryptic comments, hinted at a possibility of synthesis: "It's not about us

Alexander Levin holding forth

and them. 'Cuz they're no different to us. It's about ourselves. It's all about ourselves. Not just you and me . . but everybody . . . every fucker in the world. It's all . . . ourselves."

In addition to outlining his central philosophy Levin was keen to engage with the issue of gender equality. His position appeared to be largely liberal—"I'm not saying I've got anything against women. I love women. Y'know, women are great. I've had some gorgeous bitches in my time."

At the same time Levin did express some concerns about the viability of a feminist critique in a post-modern era—"The thing is, and I'll tell you this for nothing . . . 'cuz you're my friend . . . the thing is, women don't even like it if you treat them equally. They don't even fucking like it. They want a man to be a man. Especially in bed. They want you to give it to them. Y 'know, really give it to them. . . ."

Clark later reported that he found Levin's ideas "interesting" but is not currently planning to return to the bar.

Self Found In Neck

MADISON, WI—Scientists at the University of Wisconsin claim to have found the self—long thought to be an elusive metaphysical concept—located in the upper part of the neck, just next to the thyroid gland. "It's about half a centimeter long and made of a quite malleable material, rather like a piece of Silly Putty" said chief scientist Peter Chitty.

If true, this is certainly a ground breaking discovery, and one that will put the University of Wisconsin on the map. Previously many had questioned the very existence of a 'self'. Most famously the philosopher David Hume reported that when he went searching for the self he found nothing but a "bundle of perceptions."

Professor Peter Chitty gives meaning to "self-discovery"

Now it looks as though Hume may simply have been looking in the wrong place.

Some modern-day philosophers, however, remain skeptical. "These guys are nuts," said Professor Pat Ficken, author of *The Self and other Mysteries*. "Last year staff from their Archaeology department announced they found the remains of God and were arguing that this offered support for Nietzsche's claim that "God is dead." You have the impression that they just don't get philosophy."

But Chitty dismissed Ficken's comments as "sour grapes." "Philosophers often like to sit on the fence. But we scientists are in the business of finding hard evidence."

Chitty added that other university faculty members were in the process of establishing proof of the existence of material objects. "All these philosophers run around questioning the existence of tables and chairs, but Doug Armstrong of the Design and Technology department has rightly pointed out that there are an abundance of such items around campus. Indeed, in his workshop alone there are about twenty chairs."

"No One Has Read Hegel," Poll Concludes

CAMBRIDGE, MA—Philosophers were left red-faced yesterday when a poll found that there may well not be a single professional philosopher at any American University who has read Hegel's famous work *Phenomenology of Spirit* in its entirety. The results of the poll, which were published in the *Journal of Academic Excellence*, raise serious questions about the standards of philosophy teaching in the US and may lead to a government inquiry about the selection policy for philosophy department faculty members.

The impetus for the study came originally from a single student, Daisy Mustram, a philosophy graduate student at Massachusetts Institute of Technology. Mustram was having problems with a particular passage in the book which begins "Spirit as the essence that is *self-consciousness*—or the self conscious Being that is all truth and knows all reality as its own self—is, to begin with, only its *Notion* in contrast to the actuality which it gives itself in the movement of its consciousness."

Daisey Mustram: Has anyone read this book?

"I asked my professor for help," says Mustram, "but he told me to ignore that passage since it was not assigned on our syllabus. I said I wanted to understand it anyway since it would help place the stuff that *was* assigned in a wider context. Then he looked a bit uncomfortable and said he would get back to me. I didn't want to wait so I asked some other faculty members. None of them wanted to talk to me. One said he'd 'only really read the bit about the master and the slave.'"

Mustram then started posting messages on various online philosophy forums used by academics but had no luck with these either. She received a number of replies, but she says that most merely restated what she had already been told about Hegel in philosophy 101. Of the remaining replies one confused Hegel with Heidegger, one offered an unlikely Buddhist interpretation, and one consisted of sexual innuendo.

It was at this point that she hit on the idea of writing to the *Journal of Academic Excellence* to suggest they commission a poll to find out just how many professional philosophers had actually read the *Phenomenology of Spirit* from cover to cover. Surprisingly, the journal agreed and questionnaires were duly dispatched to campuses across America. When the results came in, Mustram says she could hardly believe her eyes. Of the 1037 responses received not one gave an unequivocal "yes" to the question "Have you read all of Hegel's *Phenomenology of Spirit?*" and only 17 could say they had read "at least half" of the book.

Added Mustram, "It's like these guys have just bluffed their way through the education system."

Madonna Converts To Philosophy

NEW YORK—At a press conference yesterday singer Madonna revealed that she was "converting to Philosophy." The revelation followed reports from insiders that for the last three months the singer has been attending sessions run by self-styled 'Philosophy Mentor' Andrew Weiss. Previous to her conversion Madonna had been a follower of both Buddhism and Judaism but she claims she has now "finally found her home in philosophy."

Andrew Weiss, philosophy mentor

Asked what impact her conversion to Philosophy would have on her daily life the singer explained "Well, I can do most of the things I did before. I mean I'm not going to stop performing, for example. But on the other hand it's important that I live my life in accordance with what Andrew calls the 'Seven Precepts of Philosophy'." The singer was reluctant to go into detail about what these seven precepts were but did reveal that they were "kind of about being yourself and having positive energy."

Grudging Respects Paid To Unexceptional Philosopher

LARAMIE, WY—A commemoration ceremony was held yesterday for philosopher Dan Weaver who died of a heart attack on Tuesday at age 62. Weaver had been Professor of Philosophy at Wyoming State University for 23 years, previous to which he had worked at several other institutions, including Nebraska Technical College.

Dick Rawson, mustering respect

Speaking at the ceremony, friend and colleague Dick Rawson said that Weaver had a "fairly adequate" career. "Dan produced a steady output in the fields of ethics and metaphysics. It cannot be said that any of this work was ground-breaking or original but it did exhibit a certain degree of competence." During the speech Rawson did not look visibly moved although he did force himself to pause once and look down at his shoes as a mark of respect.

His remarks were later echoed by comments from another colleague, Professor Sanjay Gilmi. "Dan had published endless papers outlining the difference between what he called 'moral qualities' and 'moral properties," said Gilmi, fiddling with his ear in a slightly irritated way, "Most of us couldn't really see what hung on this distinction but I guess it must have meant something to him."

I'm Sorry but Your Essay Makes No Sense

Hi Michael. Prof Dyerson here. Look, I'm just going over your essay and, to be honest, I'm having a few problems with it. I think maybe you need to work on it a little more?

The question I gave you was 'What do you think Sartre was saying in his book *Existentialism and Humanism*? Now looking at this I can't find the part where you've tackled the question head on. There's lots of stuff here about *Planet of the Apes*. I can see you go into quite some depth about *Planet of the Apes*. And I don't want to stop you writing about what interests you. But if you could just draw it together a bit? Kind of make it more relevant to the question. . . .

For example, I like your point that the original *Planet of the Apes* story was also written by a Frenchman. Maybe you could do more with that. What are the similarities between the *Planet of the Apes* story and Sartre's work? What makes them both uniquely French? These are questions you might investigate. At any rate, you will lose marks if you just talk about *Planet of the Apes* without making any reference to Sartre.

I see that later in the paper you do talk a bit more about Sartre. However, I'm a little confused by the question you pose (on p.4) "If Sartre were invisible would he be able to fly?" Really I'm not quite sure what to make of this. The likely consequences of Sartre becoming invisible do not seem to have much bearing on the question I posed, or at least you have not shown that they do. Possibly some argument could be put forward which relates existentialism to a kind of 'metaphorical invisibility'—Is that what you were getting at? But then what has invisibility got to do with flying anyway? I think maybe you have got a little muddled here.

And then there's this "Mr Horse" business. In several places you refer to Sartre as "Mr Horse." It took me quite some time to work out that that's what you were doing, and nowhere do you explain why you've done so. It really is quite important when you're writing an essay that you are consistent with names. Otherwise the reader will get lost. If you feel it is getting a bit repetitive writing "Sartre" all the time then maybe you could use another phrase such as "the author" or simply "he." Either way, you can't just make up random names....

How Often Do You Philosophize?

Current research indicates that we need to philosophize three or four times a week to maintain good health. We asked four members of the public—"How often do you philosophize?"

Stacey Cook (25)
Nurse
I like to keep fit so try to philosophize most days after breakfast if I can.

Sally and Jim Davies (38 and 39)
Small business owners
We put time aside every week to philosophize together. It's very important to our relationship.

Pat Holden (46)
Executive
I have a very busy schedule. I usually get my secretary to philosophize for me and then she'll type up a brief summary.

Neela Martin (32)
Assistant Professor of Philosophy
What the hell are you talking about?

Philososcope

Aries See page 232 of Heidegger's *Being and Time* (Blackwell, 1962).

Taurus This will be a great week to seek cab driver certification.

Gemini Your 'Talk Philosophy With Hot Teens' phone-line idea is certainly original but unlikely to succeed.

Cancer The passing of Saturn through Leo this week allows you to give free expression to your tendencies to be shy and inconsequential.

Leo I suggest you get some practice at saying the word 'phenomenology' if you don't want to make an ass of yourself again.

Virgo Why do you pretend?

Libra On Tuesday your philosophy tutor will, in a certain fleeting expression of his face, reveal to you that he hates his whole life.

Scorpio That thing you were going to do, you should do it.

Sagittarius All your ideas about 'being an individual' come from someone else.

Capricorn Your chapter for 'Pussycat Dolls and Philosophy' has been accepted.

Pisces Pisces, try not to crack your knuckles like that.

Empedocles Aries and Taurus will be real pains in the ass this week but Gemini will let you feel her up in the office supplies closet as long as you don't tell Capricorn.

"Loser" In Movie Quotes Nietzsche

HOLLYWOOD—A "loser" character in the newly released movie *My Christmas Wedding* is shown quoting philosopher Frederick Nietzsche.

The controversial decision to include a reference to Nietzsche in the film was made by director Morgan Davies. Davies explained "I

Controversial Director Morgan Davies

thought it would be a novel idea to have a character in a film who would occasionally say something 'deep' as a counterbalance to the light-hearted goings on occurring elsewhere. I then thought, Who could be deeper than Nietzsche? Nietzsche is like a byword for deepness. So I developed this character, Jo, who is a kind of amiable loser—he smokes a bit too much dope and occasionally says profound things."

In the scene in question, Jo's sister turns to him for advice about her love life. He fixes her with a meaningful stare and says, "There is always some madness in love. But there is always some reason in madness. Nietzsche." Then he trips over backwards and falls into a pond.

"I know no one has tried anything like this before," says Davies "and I guess I'm taking a risk playing with the genre in this way. But I think audiences will enjoy the intellectual challenge."

Assistant Professor Sexually Aroused On Meeting Intellectual Hero

CAMDEN, NJ—Assistant Professor Robert Stabeley admitted to getting an erection on meeting his intellectual hero Daniel Bennett for the first time last Friday. "I just couldn't help myself," said Stabeley, "It was just so amazing meeting the guy in the flesh."

The incident occurred during a two-day conference on "Mind and Consciousness" held at Rutgers University. Professor Bennett, a leading authority on philosophy of mind and author of numerous influential books, gave the plenary lecture to a packed hall of academics and graduate students. Stabeley said that even at this point he began to experience some sexual feelings.

"Just listening to the guy talk was something else. I was hanging on his every word. I mean this is the guy I wrote my thesis on. I have everything he's ever written, including some hard-to-find first editions of his early work." However it was not until a later face-to-face encounter with his hero that Stabeley achieved what he describes as "pretty much a full erection."

Stabeley states that after the plenary lecture finished there was a break for lunch in the main dining hall. "I was standing in line. I think I was waiting for the lasagne. I remember I already had an orange juice on my tray. Anyway, suddenly I hear this voice behind me. . . . (*continued, p. 289*)

Marxist Wants Capitalism To Collapse "Once Book Is Published"

EUGENE, OR—Janet Myler, a radical Marxist of some thirty years standing, claims that she still wants capitalism to collapse but is hoping it might hang around for another six months or so until her book is published.

"I've been a vehement critic of the capitalist system since my student days," said Myler, professor of political philosophy at the University of Oregon, "but I've been working on this book

Janet Myler, hoping for delayed collapse rather than imminent demise

for about four years now and it will be quite frustrating if the whole system decides to collapse just as I'm about to get it published."

Manuscript copies of the book—entitled *Why Capitalism Must End*—have been circulated to some of the major publishers with several already expressing an interest in publishing it. What worries Myler, however, is the current economic downturn, which the book itself predicted as a likely precursor to capitalism's imminent demise.

"I'm hoping that maybe capitalism is a little more resilient than I had originally thought. Otherwise I'm done for," said Myler yesterday.

Gene For Pedantry Same As Gene For Philosophy

JEFFERSON CITY, MT—Researchers at Montana Biological Institute think they may have found a genetic explanation for the development of Philosophy in some human beings and not others.

Looking at DNA samples from 72 philosophers and non philosophers they discovered that the former were more likely to

Donna Hathelwate explaining the gene for pedantry, at great length

have two copies of a particular variant of a gene known as ANL. The variant has been known to researchers in the field for some time but had previously only been linked with the expression of pedantry.

"These are early days yet," says research Team leader Donna Hathelwate, "But what our findings seem to suggest is a close connection between philosophy and pedantry in adult human beings. Indeed for all practical purposes they seem to be the same thing."

Business

13

Sarcastic Bastards, Useless Bullshit, and Murder

DAN MIORI

Congratulations! If you're reading this it means a couple of things. First, you're making your way through an enjoyable and informative book. Second, you're still alive. You already are very familiar with the upside of being alive: eating good food, listening to music, spending time with your friends getting high . . . One big downside, however, is that us alive folks (yes, I too am alive) stand about a fifty-fifty chance of dying in a hospital ICU with a bunch of tubes in us, and that possibility grows every year (you stoners stand a particularly good chance).

As a Physician Assistant on a Palliative Care service, the majority of my work is with patients near the end of their life. I know a few things based on this experience and one of the most important things I've learned is that dying in an intensive care unit is not always necessary; and it is sometimes completely avoidable; but by not planning ahead that is how we end up. Tubes will be inserted into every orifice and a few in openings that didn't previously exist. You will lie in an uncomfortable bed in a strange room with lights on round the clock, alarms beeping, staff waking you up to poke you with needles, and lots of other unpleasant things that you probably wouldn't believe if I told you.

If this picture is attractive to you, if you think all those tubes might feel interesting and are willing to trust that medical providers are good at anticipating and treating pain (they are not; something else I've learned), then please consider the fact that most of us only go to the hospital as a last resort. Some illness or injury needs to make us feel really crappy before we allow ourselves to be taken there. If you're one of those people who waited too long to come to the hospital because you rightly figured you would die there, then you probably feel really *really* crappy (especially you stoners).

Reaching an understanding of your life and its end, how decisions are made in an ICU when there are no good choices, and exploring the difference between a good death and a bad one, may help prevent you winding up in the same situation as cancer patient Russell Kunkel in the *Onion* story "Loved Ones Recall Local Man's Cowardly Battle With Cancer" (2/24/99). Russell was given four months to live but died in just one due to what his physician might have called his *exceptionally* negative attitude. Perhaps a little reflection would have helped him. Yet most of us don't spend our days walking around thinking about death. Nor should we: it would be too depressing.

The choices we make that put us into, affect our care in, and get us out of hospitals are reflected in *The Onion*'s articles concerning medical ethics. *The Onion* brings its readers to a greater understanding of those situations, maybe not every reader and maybe not all the time, but certainly far more often than I ever managed to do.

Bad News Served with a Smile

The Onion is a satirical news magazine. Ultimately, its writers' first job is to sell ad space. They do this by making fun of news journalism, but in doing so they also challenge us and help us reflect on our lives. In spite of the many articles on philosophy, death and dying, and euthanasia, *The Onion* does not have a philosophy on those topics so much as it has a philosophy on a life unexamined. *The Onion* examines those things mercilessly in the tradition of Diogenes of Sinop, a student of Socrates who liked to poke fun at the nonsensical things ancient Athenians did every day. He didn't offer them an alternative, he just pointed out their foibles with subtle little signs, like that time he masturbated in the marketplace.

Many of the articles in *The Onion* which use medical ethics or the delivery of health care as their main topic also offer us no reasonable alternative. Even the generously described libertarian philosophy of *South Park* offers us some direction once it gloriously dismantles our pre-established doctrines, but *The Onion* leaves us to stew in our own juices, to draw our own conclusions (the bastards!). So what does *The Onion* want us to do? Can there be philosophy without learning? Without some direction for our now

open mind the lesson is lost and *The Onion* becomes frank bur-
lesque with no purpose other than coarse humor at the expense of
others (the *sarcastic* bastards!).

Jonathan Swift, who wrote *Gulliver's Travels*, said that satire was
a mirror in which we see everyone's face but our own. I think Swift
was full of shit. For those of you who have spent time trying to
wring information out of a medical provider it may seem we lack
humanity, that we haven't figured out that when we talk to you
about *your* mortality, we are also talking about *our own* mortality.
In reality, you would need to be a sociopath not to think about it.
Some of us manage to have the conversation anyway because we
come to grips with the fact that we too will die. Some of us are able
to do it because we temporarily shut the reality out. Some of us
simply stop dealing with the dilemma by working in dermatology.

I believe *The Onion*'s writers and editors also feel the humanity
of the situations they deal with. They're writing about the
dichotomy of tragedy (I cut my finger) and comedy (you cut your
finger) with every story. This self-knowledge and honesty helps
them to bring the realization of their own pending cowardly death
into the story, a shared understanding that makes us think behind
the laughter.

Philosophy Is Helpful ? . . . Who Knew

A basic awareness of philosophy is useful in understanding medical ethics. As an ethics consultant in a hospital, I spend a large part
of my day counseling patients and their families on how to find a
way through the almost impossible minefield of decision-making at
the end of life. Choosing a way forward when there are no good
outcomes, only relatively less bad outcomes. This is a time when
the fundamental reason for philosophy—understanding the world
and our place in it—becomes paramount.

In Western philosophy there are three prominent theories, each
of which provides a valid path for resolving moral dilemmas. To
arrive at a decision in a situation where there's no clear right or
wrong answer is not easy, and often we simply must try to make
the least crappy choice. Which theory we use as a guide should not
make a big difference in the decision reached, but each has its
advantages and limitations. In no particular order, the theories are:
consequentialism, deontology, and virtue ethics. I will also mention
some of the philosophers associated with those schools of thought.

In part because their works are commonly discussed as examples of these ideas, but mostly because they were the ones mentioned in Monty Python's "Philosopher's Song", a catchy little tune I've been working into conversations for years.

Consequentialism

John Stuart Mill of his own free will, on half a pint of shandy was particularly ill.

John Stuart Mill (1806–1873) felt that humans are rational beings and are capable of reaching moral decisions (despite all evidence to the contrary). While recognizing reasoning as an important part of the process, he believed that the result is what counts. If the result is good, then we might overlook how it was accomplished. Mill would say that it was okay for Robin Hood to steal from the rich as long as this enabled him to help more people than he hurt. As an aside, I'm not so sure that Mill had a realistic understanding of why most people make the stupid decisions that they do, for example Derek Yothers in *The Onion's* " Man's Impending Death Alcohol-Related " (6/16/04) or "Investigators Blame Stupidity In Area Death" (5/25/05). (That moron's name was "withheld out of respect for his stupid family".) Also, Mill's belief that we are even remotely capable of anticipating all the possible outcomes of our actions simply demonstrates the fact that he never really got outside much when he was a kid (climbing a tree *always* seems like a good idea at the time). Another thing worth knowing is that shandy is a combination of beer and lemonade ('lemonade' in the British sense, meaning a lemon-and-lime-flavored soda like 7-Up).

Deontology:

Immanuel Kant was a real pissant.

Immanuel Kant (1724–1804) felt that good intentions are the glue of a society, and that we ought to abide by certain rules so that the greater good is protected. In this case, how we arrive at a decision is the focus. Abiding by rules allows everyone a fair shot and, even though some of the outcomes may not make everyone happy, the overall good is protected. Robin Hood should not steal to feed the poor because stealing is against the law. Certainly it is against the established statutes of most civilizations, but it is also against a higher moral law. The basis for that higher law is that it's rational, (to Kant) and if we just think about it hard enough we will realize that we agree with him. As with Mill, I have a few issues with Kant and this entire *higher law* thing.

Virtue Ethics

Aristotle, Aristotle was a bugger for the bottle.

Party animals from left to right: Kant, Mill, God, Aristotle!

According to Aristotle, Socrates, Plato, and even Confucius, the most important factor in making a decision is the character of the decision-maker. The individual's character has many parts, and writers have described those parts differently, but most would agree that they consist of; a natural talent for virtue, such as honesty or a willingness to do good; an intellectual virtue, like striving to understand things without judging them; and having knowledge or experience of what is bad and good. A virtue ethicist would understand the difficulty in knowing the full outcome of an act ahead of time, and that rules are only useful in straightforward situations. Aristotle Hood will have to arrive at his own decision about stealing from the rich; relying on his virtuous character and his knowledge of himself and the world he lived in (is he stealing to feed the poor or because he really just craves attention?). He would probably try to generate an alternative solution, consistent with the virtue of honesty, to balance between two bad outcomes of stealing and allowing the poor to starve.

Medical Ethics Is Not an Oxymoron

The role of medical ethics is not to decide what's right and wrong; it is to help resolve moral dilemmas. Hippocrates (of Hippocratic Oath fame) faced a moral dilemma in his time, and its name was "surgery." It seems that surgery in the third century B.C. was not as advanced as it is today. In fact, it was so unreliable that Hippocrates included a prohibition on performing surgery in his original oath (as well as forbidding sex with your patient's slaves). Much has changed over the last 2,300 years, since surgery is now an integral part of medicine (to my knowledge the sex with slaves thing is still a *big* no-no). Over time, some of what was considered ethical changed as technology changed; some of what was considered ethical stayed the same.

Virtue ethics had a good run up until about the eighteenth century; deontology and consequentialism were fairly popular from then till about the middle of the twentieth century. Over the last fifty years though, virtue ethics has made a comeback of sorts and much of current medical ethics theory is based on it. A good starting point in the discussion of contemporary medical ethics would be the work of two guys who are rather fond of virtue ethics, Tom Beauchamp and James Childress. In 1979 they literally wrote the book on medical ethics, which outlined a method of examining medical decisions using four ideas: autonomy, nonmaleficence, beneficence, and justice.

Autonomy: Freedom from Undue Influence

Giving you, as the patient, autonomy does not mean that we will ask you to make all the medical decisions for us (although we sure would like to). It means we will give you unbiased information so that you can make the value-based decisions that you should be making. While deciding which antibiotic to use would be a medical decision, deciding whether to continue antibiotics and all the potential side effects they will give, when at best they will only delay certain death by hours, is a value-based decision.

Medical providers unduly influence their patients' ability to make value-based decisions by being lousy bearers of bad news.

They overstate the good news no matter how marginal ("Your husband's decline has stabilized and we are seeing no further tumor growth or spread") and avoid talking about the bad news ("the fist sized tumor between his stomach and his liver is every bit as bad as it was yesterday, it just hasn't gotten any worse").

The Onion ridicules this tendency in "I've Got Some Bad News, And I've Got Some Hilarious News" (6/13/07). The bad news was that Uncle Murray was dead before his time, but the hilarious news was that "he died after a pair of bumbling orderlies slipped on an ill-placed mop, lost control of his gurney, and sent him rolling uncontrollably down the length of the hall and through an open stairway door. . . . it was a really funny way to go." Being able to honestly and compassionately communicate bad news is not easy; it requires constant monitoring, while allowing patients autonomy in their decision-making.

Nonmaleficence: Don't Do Bad Things

Sounds simple but it means more than it seems. While it's easy to say "Don't go out of your way to practice evil," nonmaleficence tells us that we need to take into account the possible evil that we may do just by being tired, or poorly informed, or criminally stupid. It's not evil to want to be at home in bed, but if you're ten miles away, completely drunk, and try to get home by pouring yourself into the driver's seat. . . . that's maleficent. Accepting that you are too shitfaced to drive and taking a cab home, even though it's expensive and inconvenient, is nonmaleficence. Understanding you have a difficult time breaking bad news and working on doing a better job of it is nonmaleficence.

Beneficence: Do Good Things

As with many profound thoughts, this one's fairly simple. In reality, it means you should go out of your way to do things that benefit your patient, even when you want to go home at the end of a long day. It's not the same as nonmaleficence, since you can put in the hours, not screw up, and still not be beneficent. If my dying patient wants his pet to visit him but there is a strict "We're a bunch of assholes who don't like dogs and won't let them in our hospital" policy, telling your patient "no pets" is certainly nonmaleficent, but it's not really beneficent. Working your way up the administrative ladder until you find someone with authority who will okay the visit is beneficence.

An important thing to understand, by the way, is that there are more than a few congenial and beneficent slackers out there who somehow managed to successfully stumble through their medical training, and who would gladly buy drinks for the house. They are maleficent, however, by their routine delivery of even slightly substandard care. They make great drinking buddies, but terrible medical providers.

Justice: Distribute Goods Fairly

Currently, hospitals don't ask who will or will not get the ventilator because everyone gets it, even if they don't want it. For anything more than basic care, our profit-driven healthcare system lets money decide who gets what. Pounding down the door to the room, however, is a rather frightening nine-hundred pound gorilla, namely, the forty million Americans without health insurance. Once we wake up and try to provide everyone with equitable healthcare, distributing expensive high-tech medical treatments will become a much tougher issue.

There are many ways to split those medical-ethics hairs down further, but for this conversation, the hairs are probably split just about right.

Socrates's Last Words: "I Drank WHAT?"

Euthanasia is a huge issue in medical ethics. Today we take euthanasia to mean mercy killing with just a slight stretch to physician-assisted suicide.

To the ancient Greeks, and as it is literally translated, *euthanasia* meant "good death," quite simply, a peaceful exit from this world. It focused on the spiritual aspects of death (or *existential aspects* for the atheists in the crowd) and had a lot more to do with incense, music, and family telling funny stories than it did with suicide (literally "self-killing").

On the occasion that the dying process involved painful symptoms, *which were beyond the ability of contemporary medicine to treat*, euthanasia might also have involved some hemlock tea to speed the process along. The ancient Greeks had other terms to describe death in different situations based on the events of those situations, such as *haireo thanaton*, meaning "seize death"; or *biazesthai heauton*, "flee life." Socrates was given the choice to end his life by drinking Hemlock tea or to be banished from Athens (he also had the opportunity to escape with the help of some friends but declined). His choice was to end his life, and he talked about it using the term *eulogos exagoge* or "sensible removal"

If we look to *The Onion* for a definition of physician-assisted suicide it might propose Vehicular Manslaughter, a crime in most states and the subject the story "'Vehicular Manslaughter Doctor' Assists In 23rd Doctor-Assisted Vehicular Manslaughter" (7/9/97). Physician-assisted suicide occurs when we deliberately speed up the process of death by intentionally using appropriate medicines in excessive amounts, by devices such as Jack Kervorkian's "death machine", or by 'Vehicular Manslaughter Doctor' James Munson's 1994 Ford Escort. Most Americans are against physician assisted suicide, or mercy killing, or what outside the states of Oregon and Washington is called "murder." Coincidently, one of the hold-outs on making the act of killing someone with a car a crime is Oregon, clearly not a state to be old or slow in.

Part of euthanasia's bad rap comes from organizations like The Hemlock Society, and the Final Exit Network. The Hemlock Society advocates for laws allowing physician-assisted suicide. They used to use the word "euthanasia" a lot, but now that they shit all over it they say they advocate "death with dignity." In theory, giving your medical provider permission to kill you preserves your dignity. Final Exit Network, which has been in the news a bit lately, is a different story. The Georgia Bureau of Investigation alleges that "exit guides" will actually come to your house, hold you down, put an "exit hood" over your head and run helium into your lungs until your dignity has been good and preserved. They will then clean up the evidence, and all this for just a low, low fifty-dollar membership fee.

I will borrow that term, "death with dignity," from the right-to-die fanatics (you homicidal bastards can have it back when I'm done), and in doing so will try to restore euthanasia to its original meaning of "good death." We can treat pain, air hunger, nausea, congestion, post nasal drip, halitosis. . . . almost all the symptoms of dying. There is no reason to go killing yourself to avoid them, especially not with my help.

Death with Dignity: Schiavo's Right to Die

The Onion's American Voices column is a satirical opinion poll. It uses the same six photos of average looking people every week, changing their names and occupations in ridiculously appropriate ways. Appearing three at a time in random order, these Americans serve as conduits of *Onion* commentary on actual current events. The photos even include a UPS messenger who just happened to be delivering a package to *The Onion* on the day an American face was needed. In all the issues I've read, Al Gore was a guest photo once and there was a ghost once, but the only time all six photo's were used simultaneously was for commentary on Terry Schiavo. In this unprecedented panoply of opinion, *The Onion* outdid itself in what it does best: make fun of everyone.

Statements like "If God had wanted people to die with dignity he wouldn't have created modern medical technology capable of artificially prolonging life" and "With proper treatment Terry Schiavo could have gone on to live a long and . . . long life" suggest that prolonging the life of a person in a vegetative state might not be the best way to go. Whereas "My family is currently petitioning the state for permission to remove my fat uncle's feeding spoon" suggests that artificial nutrition is the same as eating by mouth, and that stopping it would be the same as the starvation of a healthy (but fat) uncle. The comment "I've set up a living will so that, in the event I fall into a persistent vegetative state, I should be blown to death" suggests "blow me." Finally, Maria Avery's comment "And what about the feeding tube, is no one considering its feelings" suggests that she is, in fact, an asshole. Bottom line, as we said in the Sixties, question everything.

Diseased and Deformed Animal Lover as Medicine American-Style

One of *The Onion*'s strongest articles on the subject of medical ethics and euthanasia was a story told in the first person by Tricia McCory, an animal lover of truly sickening proportions ("I'm A Diseased And Deformed Animal Lover," 10/15/03).

Tricia may have been acting beneficently by caring for the diseased and deformed animals that literally filled her house, and she most certainly had the justice thing down since it seems she treated every sick animal that washed up on her bleak shore. "I'd never be so cruel as to turn away a stray dog, just because his care requires that I siphon fluid from his lungs with a plastic tube every four hours," she said. In spite of these positives her actions represent the worst of medical care today. She was making decisions based completely on her own need to keep her patients alive, with no consideration for their wishes (autonomy) or the pain she was causing by needlessly extending the inevitable process of their dying (nonmaleficence).

The moral dilemma this story presents is that kindness can be cruel. Tricia saved a mortally injured paraplegic deer by hand-feeding him "corn that I chewed up myself." You could almost see the frowsy, fanatical glow in her bloodshot eyes as she added "I kept him alive for almost a week." The problem is that, in doing so, she provides absolutely no benefit to the deer. Tricia's heroism is harmful, not only to her animals, but also to herself. She risked her own safety trying to give Señor Oink the epileptic pig a safe home. "I love little Oinky," she said, "no matter how many times he's accidentally bitten me or destroyed one of my lamps during an episode."

World Death Rate Holding Steady At 100 Percent

With very little translation, "World Death Rate Holding Steady At 100 Percent" (1/22/97) is as true as anything you would hear on CNN. In fact, it would be the most accurate story Fox ever ran. We all die; no one has cured that yet. We have some great technology to cure a few things, and we are improving all the time. We have some fairly heavy-handed medical treatment to sustain life, like feeding tubes (artificial nutrition) and ventilators (artificial respiration), which sometimes buy people enough time to recover from life threatening illness. We do not, however, possess is the ability to stop someone from dying.

There comes a point, usually a clearly identifiable point, when we know someone is going to die. We've even come up with a very clever term for it; *actively dying*.

If we mobilize all our treatments and technology we can slow down this process, but do you want us to? Although slowing things down a bit may sound like a good idea, it could be a mistake. If you're suffocating because you ran out of functioning lung, being on a ventilator simply allows you to experience your death over the course of weeks instead of days. Allowing natural death to occur in its own time is not murder. It is accepting that the death rate is still one hundred percent and until someone comes up with a really great cure for death (and please call me when you do), it will remain one hundred percent.

We can fix the *way* we die—we can recognize that there is existential pain for all of us at the end of life and open ourselves to helping others with that pain. We can plan ahead by designating someone to make decisions for us when we can no longer do so. It may seem too morbid to devote a sunny spring day to drawing up a living will, but it beats the heck out of allowing medical providers to dictate unnecessary and burdensome treatment. (In my home state of New York the document to appoint a decision making agent is called a Health Care Proxy. Whatever your state calls it, get one!).

In this age of information, we can learn about our illness and take an active part in our ongoing medical treatment. Even if we do all the right things it won't be very funny and we won't read about it in *The Onion*. We may, however, be able to take some satisfaction from the fact that we will end our lives with a good and dignified death (and now you Hemlock Society morons can have "death with dignity" back. . . . assholes).

14

The Green *Onion*

MATTHEW C. ALTMAN

It's often said that philosophy unsettles the settled mind and set-tles the unsettled mind. Literally, *philosophia* means "the love of wisdom," and the pursuit of wisdom involves first questioning what we happen to believe in order to figure out what we ought to believe. Most of us are all too certain of our convictions, so philosophers usually begin by showing just how fragile, unjustified, or inconsistent our beliefs are. This is why philosophers threaten (or should threaten) the status quo. It's why Socrates was given a hemlock cocktail. The Athenian citizens who passed judgment on Socrates were stung by his challenge to their values, his charge that they were more concerned with shallow comforts than the pursuit of the good.

Satire serves a philosophical purpose in that it calls attention to our shortcomings in an effort to transform our thinking. Unlike most professional philosophers, satirists use humor to accomplish this end, but the end is the same: to decenter us or provoke us. *The Onion* portrays our beliefs and practices in an exaggerated light so that we can see our faults more clearly. We recognize ourselves in caricature, and we don't like what we see. In response, we may take ourselves less seriously, we may adjust our views, or we may write angry letters to the editor. Denial isn't just a jury in Athens.

Like a number of contemporary philosophers, *The Onion* chal-lenges how we conceive of and relate to the natural world. Ever since its first appearance in 1783, when it was printed on paper made from recycled wigs, *The Onion* has lampooned the common belief that nature is merely a resource to be used and has put for-ward the idea that it has value in its own right. *The Onion* has also advanced ecofeminism, a theoretical framework that critiques the mutually reinforcing domination of women, animals, nature, and the Third World. At the risk of overstating its impact, without *The Onion* and the contributions it has made to our ecological consciousness, things would be a lot different: the world would be losing its rainforests and warming drastically, thousands of species would become extinct every year, and we would be stuffing landfills with tons of garbage while we eat millions of factory-farmed animals. *The Onion* is our bulwark against this.

It's Not Just about Us

Most moral theories in the history of Western philosophy are anthropocentric, meaning that we only have direct obligations to other human beings; the well-being of animals and ecosystems matters only indirectly, insofar as they affect us. For example, diminutive eighteenth-century German philosopher Immanuel Kant believed that it is wrong to torture animals only because it hardens us to suffering and makes it more likely that we will hurt other people. Following Aristotle, Catholic theologian Thomas Aquinas thought that we could use the "less perfect" objects of creation (animals and plants) however we see fit. We ought to respect the environment only if not doing so harms us—for example, if polluting the stream taints our drinking water. To hell with the fish.

The Onion has consistently satirized this kind of anthropocentric position, doing the work that the mainstream philosophical media refuses to do. For example, in "New, Delicious Species Discovered" (5/18/05), an international team of scientists comes upon a previously unknown species in the Amazon River Basin, and the animals' value is measured by how they taste to us. The "delicacy apes" are conceived as a food source; their social habits are merely a means to more delectable monkey steaks: "They often sit grooming each other for hours on end, which explains why their meat is so marbled and tender." That animals would have value in themselves is not even mentioned. No one says that they have a right to exist, or that their interests ought to be taken into account when we decide what to do with them. But the reader notices the trivial human needs that the monkeys are fulfilling, and it seems strange to consider the species only in this way.

Anthropocentrism can take many forms. In "Beauty Of National Forest Enjoyed By Logger" (2/28/01), Steve Orton smells the pines,

The primate   *The prime cut*

admires the wildlife, and is awestruck by the majesty of the old-growth forest. We are all the more appalled, then, when his sawing and stump grinding turns the area into a "pockmarked, heavily eroded field." At first, the contrast between aesthetic appreciation and heartless exploitation seems like a clear case of good versus evil. On closer examination, however, both ways of approaching the environment think only of how we are affected: the trees are valuable because we like seeing them or because we like to profit from selling the wood. The worth of the forest in each case is relative to our interest in it. Although cutting down the trees more blatantly commodifies nature, the shift in the article is jarring primarily because we come to see the underlying anthropocentrism that is at the heart even of Orton's initial reaction to it. The piece makes us uncomfortable with what is traditionally taken to be an environmentally friendly attitude: that nature is there for us to enjoy.

Granted, it may seem strange that *The Onion* would have a progressive environmentalist agenda. After all, this is the satirical newspaper that includes such ludicrous titles as "Nation's Snowmen March Against Global Warming" (1/25/06) and "Endangered Manatee Struggles To Make Self Understood to Congress" (8/15/01). Is there a serious message in these short, anything-for-a-laugh articles that lash out at everyone and everything? Certainly *The Onion* is irreverent. It's provocative. But that's the point. By lampooning our most deeply held attitudes, *The Onion* prompts us to question our anthropocentrism, thus paving the way for the idea that we have direct duties to animals and ecosystems.

Suffering Is Bad, Even for Animals

Revealing the ugly implications of anthropocentrism does not by itself establish the inherent worth of nonhuman, living things. However, it allows us to assess without bias what makes something morally considerable—that is, what makes it such that we ought to consider its interests when we make a decision. To this end, environmental ethicists often begin by discussing the value of nonhuman animals. If we could show that we ought to be concerned about our treatment of animals, then we would begin to expand the class of things to which we have direct moral obligations.

In his seminal work *Animal Liberation* (1975), Peter Singer argues that it is unjustified to restrict moral consideration to human beings. Why does a severely disabled human baby have more value than a chimpanzee with a greater mental capacity? The fact that someone is a member of a particular species is morally irrelevant. Singer coined the term "speciesism" to describe our usual attitude. Like racism, speciesism is merely a prejudice in favor of things like us.

What really matters, according to Singer, is whether the thing can suffer. A being is directly morally considerable if it has interests, and any sentient being—that is, any being who is capable of feeling pleasure and pain—has at least one interest: to avoid pain and seek pleasure. Singer's view is a form of utilitarianism, the classic ethical theory according to which we ought to maximize overall happiness. If this is true, then the effects of a given action on sentient animals ought to be considered along with its effects on human beings.

Appealing to utilitarianism, Singer criticizes both animal testing, most of which is misleading or unnecessary, and the eating of meat, which subjects animals to horrible factory farm conditions simply to satisfy our palates. Although the new Cover Girl Mascara "will leave your lashes 40 percent thicker than Elizabeth Arden mascara," such a giant leap in the development of human culture is probably not worth the excised eyelids, cauterized tear ducts, and chemical scarring described in "Lab Rabbit Strongly Recommends Cover Girl Waterproof Mascara For Sensitive Eyes" (11/29/00). Likewise, the lovable antics of Captain Bananas are described in "Funny Monkey Tested On" (4/29/98) so we are that much more disturbed when lab technicians "inject a concentrated mixture of cadmium chlorate directly into his exposed eyeball" and "force 2.7 liters of flammable lighter-fluid/paint-thinner mixture down his throat." How could they treat a captain that way?

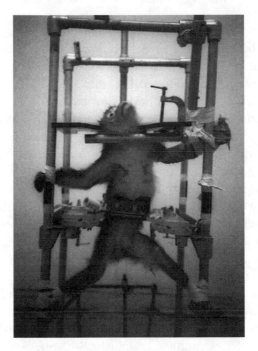

Captain Bananas, doing some prop comedy

The Onion also lampoons Americans' love for dead animal flesh: "Denny's Introduces 'Just A Humongous Bucket Of Eggs And Meat'" (1/17/01), "Meat Now America's No. 2 Condiment" (8/2/06), "Dozens Die In Chicago-Area Meatwave" (5/7/03)—the titles attest to the kind of eating habits that, in the U.S. alone, lead to the deaths of thirty-six million cows and nine billion chickens every year.

But the treatment of animals prior to slaughter is also a concern, and *The Onion* often addresses factory farm conditions through an analysis of what exactly we're putting down our throats. In "U.S. Children Getting Majority Of Antibiotics From McDonald's Meat" (4/17/02), then US Secretary of Health and Human Services Tommy Thompson notes that many low-income and uninsured children now get their medications primarily through Big Macs loaded with quinupristin-dalfopristin. Then comes the explanation as to why beef contains such drugs:

> Large-scale meat producers . . . routinely add antibiotics to the feed of
> healthy animals to prevent cross-infection in the crowded, cramped
> quarters where livestock are typically raised. In the U.S., the average
> beef steer receives eight times more antibiotics than its human coun-
> terpart.

Cows must be chemically engineered to withstand the deplorable
conditions in which they are raised and eventually killed: limited
movement (often total confinement) that leads to the animals' hurting each other, a lack of light and proper ventilation, the cramped
and cold transportation to the slaughter plant, stress when they're
not allowed to express their natural instincts, being fed in ways that
are unhealthy and unnatural (to produce larger animals more
quickly). This kind of suffering is only the beginning. Chickens and
turkeys are debeaked, pigs' tails are cut off, cows are branded, pigs
and cows are castrated, and usually animals are electrically stunned
before being hung upside down and having their throats slit.

    We do not do these things because we need the nutrients or
because it is a more efficient means of getting the necessary pro-
tein. Raising animals for food is very inefficient compared to growing crops, and a balanced vegetarian diet can give us everything
our body requires. Instead, we do these things simply because we
like how dead animals taste. We completely disregard their suffering—and this, Singer argues, is unjustifiable. Speciesism makes the
meat industry possible.

    When we do consider the suffering of animals, our concern is
erratic and inconsistent. After Congress banned the "barbaric" practice of selling horse meat, one of *The Onion*'s "American Voices"
illustrated the hypocrisy of the law: "I support this ruling. We
shouldn't be allowed to eat horses, dogs, or anything else we can
race for sport" ("Horse Meat Banned," 9/18/06). There's no good
reason why a cow's suffering is any less important than that of a
dog or a horse, yet anti-cruelty laws explicitly exclude animals
raised for food. In most states, it's illegal to leave your dog alone
in a hot car, but you can crack a pig's head open with a poleax
without even being accused of treating it abnormally.

    The Onion has worked to make animal welfare an important
moral issue by informing its readership about factory farm conditions and exposing our hypocrisy regarding animal cruelty. When
alternatives are easily available, like "I Can't Believe It's Not A Dead
Animal!" and "Tofuck You, Meat Lover," the only reason to continue

eating meat is because we prefer the taste of it ("Infographic: The Meat Substitute Boom," 3/14/01). The vast majority of animal suffering is unnecessary, and causing unnecessary suffering is the paradigm case of an immoral act. Singer concludes that vegetarianism is morally required of us. We should all be more like Pamela Anderson.

Stuff Matters for Living Things

Whether animal welfare theory ought to be considered a part of environmental ethics is a matter of debate. Singer considers non-human things only to the extent that they are like human beings—they suffer like us. Some philosophers claim that this kind of reasoning retains the spirit of anthropocentrism. Furthermore, the individualistic focus on particular sentient beings seems to contradict a concern for species, ecosystems, and nature as a whole, and this is thought by many to be the hallmark of an environmental ethic.

In 1973, Richard Sylvan published an essay with the title "Is There a Need for a New, an Environmental, Ethic?" While Singer tries to extend a traditional ethical theory (utilitarianism) to modern practices (animal experimentation and factory farming), Sylvan claims that we need an entirely different way of conceptualizing our obligations to nonhuman things, one that explains how we could have direct duties to holistic entities.

Singer draws the line of moral consideration at sentience because sentient beings have interests that can be promoted or hindered. But all living things develop teleologically—that is, they grow in certain ways, toward certain ends. An acorn grows into an oak tree; an animal tries to survive and remain healthy. When we cut down a plant or poison its soil, we are thwarting its development. When we clear cut a forest and remove animals' habitat and food source, we are impacting their chances of survival. When we negatively impact the health of plants or animals, we are harming them. But if right actions promote the good and minimize harm, then we have moral obligations to all living things. We arrive at a biocentric, or life-centered, ethic.

Biocentrism looks at the big picture. When a species is culled of its old and weak members, either through disease or predation, the individuals suffer, to be sure, but the species becomes healthier and less susceptible to such threats in the future. In addition,

biodiversity is a sign of a healthy ecosystem; species extinction usually constitutes a harm to the environment. Thus we are morally
obligated to prevent species extinction when we can, not because
of the harm suffered by individual animals, but because we ought
to maintain ecosystems.

The Onion is particularly concerned about the loss of biodiversity. In "Stuffed-Animal Biodiversity Rising" (4/18/01), *The Onion*
charts the loss of biodiversity relative to the variety of available
plush toys. Attributing the popularity of stuffed animals to "humans'
growing interest in environmental issues" is ironic given that, at the
same time, "rainforests continue to disappear at a rate of one and
a half acres every second"—and various animal species along with
them. Similarly, in "Consumer-Product Diversity Now Exceeds
Biodiversity" (10/21/98), *The Onion* contrasts the plethora of consumer products with the dwindling number of animal and plant
species. The idea that the production of new commodities could
distract us from "the crumbling global ecosystem" both satirizes the
fact that we remain "optimistic" despite "one of the worst episodes
of mass extinction in history," and emphasizes the extent of
American consumerism. As refreshing as it is, having 2,794 kinds of
soda to drink is not going to stop the march of global extinctions.

Ecological Consciousness + Feminism = Ecofeminism

Even if we grant that all living things have value and that our
unchecked exploitation of nature is morally wrong, we still don't
get at the root of our environmental attitudes. Why is it that we typically view nature as something to be used and dominated? One of
the most prominent and influential theoretical approaches to this
question is ecofeminism.

Of course, the feminist movement is well-known. Feminists
believe that women have been oppressed on the basis of their gender, and they work to correct this injustice. But it is less clear how
feminism is related to our treatment of nature. Why should there be
a distinct kind of environmental philosophy known as ecofeminism?

According to ecofeminists, the subordination of women is not
an isolated phenomenon. In her groundbreaking work *Ecofeminist
Philosophy* (2000), Karen Warren claims that sexism is one of the
many "isms of domination" that includes racism and anthropocentrism. By largely ignoring environmental issues, the mainstream

feminist movement in the United States is addressing only one symptom of a larger problem. A consideration of subordinated humans should lead to a consideration of other subordinated classes, including animals and the land. Feminists ought to oppose *all* systems of domination.

Ecofeminists challenge the traditional way that philosophical theorizing is structured — namely, according to a series of normative dualisms. These are distinctions that are hierarchically ordered, a two-term set in which one of the terms is valued over the other one. For example, the mind is privileged over the body, reason is privileged over feeling, and culture is privileged over nature. Historically, women have been associated with the devalued halves of these dualisms. Women are considered more emotional and more tied to the vicissitudes of nature and the body. Thus social inequality and environmental degradation can ultimately be traced to the same kind of dualistic thinking that subjects nonrational or less rational things (like women and nature) to the demands of rational civilization.

Some Normative Dualisms

Mind	Body
Reason	Feeling
Culture	Nature
Human	Animal
Man	Woman
White	Nonwhite
West	East
First World	Third World

One way to subordinate something or someone, then, is to feminize it or naturalize it, to describe it in terms that make it less than fully rational or less than fully human. *The Onion* exposes this conceptual process in "Raped Environment Led Polluters On, Defense Attorneys Argue" (1/21/98). The article describes how the "red-blooded American developer" was enticed by the forest's "eager display of its rich, fertile bounty." The "virgin forest" flaunted its "abundant natural resources" until its "forced ravaging."

What makes this article so important is that it traces the root of our environmental problems to the same kind of attitude at the heart of sexism. The use of the forest as merely a natural resource depends on making it into a thing to be used rather than a living ecosystem with value of its own, so the forest is transformed into an alluring woman. This is ironic, because it would seem that comparing nature to a woman would make it more morally considerable. After all, chicks are human beings. However, women's capacity to reason, and thus their humanity, is frequently dismissed by comparing them with animals—calling them "bitches," "cows," or other names that escape me right now. In this cultural context, the idea that the forest is merely a thing to be used is best captured by feminizing it. By comparing exploited nature to an exploited woman, *The Onion* links environmental degradation to sexism. If we resist the dehumanizing effects of sexism, we also ought to resist the commodification of nature, and vice versa.

Mother Nature? That Birch Was Asking for It

In addition, this story gets at the thorny issue of consent by talking about how the loggers felt that they were "led on" by nature. Like a flirtatious woman, the forest gave off "mixed signals" and set out "to tease and encourage" the development company. This kind of attitude toward women attempts to justify the crime of sexual assault by claiming that they actually consent to it, despite their protests to the contrary. Although women resist, at some level they really want it, and they are asking for it. This is a strategy designed to relieve the attacker of responsibility, despite all appearances of violence. It is the woman's fault for attracting the rapist.

The attempt to shift responsibility to the one victimized by violence also shows up in a commonplace response to environmentalist claims: natural things are useful to us, so of course we would treat them as resources for our own gratification. Indeed, this is human nature, dictated by nature herself. Many people say that it is natural for us to cut down trees and eat animals—it is the result of a long evolutionary process of shaping the environment to meet our needs—so we are not responsible for environmental degradation. We attribute environmental harm to nature in us, and thus we blame it for what we do.

Ultimately, this strategy fails because, although we are part of nature, we are capable of reflecting on and evaluating our actions. Noting that we are natural beings does not rule out the need for reason-giving. As beings who can hold each other to account, we are responsible for our environmental policies. Neither our evolutionary history nor nature itself decides for us, any more than the rape victim is responsible for what happens to her. Knowing what we know now about how we are harming the natural world, if we choose to continue with the same careless environmental policies, we are acting immorally.

Famous Ecofeminists

Karen Warren   **H. Ulysses Zweibel,**   **Vandana Shiva**

founder of *The Mercantile-Onion*,
attending the Seneca Falls Convention
in 1848

Ecofeminism Goes Global

Resistance to victim-blaming tendencies in ethics and politics constitutes a major task of the global ecofeminist movement worldwide. Since ecofeminists oppose all forms of domination, many ecofeminists also confront our attitudes toward the so-called Third

World, and how those attitudes express themselves even within mainstream environmentalism.

Often environmentalists cite overpopulation as a threat to ecological stability. The worry is that the use of more and more land for food production, living space, and infrastructure (such as roads) interferes with nature's functioning. If we depend on large monocultures such as corn or we clear cut the world's rainforests in order to have grazing lands for beef cattle, there will be less biodiversity and more species extinction. The growing demand for fresh water also leads to water scarcity and subsequent droughts, followed by lower food production. Paul Ehrlich argues, in both *The Population Bomb* (1968) and *The Population Explosion* (1991), that there will be widespread famine when the growing population outstrips our capacity to feed everyone. He mentions Africa in particular as a place where poverty and lack of food are due to overpopulation.

Ecofeminists such as Vandana Shiva have challenged Ehrlich's explanation. Shiva traces poverty and famine in the Third World to the mismanagement of resources, usually as a result of continuing colonial-era practices and economic pressures from the West. Agricultural development programs in many Third-World countries often divert land to the growth of export crops, supposedly in order to compete in the global economy. This displaces peasant farmers who rely on the land to grow a diverse set of crops to feed themselves. While governments profit from exports, the growth of nonindigenous crops and poor land-use planning lead to erosion and widespread malnutrition. Women are hit hardest by this. Because women are considered marginal in the production of food for export, what little food there is often is given preferentially to men, leading to a number of health problems for women, including complications during pregnancy.

The *Onion* article "Thousands Feared Born In Nigerian Population Explosion" (6/7/06) serves a dual purpose: both to depict the deplorable living conditions experienced by many people in the Third World, and to exploit our racist attitudes as they express themselves in our concern with overpopulation. The birth of African children is considered "an unparalleled natural disaster" because they must try to survive despite "continuing devastation of the nation's crops," "already-inadequate drinking water," and "a vanishing rainforest," all of which are the result of Western economic policies toward nonindustrialized nations. Land and resources that had been used to sustain people is transformed into land to produce crops for export.

In addition, ecofeminists note that concerns about overpopulation often obscure the real issue—namely, the disproportionate environmental damage done by Western industrialized nations like the United States. Because the U.S. consumes much more and produces much more waste, slowing the U.S. population growth even a little would have a much bigger impact than a great change in foreign countries' growth. If the crises predicted by environmentalists like Ehrlich were to occur, they would be the result not of overpopulation in the Third World, but of overconsumption in the West.

The neglect of non-Western nations is a form of domination that subjects them disproportionately to the hidden costs of Western consumerism. For instance, although global warming is largely the result of Americans' use (or overuse) of fossil fuels, the environmental impact of global warming will be felt mostly along the coasts of the Pacific and Indian oceans and in sub-Saharan Africa. Higher temperatures affect the spread of infectious diseases like malaria, increase flooding in low-lying areas, and worsen droughts and malnutrition. Environmental philosopher Stephen Gardiner has called global warming "a perfect moral storm." Global warming cannot be blamed on a particular agent or set of agents, its effects are dispersed to those who did not produce the greenhouse gas emissions, and the negative impact is felt primarily by future generations. Because of this, Gardiner worries that we will not have the willpower to do what we ought to do. It is easy to ignore the global warming crisis because we are not the ones who are most harmed by it, and we are not solely responsible for it.

In the context of this ethical problem, the *Onion* story "Addressing Climate Crisis, Bush Calls For Development Of National Air Conditioner" (6/20/07) can be read as an indictment of American consumerism. In the article, a concern for future generations is equated with a concern for future generations *of Americans*. But the most subversive element of the piece is that a national air conditioner would actually increase the rise in global temperatures felt by the rest of the world. "The plan . . . would stimulate additional exploration and production of oil and gas to satisfy the machine's staggering energy needs," thus producing carbon dioxide. In addition, the refrigerants used in air conditioners produce hydrofluorocarbons (HFCs). Because both CO_2 and HFCs are greenhouse gases, one of the things that makes this story so funny is not only that President Bush thinks this is the way to give our children's children "a world where they don't get sweaty and have to change their shirts all the time," but that this "solution" to America's global warming problem would actually exacerbate the problem for the rest of the world. Addressing the climate crisis means addressing Americans' discomfort. In a final jab at the hypocrisy of American environmental groups, *The Onion* reports that the Sierra Club has demanded only that the air conditioner be "switched to a special energy-conserving 'sleep' setting when the country cools off at night."

The Pitfalls of Self-Satisfaction

Lab-coated technicians who poison a cute monkey, scientists who feast on a Brazilian primate, loggers who sexualize trees, George W. Bush—these are ludicrously comic figures from whom most of us can distance ourselves. But *The Onion* is perhaps at its most provocative and most progressive when it satirizes the complacency of the everyday environmentalist. It is here where the typical *Onion* reader, whom I picture as a cross between Jim Anchower and Ira Glass, is most likely to be challenged.

Ironically, environmentalism itself can become a means of advancing our own selfish interests, as when we barely adjust our lifestyles in order to feel a disproportionately strong sense of smugness. *The Onion* tells us that Americans' recycling efforts in 1996 reduced landfill waste by 0.00004 percent, but "Americans themselves experienced a whopping 47 percent drop in guilt" ("EPA: Recycling Eliminated More Than 50 Million Tons Of Guilt In '96," 3/12/97). Attempts to contain the smug over San Francisco were unsuccessful and led to the complete annihilation of South Park, Colorado. Luckily, they were able to rebuild—unlike Beaverton, which was an early casualty of global warming. (We didn't listen!)

Peter Keim's opinion piece, "I'm Doing My Inconsequential Part for the Environment" (5/10/06), is particularly challenging to the environmentalist mindset. By recycling and composting, buying "earth-friendly" paper products, growing his own organic vegetables, boycotting oil and gas companies that neglect the global warming issue, demonstrating against the draining of local wetlands, minimizing his consumption of fossil fuels by using mass transit and riding his bike, restricting his energy use to non-peak hours, and using a low-flow toilet, Keim is doing more to reduce his environmental impact than the vast majority of the U.S. population. Despite the fact that his "quixotic, Sisyphean efforts" do nothing to stave off the "inevitable global death-age," Keim takes pleasure in his own goodness:

> At the very least, I know with absolute certainty that I have done everything I can to nurture and protect the environment, through genuinely well-intentioned albeit minuscule actions, tragically destined to have absolutely no substantive effect. For I sleep better at night knowing that I have as much influence on global environmental policy as I would had I never been born.

If a well-intentioned environmentalism does nothing for nature, it only has anthropocentric value: its contribution to the environmentalist's sense of self-satisfaction.

Although *The Onion* usually focuses on the everyday consumer, hardcore environmentalists sometimes receive their own word-lashing. "Heroic PETA Commandos Kill 49, Save Rabbit" (3/19/97) depicts how misguided it is to express a concern for animal suffering by brutally executing 49 human animals. When "Animal-Rights Activists Release 71,000 Cows Into Wild" (12/16/98) and the cows are hit by cars, fall off bridges, and electrocute themselves by chewing on power lines, we are supposed to laugh at the Animal Liberation Front's naïveté and thoughtless idealism. The intent of animal liberation is to minimize suffering, and that purpose is corrupted by militant animal-rights activists. Peter Singer is rolling over in his grave—or at least he would be if he were dead.

Peter Singer: Not Dead

The Onion's New Environmental Ethic

It's estimated that a stretch of forest the size of Washington state has been felled in order to publish *The Onion* over the course of its long history. Greenpeace is suing *Onion* publisher emeritus T. Herman Zweibel for depriving citizens of their right to shade.

For a moment, though, forget about all the trees that have been killed to produce the newspaper. *The Onion* is at the forefront of environmental ethics. By demonstrating the moral bankruptcy of anthropocentrism, *The Onion* works to advance the interests of animals, species, and ecosystems. Nonhuman animals ought not to be harmed unnecessarily; their suffering matters because it is bad for them. The extinction of species is morally troubling not only because of how it affects us, but because biodiversity and the health of the environment is important in its own right. Ultimately, the treatment of nature as merely a resource is part of a pattern of subordination that includes women and people of the Third World. In this intellectual landscape, it is not enough for us to change our behavior slightly by buying "green" products and recycling. Rather, we first need to transform our way of thinking about how we are related to nature. Through its satire, *The Onion* tries to effect this transformation by exposing the limitations of the anthropocentric environmentalism that is now the norm. Once we adopt a new ethic, an environmental ethic, we will finally recognize our direct obligations to all living things. To be good environmentalists, we should distribute copies of *The Onion* to everyone, until every garbage can in America is stuffed with them.

There are limits to what a satirical newspaper can do. Socrates used rational arguments to criticize those in power, and his direct attempts to question the prevailing Greek values largely failed to change minds. The jury voted to execute Socrates because he was perceived as a threat. By contrast, *The Onion* uses satire to challenge us, and it makes fun of anyone who takes him- or herself too seriously. Thus it avoids the kind of resistance that people have to direct and serious criticisms. The risk is that people will too easily be able to laugh it off, that the political significance is entirely contained within the joke and is therefore unable to transform our thinking or to make us truly uncomfortable in our own skin. *The Onion* has value in reflecting our faults back to us. We can gauge its philosophical importance, however, by how dangerous it is. And on that count, it has some way to go.

Local

15

Area Man Realizes Error Of Ways After Reading *Onion* Article

NOAH LEVIN

BOWLING GREEN, OH—Graduate Student and spicy food fanatic Noah Levin has changed his life for the better, his friends hope, after reading an article in *The Onion*.

"So I read this article in *The Onion* the other day about some chump's quest to be 'the spicy food guy,'" Levin said, referring to the story on Royce Flankingston, "Area Man Committed To Being Spicy Food Guy" (9/18/08).

"At first I thought, 'this guy probably can't even handle the Blazin' Sauce at Buffalo Wild Wings.'" Levin continued. "But then the article explained how he can eat some wicked hot stuff and enjoyed showing off. By the time I finished the article, I thought, 'Wow, this guy's a real dick.'"

A friend of Levin who wishes to remain anonymous confirmed Levin's claim to fame as spicy food guy.

"He knows he can eat stuff hotter than everyone else and lets us know it when he tells us that we wouldn't want to try his dishes because we're too wussy to handle it," the friend said.

Levin has been known to order dishes "as hot as you can possibly make them" or "hotter than the flames of hell." He has to convince waiters and waitresses at Thai and Indian restaurants that he knows what he's getting himself into.

"Just because I'm white they think I can't handle it and that I will have to send it back. Once they see me eat, then they know what I'm made of," Levin said.

Levin is the best person he knows at eating hot food. He was ecstatic when he got his hands on the newly crowned World's Hottest Pepper, the bhut jolokia. Hot peppers are something he always enjoys eating, unless he gets the 'ring of fire' or the 'flame-thrower' as a result.

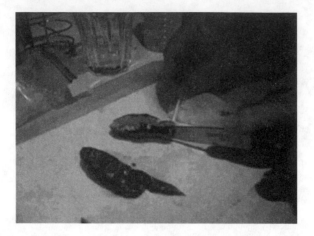

Noah Levin Preparing a Hot Pepper for Consumption

Dining companions have noted that Levin has been disappointed at the levels of heat in most of the "extra spicy" meals he has been served. They also have stopped listening to him when he recommends a favorite dish. He has been known to enjoy it when his recommendations cause them to guzzle down water.

"I've never tricked anyone into eating something *insanely* hot. Okay, only once, and I realized how much of a douchebag I was for doing that," added Levin.

But when Levin read the article about Royce Flankingston he found himself wishing he didn't bear such a striking resemblance to the man. The article hit too close to home. As a result, he has begun to think maybe he should be a little subtler about his mad skills.

"Perhaps I'll even agree when someone says, 'Wow, this is really spicy,' even though it isn't," Levin said. "Well, maybe I won't go that far. But I will hold back on my insults for those with no tolerance for flavor. And if someone wants to brag to me about how they can eat spicy food, I'm still going to unleash my mouth."

There are a bunch of ways my friends could have told me that I was annoying about hot food—but they never did. I'm sure I really wasn't that bad and didn't rub in my culinary ability that often. Since my level of annoyance wasn't at unbearable levels, no one said anything. I was a little aware of some of the things I did, but I didn't give much thought to it. Until I read that little article in *The Onion*.

When I read the article on the "spicy food guy" that my friend Michael Mullins sent me, I laughed because it was funny. And then

I thought about why he sent it to me—one reason was clearly that I was the local "spicy food guy." Perhaps that was the only reason he sent it to me, but I noticed a little bit of myself in auto salesman Royce Flankingston. Sometimes I had done things similar to Royce, and so I stopped to reflect on my feelings about Royce and if I was ever like him.

It didn't take me long to realize that, no, I wasn't as much of an annoying ass as Royce appeared to be. I also realized that sometimes I was like a milder version of him and that I should be more aware of my actions in that regard. Since reading the article, I have been more conscious of statements and actions about hot food, and I like to think it's made me a better person (well, at least a less annoying person).

Sarcasm as a Method of Argumentation

Why did the article speak to me so vividly and convince me to modify my life (slightly)? It was because of the subtle—yet forceful—method of argumentation that it disguisedly employed. *The Onion* is meant to be funny and give us hilarious fake news stories that mock current politics, business, or someone we might know. Some classic articles in this vein include "Bush Regales Dinner Guests With Impromptu Oratory On Virgil's Minor Works" (4/18/01) and "Pope Died As He Lived, Propped Up For Public Viewing" (12/28/05). But this time, that someone we might know was me. *I* was being mocked. In a not-so-subtle way, I was being told that I might be annoying.

When executed properly, sarcastic statements make an effective form of criticism. They are best employed in spoken language because the tone of one's voice is often what makes the statement sarcastic (as in, *"Good job"*). According to *The Onion*, *"Nice one, Einstein"* is sarcastic 99% of the time ("Report: 70 Percent of all Praise Sarcastic," 4/30/07). "Wow, this meatloaf is *delicious*" is another favorite. Right now, you might be thinking, "Please tell me something I *don't know*," which I will take as my cue to stop explaining sarcasm and assume you are familiar with it. But you might not be as familiar with it as you think.

Are *Onion* articles sarcastic? *Onion* writers are probably aiming not for sarcasm but for satire and parody. Although sarcasm, satire, and parody are very closely related, they are distinct.

A parody is a comical imitation of some other work. *The Onion's* book, *Our Dumb World,* for example, is a parody of picture desk atlases like MacMillan's *My Big World.*

Satire points out a foible in a humorous way with the intent of changing someone's behavior. The *Onion* article "Parody Movie Script One Crotch-Hitting Joke Short Of Being Greenlit" (9/18/08) helps to illustrate the distinction between parody and satire: the movie itself parodies other films while the article satirizes Hollywood.

But then what is sarcasm?

Like satire, sarcasm points out short-comings. Where satire is meant merely to "poke fun," however, sarcasm is meant to wound. Satire is comical in nature while sarcasm is malicious in nature. So why do I say that the article on the spicy food guy is sarcastic?

Well, I don't really want to say that—the writers probably intended merely to be funny. They describe the actions of a person who is a bit of an asshole and spark a good laugh about someone we might know who likes to gloat about his odd expertise. The article certainly could be seen as satirical, and perhaps it was meant to be satirical—but I didn't take it that way.

For a contrast, consider the classic article, "Guy In Philosophy Class Needs To Shut The Fuck Up" (9/28/05). It's a clear case of satire. It pokes fun at know-it-alls, showing them how they come across to everyone else, and thereby providing possible motivation for change.

But I read the "spicy food guy" article and got something more subtle and disturbing out of it. It was saying to me, "You're a spicy food guy just like Royce Flankingston."

The difference between the articles lies both in how I came to read it and in the number of people targeted. Mike recommended the article to me as something I might enjoy through a friendly, "Hcy, check this out—you'll like it" e-mail. But my enjoyment quickly turned to disappointment in the same way I feel an instant of triumph when someone says "Good job!" just before the truth sets in. I felt the opposite of what was implied by the e-mail. Additionally, while a lot of people have a know-it-all moment in class or life not a lot of people have an obsession with spicy food. An innocent article that readers enjoy as a description of one man's quest spoke directly to me in the truest of sarcastic fashions: it was saying to me, "*you* are a dick because you let people know how much you like spicy food." Ouch.

Despite their subtle differences, satire and sarcasm both work as arguments by presenting the reader or listener with three questions as follows:

1. What characteristics are being targeted?

2. Do I exhibit those characteristics?

3. Should I change?

We recognize the foible being presented, realize we dislike it, and consequently make changes to our lives. This is the self-help side of philosophy, a venerable tradition going all the way back to Socrates when he said, "Know thyself."

Satire and sarcasm are often better than the direct approach because humor makes criticism easier to take. By poking fun or ridiculing, one makes a clear and obvious point without being overly harsh. This is especially true of sarcasm. It is as though the laugh somehow makes up for the wound. To understand how and why sarcastic arguments are effective, we can reconstruct them in terms of a formal method of argumentation.

Sarcasm and Reductio ad Absurdum

Sarcasm is a type of *reductio ad absurdum* argument. *Reductio ad absurdum* (which I will abbreviate to just *reductio*) means "reduction to the absurd" in Latin and denotes a specific type of argument. A *reductio* argument is one in which the logical implications of a statement are carried out to their conclusion with the aim of showing that the conclusion is untenable, which then causes us to reject the initial statement. The conclusion can result in a contradiction, an impossibility, something implausible, something undesirable, or anything else we might find untenable. The *reductio* is best—and most often—employed to discredit statements that appear, at first, to be sound.

For an example of a *reductio* argument, we can examine the *Onion* article, "RIAA Sues Radio Stations For Giving Away Free Music" (10/2/02). While this might seem like pure fiction, it is actually something the RIAA (Recording Industry Association of America) has considered doing.[1] So the title is presenting a possible situation. What if we follow this possibility to its logical conclusion?

---

[1] Jim Puzzanghera, "Artists and Labels Seek Royalties from Radio," *Los Angeles Times* (05/21/07).

Radio stations broadcast music for people to listen to. They do not pay royalties because the musicians get publicity through the many listeners who might not otherwise hear the music. The music is distributed via airwaves to people for free.

The underlying principle in the *Onion*'s possible scenario is that musicians should be able to charge anyone who is distributing their music. There are many ways music can be distributed—through CDs, over the internet, or on the radio. The method of distribution is irrelevant. So, if musicians should be able to charge for commercial distribution, then they should be able to charge for private distribution. People driving down the street playing a CD with their windows down are distributing the music to anyone within earshot of their car. Therefore, musicians should be able to charge them.

To formalize this argument, we can lay it out in the following way:

1. **Musicians should be able to charge anyone who distributes their music.**

2. **People who play music in their cars with the windows down distribute music.**

3. **Therefore, musicians should be able to charge people who play music in their cars with the windows down.**

Statement 3 follows from statements 1 and 2 by logical necessity. And yet, statement three is quite absurd. In order to deny it, we must deny either statement 1 or statement 2. Since it's true that people playing music in their cars with the windows down distribute music, we can't deny statement 2. So we must deny statement 1, the claim that musicians should be able to charge anyone who distributes their music. To get to the final conclusion of this *reductio* argument, we add:

1. **We don't want musicians to be able to charge people who play music in their cars with the windows down.**

2. **Therefore, it is not the case that musicians should be able to charge anyone who distributes their music.**

This is a powerful refutation of the RIAA's proposal. And it comes to us straight from *Onion* satire.

Sarcasm works in the same way. For example, let's examine the *Onion* article "That Teen-Abstinence Rally Totally Rocked!" (5/17/00). In it Brian "Bri" Knoepke tries to convince us that "praising God and resisting your body's sinful urges" is cool. Brian describes the fun he and his pals from the Springdale Youth Ministry had at the rally.

Suppose, however, that one of the teens in this group was a normal horny teenager and did not actually enjoy the rally. And suppose that afterwards he told his friends "That teen-abstinence rally totally rocked!" What he's really saying is that teen-abstinence rallies do not rock. I contend that he is making an implicit *reductio* argument.

How is this argument being made? It can be formalized in the following way:

1. **Teen-abstinence rallies totally rock.**

2. **If teen-abstinence rallies totally rock, then I enjoyed the rally.**

3. **Therefore, I enjoyed the rally.**

4. **But I did not enjoy the rally.**

5. **Therefore, it's not the case that teen-abstinence rallies totally rock.**

While formalization spoils the fun, it clearly shows how a sarcastic statement makes a *reductio* argument.

We're now ready to return to the spicy food issue. We can lay out two types of arguments aimed at altering my actions: a direct argument and a sarcastic one. Someone could make a direct argument against my tastebud touting by saying, "Noah, people who boast about eating spicy food are really annoying. You boast about eating spicy foods. Therefore, you are really annoying. Annoying people are not fun to be around. But you want to be fun to be around. Therefore, you should stop boasting about eating spicy foods." Or, as an alternative, my friend could take the sarcastic approach, and say, "Wow, I *really love* hearing about how awesome you are at eating spicy foods!" Better still, he could simply send me the *Onion* article about Royce Flankingston.

There are advantages to each approach, but I think the sarcastic method wins the fight. The direct argument (which can be laid out formally just like the others—I'll leave this as an exercise for the reader), if actually given, would turn the tables and make the person giving it into the annoying person. It is not the sort of the thing that I would enjoy my friends doing. The reason for this is two-fold: the argument is excruciatingly detailed and it is too strong for my spicy-food transgressions. It would create an unpleasant moment.

The sarcastic approach, in contrast, might give both of us a small laugh, which is always a good thing. It would also be very clear that my friend is expressing displeasure – and, as we have seen, implicitly making a *reductio* argument. By not spelling out every detail of the argument, he makes me run through the three steps outlined above: I identify the characteristics targeted, judge whether I exhibit those characteristics, and then decide whether or not I want to change. Thus I am an active participant in a conversation rather than a passive recipient of criticism.

As mentioned, this experience actually happened to me. Realizing my friend went out of his way to soften the blow, I refrained from touting my tastebuds the next time we ate together. But I did spike his food with some really hot hot sauce. Bastard had it coming, trying to tell me what to do.

The Onion, Sarcasm, and the Good of Mankind

The Onion is, most importantly, a hilarious read. The primary purpose of most, if not all, of its articles is humor. Many of the articles are satirical, and in some cases, they might be sarcastic. Satire and sarcasm, when done properly, can help people notice foibles, either in themselves or others. This might motivate them to change things for the better.

When we come to a personal realization through such a humorous medium, the motivation for change is powerful. I never thought I would be one of those people an *Onion* article was about—but I was. And I ended up changing a little for it. If you see yourself in an *Onion* article, take a look at yourself and at the argument it's making, and see if you can make the world a better place. Or, at the very least, a less annoying place.

16

Guy In Philosophy Class Needs To Shut The Fuck Up

MATT LAUBENTHAL

Dartmouth freshman Darrin Floen participates to excess in Philosophy 101 discussions. In his undying quest for the truth, and perhaps a few other tangents, he has managed to turn his entire class against him ("Guy In Philosophy Class Needs To Shut The Fuck Up," 09/28/05).

I'll be honest. For a large chunk of my college career, I was that guy: the guy who talks to talk, the guy who makes everything a story, the guy who'd rather listen to himself than to the teacher. I'm certain my classmates wanted to beat me up. Sophomore year, as I lay on a hospitable bed recovering from a severe concussion and pondering how I might make the most of a life I nearly lost, it occurred to me that perhaps I should be less dominant in class discussions. I tried it and liked it. I'm proud to report that I've been logorrhea-free now for two semesters.

Although I would never go back to being a Darrin, and although I definitely don't want him in my class, I think the poor guy deserves some consideration.

The Nature of The Guy

Darrin's professor says that Darrin's "tendency to question and challenge everything before him captures the very essence of philosophy itself." Don't let this statement make you think philosophy argues blindly just for the sake of argument. Philosophy asks the questions it does and challenges everything in an effort to develop an understanding of the world. The world is an incredibly strange and interesting place if you think about it. Therefore no question could be too deep, too long, or too boring for a philosopher. Philosophers even question the questions. And, to be consistent, they question those that question the questions, namely themselves.

For every answer there is a new question to ask. Philosophical inquiry is endless and you can always see another level just beyond your grasp. These qualities explain why philosophy gets on some people's nerves. Darrin's enthusiasm for the same qualities explains why his classmates think he's an ass.

Ass or not, Darrin is right about philosophy being important. If you don't think philosophy is important, then I ask you: what would our concepts of self, love, freedom, justice, and peace be without careful deliberation, without an effort to define and understand them? Such concepts directly affect all of our lives. Failing to think about them good and hard would be a travesty. *The Onion* regularly provides examples of terrible injustices that could have been prevented with a little more thought.

Take, for example, Kafka International Airport. Designed according to the principles of existentialism, this airport has caused debilitating levels of alienation among travelers passing through.

Franz Kafka is the author of the story *The Metamorphosis*. Telling the tale of a man called "S" who inexplicably changes into a beetle, it explores the favorite existentialist theme of the absurdity of life. Not a good theme for an airport.

The Onion reported the travails of traveler Bob Fryer: "The security guard asked me for like, eighty minutes, 'Are you who you say you are? Are you who you say you are?', and finally, he writes 'liar' on the back of my hand and lets me pass." ("Prague's Franz Kafka International Named World's Most Alienating Airport" [3/24/09])

According to the newscast, travelers also reported frustration at the airport's unusual security procedure, which includes a time-consuming personal interview as follows:

1. **Who are you?**

2. **If not, who are you?**

3. **Is it not true that you are whoever we say you are?**

4. **You are disgusting.**

5. **Have you lied to us?**

6. **Have you lied to us?**

7. Have you lied to us?

xx. Will you lie to us?

28. We believe you have lied to us. Does it matter whether you've truly lied to us?

28. Have you renounced your god?

A survey like this might not only cause you to miss your flight; it might cause mental illness.

Traveler Jim Cassoti was rattled to the core by his experience at the airport: "I asked the ticket person what gate my flight was at, and they said that the airline I was flying didn't exist, and everyone keeps calling me 'S.'"

What were the airport designers thinking? Gate B2 is next to gate B11, and gate B14 is in the F terminal. The curbside shuttle service loops around the airport before depositing passengers back at their starting point. There are extremely long corridors leading to dead ends. Worst of all, the employees are "completely indifferent to travelers' needs."

Trained philosophers can no doubt navigate this nightmare much more easily than the average person. The solution is to either take existentialism to its logical extreme—in which case nothing matters because life is absurd—or to reject existentialism.

Darrin, no doubt, could run circles around my analysis of Kafka International Airport. In capturing the very essence of philosophy itself, Darrin harkens back to Socrates—the father of philosophy. Socrates challenged his fellow Athenians to such an extent that he considered himself a gadfly.

Darrin is a gadfly all right, though we don't call flies "gad" anymore. Darrin is the fly buzzing around your bedroom when all you want to do is sleep. Darrin over-animates the classroom, constantly arguing for or against ideas without caring about what's going to be on the exam. In so doing he is reviving religious fervor on campus (at the start of a 'Darrin-tangent' many classmates find themselves pleading for the intervention of a higher power).

Darrin receives nothing but hostility for his efforts. "I have no idea what Plato's ideal reality is," says classmate Julia Wald, "but I bet it doesn't include know-it-all little shits." The Athenians sentenced Socrates to death for refusing to cease his questioning. You can bet Julia and company would love to do the same to Darrin.

The Problem with The Guy

"Guy in Philosophy Class" is significant philosophically because it brings to light the stereotype of philosophers as windbags. This is where all of the humor in this article is found—in its attack on people who go on and on without saying anything.

Darrin is first described as "the one who sits at the back of the class and acts like he's Aristotle." His comments are labeled as "frequent," "eager," "incredibly annoying," and "insufferable." He is "unfamiliar with the theory of cramming it for a change and giving someone else a chance to speak." Sophomore Miriam Blank describes Darrin as "unbearable." Even the course instructor says that he wishes Darrin would shut his "damn cake hole."

Freshman William Deekes, who "has endured the most suffering," lets us know just how far Darrin's excesses extend—"Some people know Darrin as just 'that guy in philosophy class who needs to shut the hell up.' I, however, also know him as 'the douche in African history who seriously needs to chill' and 'the a-hole in environmental sciences who could really use a girlfriend.'"

If Darrin represents all philosophers, the image he presents is unpleasant. The main complaint against Darrin is that he talks too much—which could be annoying to his classmates for many reasons. Maybe they want to be able to say something. Maybe they don't like what he says. Or maybe they don't like how he says it ("I hate his voice, and I hate the way he only half raises his hand, like he's so laid back," says freshman Duane Herring).

Although Darrin's classmates pin their irritation on Darrin, a little self-examination might reveal that its true source is philosophy itself. Is it not unpleasant to find an idea you've based your life on is flawed? Perhaps some of Darrin's questions have hit just a little too close to home—as do so many *Onion* articles, such as "Area Woman Wouldn't Mind Feeding Your Cats" (12/06/08), or "Superintendent Draws Up 'Dream School Board' Of All-Time Greats," (08/23/08).

It's depressing to think that "Guy in Philosophy Class," though fictional, might actually reflect the public's opinion of philosophy—which would ultimately imply a negative opinion of intellectuals, the pursuit of truth, and creative thought in general.

However, the popularity of *The Onion* seems to counter this argument. *The Onion* is itself philosophical in so far as it questions and challenges everything stupid in our society. That such a publication exists and is so wildly popular is evidence of the public's appreciation of intelligence.

The Guy's Point

While Darrin may go on and on, it would be hasty to conclude that he isn't saying anything. In fact, classmate James Luers mentions a particularly interesting argument that Darrin makes:

> Just last week Professor Rosenthal was talking about Russell's Paradox, and that jackass starts going off: "But what about Heraclitus' aphorism: Everything flows, nothing stands still?" . . . . At first I was like, "That's totally irrelevant," but then I was like, "Well, actually, it does apply to the nonstop flapping of your trap."

Ignoring Luer's gratuitous insult, we can reconstruct Darrin's logic.

Russell's Paradox is a famous problem that arises in set theory and can be defined as follows:

1. Some sets, such as the set of all teacups, are not members of themselves.

2. Other sets, such as the set of all non-teacups, are members of themselves.

3. Call the set of all sets that are not members of themselves "R." If R is a member of itself, then by definition it must not be a member of itself. Similarly, if R is not a member of itself, then by definition it must be a member of itself.

This definition is a little confusing at first glance, perhaps because it involves teacups, which modern Americans aren't too familiar with. Instead, we'll rework the example a little with help from the fast food industry.

A set is defined as the collection of a group of something—so the set of all Whoppers would contain every Whopper.[1] However, by defining this set, we have immediately defined another set: the set of all non-Whoppers. Thus we have two sets: the set of all Whoppers, and the set of all non-Whoppers. The set of all

---

[1] I may or may not have given essay space to Burger King in exchange for a life-time supply of shakes.

Whoppers contains all Whoppers but is not itself a Whopper; it is merely an abstract collection of them. The set of all non-Whoppers, in being a set, is also an abstract collection of things like the set of all Whoppers. However, the set of all non-Whoppers (something abstract) is *not* a Whopper (something concrete, affordable, and quite tasty, too); therefore it is a member of itself. As we can see, we have sets that are members of themselves, and sets that aren't members of themselves.

The paradox arises when we consider the following:

1. **Put every set that isn't a member of itself into the same new set, the "So-huge-it's-tremendous load," (s.h.i.t. load).**

2. **Answer the question: is the s.h.i.t. load a member of itself, or not?**

3. **Buy delicious food from your nearest Burger King.**[2]

If the s.h.i.t. load is *not* a member of itself, that is, if the s.h.i.t. load is a set that is not a member of itself, then it *must* be a member of itself, because by definition the s.h.i.t. load contains all sets that are not members of themselves. This, however, is contradictory. If the s.h.i.t. load *is* a member of itself, that is, if the s.h.i.t. load is a set that is a member of itself, then it *cannot* be a member of itself, because the s.h.i.t. load only contains sets that are not members of themselves, which is also contradictory. Thus we are led to the paradox of the s.h.i.t. load being unable to be or not be a member of itself.

Now that we understand Russell's Paradox, we can begin to see how it might be related to Heraclitus's aphorism, that "everything is in flux." By "flux" Heraclitus means that everything is always flowing in some respects. He made the same point more graphically when he said you can't step into the same river twice. In a sense, yes, you can step into the Mississippi twice because, by location, the river you are stepping into *is* the Mississippi. However, as a conduit of water, the Mississippi is made of a succession of molecules. Since the molecules passing by at any given location are never the same, you can't step into them twice.

---

[2] Optional, though I get free onion rings for every referral. Tell them that Matt sent you.

Prodding us to question our notion of identity, Heraclitus's aphorism makes an interesting counter to Russell's paradox. Darrin's objection to the paradox was that "Everything flows, nothing stands still." He is undoubtedly referencing Heraclitus's notion of a river in constant flux, and his point is probably this: if we can consider something that is in constant change to be static, then perhaps we can consider something to both be and not be a certain way; thus the s.h.i.t. load in Russell's paradox could both be and not be a member of itself without any contradiction.

It could also be that, in referencing Heraclitus's river, Darrin is proposing a third alternative to Russell's paradox: the s.h.i.t. load is neither a member of itself nor is it not a member of itself—it is a perfect neutrality. Like a flowing river it cannot be said to change or remain the same. It can be said only to exist, beyond all category.

Someone might object, "But this neutrality is non-sense! A set must either be a member of itself or not be a member of itself. A set must fit into one of these categories!" Darrin, of course, would probably reply as follows: "'Non-sense?' Name-calling is not only a form of *ad hominem* but an expression of poor rhetorical form. Must you debase my assertion in lieu of challenging the reasoning behind its premises or conclusion? But, I digress. . . In answer to your question I am of course reminded of a debate on God's existence between Bertrand Russell and the Thomist Jesuit Frederick Copleston. I think the debate aired as a BBC radio broadcast in 1948, but I could be mistaken; maybe it was '47. Regardless, they got to talking about the world, or all existence, having a first cause, which Copleston asserted there was. Russell denied it, saying that there wasn't good enough reason to suppose that there was indeed a first cause of the world, and he went on to say something like 'the universe simply is; that's it.' My objection is his objection: there needn't be a 'first cause' of the world, just like there needn't be the categorization of a set into one of two all-encompassing sets. . . . "

Not long after Darrin began this monologue eyes would roll, sighs would be heard, and everyone would start tuning him out, while some of the more imaginative individuals might wish for Darrin to spontaneously combust.

Someone brave enough to risk hearing another long-winded response might raise a new objection to Darrin's objection: "If something could be both what it is and what it is not, how would we be able to distinguish anything from anything else? A world like this would be madness. Therefore, it must be that something cannot be both what it is and what it is not."

Darrin would then probably say this: "'Must be' or 'must not be' are superficial notions that we impose unsuccessfully upon the world around us. Why must a set either be or not be a member of itself? It is true that we cannot say that something both is and is not, but how do we know that what we can say reflects reality? Is there even anything? If everything truly is in constant flux, like Heraclitus said, then it would seem impossible for us to reach any solid philosophical ground through reasoning; nothing would stay the same long enough for us to quantify it, and what good would such quantifications do if we made them—things would continually change and render our quantifications useless. To that end, if all things *are* constantly changing, identity is useless. Categories, which must be static, are futile when applied to a dynamic world, and as this *is* a dynamic world, Russell's Paradox—itself an effort to make the dynamic as static—is no longer a problem."

As you can see, I'm a little too good at playing Darrin. But I hope you can also see that, regardless of being annoying, he does have a point.

The Guy Is Not Alone. . .

I love when popular culture intersects with philosophy and explores it. One excellent example is *Star Trek: Voyager*, the story of a federation starship that accidentally gets pulled into the Delta Quadrant of space and attempts to return to Earth.

On one episode, a computer program is initialized to act as the Voyager crew's interim Chief Medical Officer. This "Emergency Medical Hologram" is outfitted with a holographic body capable of touch, sight, hearing, intelligence, and emotions. It even has a personality. Of course, this raises philosophical questions. Is the Doctor a being? If he is a being, what is it that makes him a being? What if the Doctor is *both* a being *and* a computer program? If he is both, then he is both a being and a construct created through the complex arrangement of mathematical codes. Would this then mean that emotion, personality, the mind, sentience, humanity, and self-hood could be contained in a mathematical code, a sequence of numbers? If yes, then are we anything more than organic computers ourselves? And is there a helpline?

I bet my little *Voyager* joke didn't make you laugh. That's fine. It's also my point: *The Onion* intersects and explores philosophy, but it's funny in a way that *Voyager* isn't. *Voyager's* humor is confined to situations that could possibly occur on a ship during a fantastic voyage. And, being on TV, there's a line that *Voyager* can't cross. *The Onion's* humor, however, is not restricted—just about anything's fair game. It's this comedic freedom, coupled with the quality of the humor itself, that gives *The Onion* staying power and appeal.

Now, I think I'll do us all a favor by shutting my "damn cake hole."

News Archive

17

Area God Hospitalized, Slowly Dying

DAVID KYLE JOHNSON

The Onion constantly portrays religious people as idiots. Consider its story "Paleontology Class Winces Whenever Fundamentalist Kid Raises Hand" (3/6/02) or its story "Fellow Dormmates Warned About Christian In 462" (9/2/98). In their unabashed satire, these stories reflect what Pat Robertson would call "the secularization of our society." Although I am no fan of Pat Robertson, I think he is onto something here. In line with the famous suggestion of Friedrich Nietzsche (1844–1900), God seems to be slowly dying—more and more people are refusing to take religion seriously. According to the most recent American Religious Identification Survey, atheism was the only religious identification to gain ground in all fifty states.

Of course, Pat greatly exaggerates the plight of religious believers. After all, you could hardly be elected to a major political office in this country if you admitted to being an atheist. (In fact, if you're not a Christian or a Jew, your chances are pretty low.) But our culture has become much less concerned with religion. You're much more likely to listen to one's doctor than to one's pastor. You might pray when an accident happens, but you call 911 first. Most people believe the Discovery Channel more than The Bible and it's rare to find an individual like Onion writer Gladys Parker who is content to trust in Jesus for her health insurance (5/23/07).

In general, most people are more like Kyle Richman than Melinda Tulle. The Onion reports that Kyle bailed on his first date with Melinda when he saw all the religious paraphernalia in her apartment and realized that she wasn't just a Christian, but a "Christian Christian," "one who actually 'lived her faith'"

("Apartment Full Of Jesus Stuff Brings Date To Screeching Halt," 3/22/00).

On the cutting edge of modern culture, *The Onion* suggests that science is slowly winning out as we become a secular society.

But is this fair? Is there an inevitable conflict between science and religion, and will science inevitably emerge as the victor, finally killing God off? Or is *The Onion* not giving both sides their due?

You Gotta Have Faith

Faith might be inevitable—hardwired into our brains. According to an *Onion* report, this "could explain why people with brain tumors believe there is no God" ("Humans Hardwired for Faith," (7/16/07). Regardless of whether it is inevitable, is it justified?

The way it is usually used, the term "faith" refers to "belief without sufficient evidence." Young kids, when they first believe in Santa Claus, do so with this kind of faith. Seeing presents under the Christmas tree doesn't even come close to being *sufficient evidence* for Santa—after all, anyone could have put them there. But no little kid demands proof of Santa's existence. This is why, according to *The Onion*, Santa would make a better god than God ("Ho! Ho! Ho! I Am God: The True Meaning of Christmas, by Santa Claus," 12/17/96).

Sufficient evidence is a matter of degree. How much evidence do you have to have for it to be sufficient? If you have enough evidence to make something fifty-one percent likely, is that sufficient? What about seventy-five percent? Since there is no universally accepted place to draw the line, there isn't universal agreement about when to call something "faith." But there can still be obvious cases, and when it is obvious that there is insufficient evidence for a certain belief, it will be obvious that those who believe it do so by faith.

The term "faith" is often misused to refer to "belief *despite evidence to the contrary*"—when someone can't dismiss the evidence against a belief, but holds the belief anyway. This we could call "blind faith," since the person is blind to the evidence.

A good example of blind faith is an older child who continues to believe in Santa despite clues to the contrary. "How does Santa visit everyone in one night? Who cares? I don't wanna miss out on the presents. I just hope Santa didn't see me being bad." ("Ho, Ho, Ho! I Saw You Masturbating! A Special Message From Santa Claus," 12/12/06).

Another good example is the person who takes his friend to the faith healer instead of the hospital and then believes the faith healer's excuse when his friend dies. "I invoked the name of the Holy Trinity to drive the sickness out from the poor sinner's heart, but sadly, a blockage in the sinner's pulmonary artery stopped God's love, and much blood, from getting through" ("Faith Healer Loses Patient During Routine Miracle," 11/9/05).

The same blind faith is exhibited by Beatrice Sewell, who believes her marriage to Davey will last, despite the fact that she has divorced him three times already. ("Middle-Aged Woman Believes In Fourth Marriage, Angels," 7/23/97).

Perhaps the best illustration of the concept is Bush's Blind-Faith-Based Initiative "founded on the unquestioned assumption that the Bush Administration will 'take care of everything.'" ("Bush Unveils New Blind-Faith-Based Initiatives," 1/5/05). You'd *have to be* blind to not catch the evidence against that one.

But blind-faith isn't really faith—it's just "irrationality." If X entails that Y is false, one cannot believe both X and Y without believing two contradictory things. So if solid evidence entails that a belief of yours is false, you can't continue to hold that belief without being irrational. And even though faith is often called a virtue, I think most would be hard pressed to say irrationality is virtuous. Refusing to give up a falsified belief is just stubborn.

Consequently, few embrace blind-faith—not even religious believers. Consider one of the earliest clashes between science and religion: the Copernican revolution. Before Copernicus and Galileo, everyone believed that the earth was the center of the universe, and that the sun revolved around it. Observers of the planets did notice retrogrades (the planets seemed to "double back" in the sky, every now and again) but most thought this meant the planets had epicycles (tiny circles) on their larger orbits around the Earth. But Copernicus and Galileo challenged this idea, suggesting the hypothesis that, along with the other planets, the earth revolves around the Sun better accounts for the planetary motions. The church called this heresy, insisting that the Bible entails that the sun revolves around the Earth. (Which, by the way, it does. For example, in Joshua 10, Joshua stops the sun in the sky—"The sun stood still," verse 13—not the earth from rotating.)

This was a tumultuous time for the church; many of their views were under attack by science. They did many things to keep these new ideas down. They banned Copernicus's work and placed

Galileo under a lifetime house arrest. They burned others, like Giordano Bruno, at the stake. But something they didn't do is ignore evidence. They didn't deny the existence of planetary retrogrades; they thought their theory made sense of the evidence—like the fact that from our point of view the earth seems to be stationary, and that the Bible says so—better than the other theories.

Of course, they were wrong. The church reinterpreted the Bible and rejected the old theories and finally apologized for Galileo's house arrest in 1992 (none, to date, for Copernicus or Bruno). But the point is, not even the Church in the midst of the scientific revolution had blind-faith. Ignoring evidence is not an admirable thing.

But genuine faith—*belief without sufficient evidence*—is a different matter. Genuine faith is often viewed as virtuous and is the kind of faith most religions promote. For example, it is acknowledged by nearly all philosophers, both those who believe in God and those who don't, that it's impossible to prove that God exists. In fact, any argument for God's existence provides less than adequate support for the existence of an all-knowing, all-powerful, all-loving creator that punishes sinners and rewards the rest. At best, they point to a "first cause" or "universe designer" (which, after all could be the big-bang or a multi-dimensional mad scientist, respectively). So if you believe in God, you do so without sufficient evidence. You have the childlike faith that is revered in religious circles. But is it really a good thing? And is it unique to religious believers?

Religion as Science

One of the common claims made from both sides of the science vs. religion debate is that each is the other. Those who favor science suggest that religion is just bad science. Those who favor religion suggest that science is just another form of religion. They are actually both right, in their own way.

Religion is very much like science, in some respects. For one thing, both are hard. According to *The Onion*, the theory that science is hard "gathered momentum following the 1997 publication of physicist Stephen Hawking's breakthrough paper, "Lorentz Variation And Gravitation Is Just About The Hardest Friggin' Thing In The Known Universe" ("National Science Foundation: Science Hard," 6/5/02). Anyone who has taken a theology class knows the same can be true of religion.

But religion and science also have a similar goal: to explain and make sense of the world. This was the main thing religion did for millennia. It posited a creator to explain the existence of the earth; it posited demons to explain disease; it posited divine wrath to explain lightning. Judaism explained child-birthing pains with its "Eve and the Talking Snake" story. Hinduism explained the existence of the river Ganges with a story about the goddess Ganga coming from heaven to purify the ancestors of King Bhagirath. Of course, since science seeks explanations for the same things, this is clearly where religion and science have conflicted.

And religion is losing the battle. We don't try to predict bad weather by determining which city has the most sinners; we listen to the meteorologist. We don't perform exorcisms to cure disease; we do medical research. We don't sacrifice animals for good crops; we spray and irrigate them.

There are a few holdouts. Some people still read The Bible's creation story literally, even though it contradicts the findings of science. With this in mind let's turn to another aspect of the conflict between science and religion—when religion tries to do science.

When Religion Does Science

When religion tries to do science, it almost always does it badly. Good scientists do not protect their theories from falsification. They certainly don't do it by banning works, house arrests and burning people at the stake. But they also don't do it by tweaking their theories to match the evidence, after the evidence comes in. The scientific method is: a. form a hypothesis; b. make predictions based on that hypothesis; and c. see if the predictions are right; and if the evidence is not what the hypothesis predicts, you reject that hypothesis and try another.

We saw how the church protected its theories during the scientific revolution, but we need not go to history to find examples of "theory protecting." Today's creationists could get the gold medal in the bad-science Olympics. Young-Earth-Creationists believe that the earth was created, pretty much as it is (humans and all), about six thousand to ten thousand years ago; that is what The Bible (taken literally) entails. But when convincing evidence was presented against their theory by scientists—like Sir Charles Lyell (1797–1875) who argued that the universe is billions, not thousands of years old and Charles Darwin (1809–1882) who argued that humans were not created in the Garden of Eden "as-is" but evolved from less developed life forms—creationists refused to it give up. Instead, they protected it. According to *The Onion*, they outlawed the practice of evolution in Kansas (11/28/06) and acquired a five-thousand-year-old *T. Rex* skeleton for their museum (1/15/03). But the main way they protected it is by trying to dismiss the evidence against it.

When million-year-old fossils were found, they questioned the method for dating the fossils, carbon dating, by cooking up reasons for thinking it flawed—classic bad science. If your hypothesis about the boiling temperature of water is wrong, you don't blame the thermometer. And when it was pointed out that the stars we can see must have existed billions of years ago in order for their light to have enough time to get to earth, creationists scrambled for an explanation. First it was "God must have created those stars with their light already on the way to earth." Later it was "Light used to travel a lot faster." Of course, both were debunked almost as soon as they were proposed. Amazingly, *The Onion* has not done a story on either of these brilliant hypotheses.

Kansas is the hotbed for religious "science." According to *The Onion* (9/6/00), Christian fundamentalists there lobbied to overturn the Second Law of Thermodynamics, arguing:

> What do these scientists want us teaching our children? That the universe will continue to expand until it reaches eventual heat death? That's hardly an optimistic view of a world the Lord created for mankind.
>
> Why can't disorder decrease over time instead of everything decaying? . . . Is that too much to ask? This is our children's future we're talking about.
>
> . . . it's a deeply disturbing scientific principle that threatens our children's understanding of God's universe as a benevolent and loving place . . .
>
> . . . it's a direct contradiction of what it says in the Bible, about how everything is going to get better, and we'll all live happily up in heaven after the End Times.

These individuals want the law repealed, not because it can be shown to be false, but because it isn't good for the children. Just like creationists, they refuse to believe anything contrary to The Bible. The evidence doesn't matter. Worst science ever!

Science as Religion

Many scientists, such as the British biologist Richard Dawkins, claim that any kind of faith is irrational. The Santa Claus story might be cute and useful for promoting selfishly-motivated good behavior, but in the end, it's nothing but a lie. We are teaching our children to believe in things without sufficient evidence—a bad habit that contributes to so many of our society's problems.

For example, why did so many people believe the Bush administration when it blamed 9/11 on Iraq? According to *The Onion*, the search for WMDs only turned up a Remington 7mm Magnum rifle engraved "To President Hussein, From Vice-President Bush, Independence Day 1982" and a suspiciously long extension cord (Infographic, 4/16/03). Bush and our country at large had a child-like faith in the existence of Iraqi WMDs.

But faith is not entirely absent from science. For example, scientists assume Ockham's Razor—the principle that the simplest explanation should always be preferred. But where's the evidence for that? There are also certain philosophical problems that scientists dismiss by faith. For example, it's impossible to prove that the world is real rather than a dream. This is called the Skeptical Problem and was most famously presented by the philosopher René Descartes (1596–1650). Any evidence gathered for the world being real would also be evidence that we are stuck in a vivid dream. But if the world wasn't real, what would science be studying? So the scientist must assume, on faith, that the world exists.

Scientists might object that they do have evidence for Ockham's Razor and for the existence of the world. After all, these beliefs work. People who believe them are successful in life, and those who don't end up in mental hospitals.

But that brings me to the main thing science has faith in: induction. Induction is a kind of reasoning that uses observations about the past to make predictions about the future. It relies upon the assumption that that the future will resemble the past. All scientific reasoning is based on it. (If copper has conducted electricity in the past, it will in the future.)

But what argument can scientists put forth for the assumption that the future will resemble the past? They could point out that this assumption has always worked in the past, and conclude that it will work in the future. But this is just another inductive argument! You can't prove induction with induction. That would be arguing in a circle, as was famously demonstrated by the philosopher David Hume (1711–1776). So scientists must assume, without sufficient evidence, that induction works—they must take it on faith.

But science is like religion in another way pointed out by the philosopher Ludwig Wittgenstein (1889–1951). He argued (in his earlier years) that unless an explanation refers to a physical state of affairs in the world, it's meaningless. He is especially critical of science's appeal to "physical laws" as explanations for the behavior of matter; he didn't think they were explanations at all.

Consider the physical law known as "strong nuclear force." Usually protons and neutrons repel each other. But when they get really close (as close as they are in the nucleus of an atom) they attract each other—so much so that it is nearly impossible to tear them apart. Why does this happen? "Strong nuclear force" the scientists say. But what is strong nuclear force? Well, it's whatever keeps the nucleus of an atom from flying apart. See, scientists assume (again, on faith) that nothing happens without a cause. So the nucleus of an atom can't hold together for "no reason." But they don't really know what that reason is—so they just assume it's there and give it a name.

Wittgenstein would scoff at "strong nuclear force." Giving something a name doesn't explain anything. Maybe proton-neutron attraction occurs for no reason at all. We might as well just say it has no cause, or that it's just "magic."

According to *The Onion*, scientists from the Evangelical Center For Faith-Based Reasoning tried to replace gravity with God. "Things fall not because they are acted upon by some gravitational force, but because a higher intelligence, 'God' if you will, is pushing them down" ("Evangelical Scientists Refute Gravity With New 'Intelligent Falling' Theory," (8/17/05.) Sure, go ahead and laugh. But are these "faith-based scientists" any different from conventional scientists? Conventional scientists assume that things can't fall for no reason and so they hypothesize something abstract (nonphysical) to explain it—The Law of Gravity. How is The Law of Gravity any different from God pushing things down? Wittgenstein would say it's just a different name. Neither name does any real explaining at all.

Who Wins?

The existence of our universe may one day be explained by something outside our universe (like an extra-dimensional universe creating machine). But, if it is, that itself will need to be explained. And if it is, that explanation will need explaining . . . and so on. No matter how many explanations science gives, there will always be a stopping point at which the atheistic scientist has to just say "There is no explanation; this is just the way things are." At that point, the religious believer could interject God as an explanation for the whole thing—and science would have no way of falsifying the claim.

Some might think this means the religious believers win. Atheists have no ultimate explanation, while the believers have God.

But the believers are not immune to their own criticism. If one asks them why God exists and why he is like he is, they must simply say "There is no explanation; this is just the way things are." But if religious believers are allowed to say God is unexplained, it would seem they must allow atheists to say the same thing about the universe.

So, is it a tie?

Maybe not. Contrary to Gillette—which, as *The Onion* reports, embraces complexity with their five bladed razors ("Fuck Everything, We're Doing Five Blades," 2/18/04)—Ockham and his razor tells us that complexity is a mistake; if two theories aim to explain the same thing, you should always prefer the simpler one—literally, the one with the least amount of stuff in it. (Ockham would have stuck with his single bladed Bic.) So compare these two theories:

Theory 1.   The universe and its laws simply exist, without explanation.

Theory 2.   The universe and its laws are explained by God, whose existence and properties are without explanation.

Obviously, theory 1 is simpler—it has less stuff. Thus, if you're purely scientific and only accept things on purely scientific grounds, you'd have to be an atheist.

But here's the thing. Science cannot be the final word on rational acceptability because all of morality falls outside the realm of science.

You probably believe it's wrong to harm other human beings for no reason. You probably also believe that liberty is a fundamental human right. But what's the basis for these beliefs? Have clinical trials proven them true? On the contrary, no experiment could. For right and wrong we just rely on our gut feelings.

And that's okay. The philosopher William James (1842–1910) taught us that, if you are in a situation where believing without sufficient evidence is unavoidable, it must be okay to believe without sufficient evidence. And since you really aren't ever going to have sufficient evidence to back your moral beliefs, it's okay to believe them without sufficient evidence.

Couldn't belief in God be like that too? Maybe. But we have to be careful. Just because it's okay to believe in some things without evidence doesn't mean that it is okay to believe in anything without evidence. Faith in induction seems rational, but faith in ghosts doesn't. Which is belief in God more like? I'll leave that question open.

Get Serious

We've seen that, when religion makes claims that can be tested, it conflicts with science, and science always wins. But when religion makes claims that can't be tested—about the existence of God or about morality—science seems to have nothing to say.

A growing number of people therefore want the best of both worlds: they embrace science for its ability to explain and predict but at the same time embrace religion for its ability to supply comfort and meaning.

The Onion reports that Doug Kamin, upon hearing the jubilant gospel singing that pours forth each Sunday from Bethel African Methodist Episcopal Church, wishes he believed in "all that God bullshit."

> It must be so life-affirming to be in there, connecting with fellow human beings and celebrating your faith while making that joyful noise. . . . I still say it's a big, delusional fairy tale, this whole religion thing, but what's the harm in believing in a 2,000-year-old carpenter and some 'holy ghost' if it makes you happy? ("Black Gospel Choir Makes Man Wish He Believed In All That God Bullshit," 1/16/06)

Many people want to enjoy religion without using it to make controversial physical or historical claims.

But there are objections to this approach. The philosopher William Clifford (1845–1879) argued that it is morally wrong to hold without evidence a belief that could harm others. Clifford went so far as to contend that any belief could harm others; so he concluded that it is always wrong to believe without evidence. This part seems a bit extreme. But the first part seems correct. According to Clifford, it would be wrong to believe children are sex toys because this would lead to pedophilia. Who would disagree with that?

Yet Clifford's thesis presents a problem for religious believers because no belief has harmed people more efficiently and systematically than religious belief. Obvious examples are the Crusades, the Inquisition, the Salem witch trials, and the Israeli-Palestinian conflict. According to *The Onion*, religious strife has gotten so bad in the Middle East that people are seeking solace in religion (8/24/06). All religions mistreat women and have held back scientific progress. The church was the last to let go of slavery, it was the last hold out against interracial marriage, and will be the last to accept homosexuality.

Some religious believers have gotten so out of hand that God felt the need to speak out about it. According to *The Onion*, God held a press conference shortly after the 911 attacks, in which he stated:

> Somehow, people keep coming up with the idea that I want them to kill their neighbor. Well, I don't. And to be honest, I'm really getting sick and tired of it. Get it straight. Not only do I not want anybody to kill anyone, but I specifically *commanded* you not to, in really simple terms that anybody ought to be able to understand. . . . I don't care how holy somebody claims to be. . . . If a person tells you it's My will that they kill someone, they're wrong. Got it? I don't care what religion you are, or who you think your enemy is, here it is one more time: No killing, in My name or anyone else's, ever again. ("God Angrily Clarifies 'Don't Kill' Rule," 9/26/01)

Too bad God doesn't talk sense like this more often.

Oh yeah—he can't talk at all any more now that he's in a coma. Thanks to a bold generation of satires like *The Onion*, people are beginning to see through the hypocrisy. Every time religion does something harmful—promotes stereotypes, spreads fear, or encourages superstition—God dies just a little bit more.

18
Peeling the Layers of Truth

GREGORY D. GILSON

We expect, or at least we hope, that the stories we read in a newspaper or hear on the TV news are true—that they correspond with reality. But we don't expect, or even hope, that the stories in *The Onion* are true. That would defeat the whole point of *The Onion*.

The Onion does not follow the standard journalistic convention of reporting empirical truths. *Onion* stories such as "New Starbucks Opens In Rest Room Of Existing Starbucks" (6/27/98) and "ACLU Defends Nazi's Right To Burn Down ACLU Headquarters" (10/14/03) are not true in the ordinary sense that they report facts. Nevertheless this doesn't mean they disregard the Truth. On the contrary, *Onion* journalism displays the unorthodox theory of Truth inherent in postmodernism. In fact, a careful look at *The Onion* reveals that it is *more true* than standard newspapers in many ways.

Traditional Newspapers and the Correspondence Theory of Truth

Traditional newspapers reflect the correspondence theory of truth, according to which a belief or assertion is true just in case its meaning corresponds to a fact. The belief or assertion expressed by the sentence "There are weapons of mass destruction in Iraq" is true if and only if it is a fact that there are weapons of mass destruction in Iraq. Facts are objective states of affairs in the world that do not depend on what anybody believes or decrees. Even when it was widely believed that the earth is flat, this did not alter the *fact* that the earth is spherical.

Beliefs necessarily aim at facts. Just try to believe something that you know is contradicted by a fact. For example, try for a moment to make yourself believe that the earth is flat. You can't, and that's a good thing. People who do not match their beliefs to known facts are not taken seriously.

Assertions are further removed from facts in that it is not impossible or even uncommon for people to make assertions that are contrary to known facts. These are commonly known as *lies*. Just as false beliefs have no effect on the truth, neither do lies. The *Onion* headline, "I Lied About Making $80,000 From Home . . . And So Can You" (5/1/02) illustrates this point nicely. Nevertheless, in typical circumstances, assertions, like beliefs, are expected to aim at truth. False assertions are condemned in society at large and especially in conventional journalism.

Conventional journalism serves the needs of society by disseminating truths. Democracy flourishes when citizens have access to accurate information about the activities of government leaders. Capitalism thrives when consumers have access to accurate information about products and services. The public good depends on honest reporting and thoughtful analysis of basic facts.

Flying in the face of this principle, *The Onion* deliberately reports falsehoods, presenting a distorted view of society. *Onion* headlines "Bush Calls For Panic" (10/15/08) and "U.S. Consumer Confidence Down, Says Guy Trying to Sell Van" (11/20/02) never would have seen the light of day on CNN.

In addition to discovering what might be called "plain facts," conventional journalists spin those facts into interesting news stories. It's not forbidden, and sometimes even seen as a good thing, for a newspaper to have a partisan point of view. There are conservative, liberal, libertarian, and even communist newspapers. There are also newspapers—tabloids—that spin facts into prurient tales.

The Onion, though not a tabloid, routinely violates or simply ignores any reasonable standard of decency. It is completely unconcerned to present issues truly, fairly, or even coherently. Nor does *The Onion* promote any partisan point of view. It dishes out abuse to conservatives, liberals, libertarians, communists, and capitalists with equal fervor: "Limbaugh Says Drug Addiction A Remnant Of Clinton Administration" (10/22/03), "Nation's Liberals Suffering From Outrage Fatigue" (7/7/04), "Libertarian Reluctantly Calls Fire Department" (4/21/04), "Communists Least Threatening

Group In U.S." (10/20/00), and "Widening Gap Between Rich And Super-Rich Threatening The American Dream" (11/19/96).

Knowledge for Sale

The Onion systematically deviates from conventional journalism's commitment to truth and Truth in exactly the way predicted by the postmodern philosopher Jean-Francois Lyotard (1924–1998). Lyotard maintains that the rise of mass communication, computerization, and the post-industrialization of society has transformed the nature and value of knowledge.[1]

Prior to the end of the Second World War, people valued knowledge for the sake of information. They therefore adhered to the correspondence theory of truth, according to which truth is based on facts. Today, however, we value knowledge as a means of augmenting wealth and power. Governments produce "facts" in order to consolidate power and corporations produce "facts" in order to sell their products. Lyotard calls this process the "mercantilization" of knowledge.

The Onion wholeheartedly embraces the mercantilization of knowledge. In the fictional October 6th, 1783, founding issue of *The Onion*, the editor, H. Ulysses Zweibel, claims to have invented the notion of directly integrating advertising with the content of the news.

> The Onion herewith rises beyonde its competitors throo a great INNOVATION in ink-printing known here-to-fore as ADVERTISING; a concept of my design; which is a FEATURE ARTICKLE composed, not by the press-man but by a prominent SELLER OF WARES.

Thus *The Onion* set precedent for postmodernism by explicitly and intentionally mixing news stories and the "facts" they contain with advertising propaganda.

Dominant Narratives and Language Games

In order to generate meaningful debate, a society must maintain certain background assumptions that function as the conceptual

---

[1] Jean-Francois Lyotard, "The Postmodern Condition: A Report on Knowledge," *Theory and History of Literature* 10 (1984).

framework for that debate. For example, in the US media, it is almost universally accepted that democracy, free speech, free markets, and scientific progress are good. Hence anything Americans deem true must be built upon these concepts.

Traditional mass media has played a significant role in establishing the background assumptions for our debates by organizing news stories around narratives that assume their truth. Consider the portrayal of American exceptionalism. Frequent stories about the U.S. as superpower create the impression that the normal rules of behavior don't apply to the U.S. For example, when *The Onion* asked average American "Scott Watkins" what he thought about the continuing skirmishes between U.S. troops and Iraqi protesters, he said, "I don't understand why these wackos won't simply face facts and accept that they're under the control of a foreign superpower's occupational force" (5/7/03). Dominant narratives like American exceptionalism legitimate the discourse that takes place within it.

Lyotard argues that the traditional dominant narratives of democracy, free speech, free markets, and scientific progress are no longer credible and therefore no longer legitimate their respective discourses. The result has been strict separation of the various narratives into distinct and isolated language games.

A language game is an unspoken set of rules for conversation. When combined with social practices, language games structure one's reality. Differing language games often account for lack of understanding between different groups. For example, teenagers and adults typically play different language games. This difference often results in mutual revulsion, as depicted in the *Onion* story "Area Teen Accidentally Enters Teen Center" (1/7/09).

The language game of science is based on empirical verification. In contrast, the language game of religion is based on emotional and spiritual needs. Religious claims cannot be explained by science and scientific claims cannot be explained by religion. The result of the gap between fact and value has been fragmentation and isolation of our society's dominant narratives.

According to an *Onion* report, this fragmentation and isolation worsened to such an extent by the end of the twentieth-century that the condition of humanity was officially upgraded to "pre-apocalyptic." The report cited new findings from leading postmodern philosopher Richard Rorty, who said,

I was flipping through the cable channels the other night, trying to get an abstract sense of the way emergent processes of change and transformation generated by contemporary high-tech society are challenging cultural assumptions regarding diverse aesthetic forms to create a novel state of history . . . when, all of a sudden, I realized that everything I was looking at was the biggest load of unimaginably horrific crap ever.

Rorty went on to say that, at this point in the socio-cultural discourse, the key question is no longer whether or not social fragmentation, cultural meta-juxtaposition and socioeconomic problematics require new modes of experience and interpretation, but rather, "When will the seven-headed dragon of the End Times descend upon us all in unholy fury?" ("Post-Modern Condition Upgraded To Pre-Apocalyptic," 7/28/99).

Hyper-Reality, Disneyworld, and Simulacra

The French philosopher Jean Baudrillad (1929–2007) applies Lyotard's analysis of truth to contemporary mass media. According to Baudrillard, the mass media is a completely self-contained informational system that no longer makes any direct reference to reality. Its only reference is to what Baudrillard calls "hyper-reality."

Baudrillard uses Disneyworld as an example of hyper-reality. Disneyworld is more real, more true, than "real America" in the sense that "All its values are exalted here, in miniature and comic strip form. Embalmed and pacified."[2]

Though Disneyworld was designed specifically for amusement, it defines America's view of itself and the rest of the world. The fact that Disneyworld is based on imagination makes the rest of America seem real when, in fact, America itself has long since become what Baudrillard calls a "simulacrum": a self-perpetuating system of simulation that makes no reference to an objective reality. At first glance, Disneyworld seems to legitimate the rest of America as genuine reality; on closer inspection, however, both Disneyworld and America are illusions that feed off each other. Like America itself, Disneyworld has become too hyper-real for some people to take, as reported in the *Onion* article,

---

[2] Jean Baudrillard, "Simulacra and Simulations," *Selected Writings* (Stanford University Press, 1998), p. 71.

"Disney Family Vacation Ruined By Walt Disney Corporation" (6/18/03).

Baudrillard claims that all contemporary mass media is a simulacrum, referencing only the hyper-real. Consider the Watergate affair. It was created by the mainstream media to disguise the fact that nearly all political activity is scandalous, or would be if publicly known. By isolating the Watergate affair as an extraordinary instance of political deviance, we conceal the fact that scandalous behavior is the norm in politics. *The Onion* highlights this problem in the story, "President Creates Cabinet-Level Position To Coordinate Scandals" (2/1/06).

The Onion as Simulacrum of the Hyper-Real

The Onion may be an obvious spoof of mainstream media, but it also legitimates that media. In the same way that branding Disneyworld imaginary makes the rest of America real, branding the *The Onion* fake makes mainstream media genuine.

Nevertheless, by postmodern standards, *The Onion*'s stories are more authentic than the mainstream media it parodies. The entire media has become a simulacrum because its goal is to capture our attention rather than convey information. *The Onion* is unique only in that it wears this fact on its sleeve. If the point of media is spectacle, *The Onion*, it would seem, is Baudrillard's simulacrum gone self-conscious.

Stories in *The Onion* do not aim at truth in the traditional sense of making accurate statements of fact that correspond to reality. In the reverse of standard journalistic practice, *The Onion*'s editorial staff first writes headlines and then assigns writers the task of inventing stories to go with them.[3] Editors formulate headlines based solely on absurd representations of mainstream news. Hence, the resulting stories are direct reflections of currents, topics, and trends in mass media and bear no direct relation to external reality. There is obviously no fact-checking procedure at *The Onion*.

---

[3] The Editorial Manager Chet Clem and President Sean Mills discuss this reversal of editorial procedure in an interview conducted by David Shankbone, "*The Onion*: An Interview with 'America's Finest News Source'" - Wikinews, November 25th, 2007.

Onion stories are not produced to promote knowledge. Since the stories are entirely made-up, their value cannot lie in the usefulness of the information they provide. Rather, the value of the stories lies entirely in their ability to amuse readers and make them question what is true and what is True. In this way, *The Onion* is thoroughly postmodern.

The Onion's Treatment of Dominant Narratives

The Onion systematically deviates from the language games that govern our dominant narratives. The result is at the very least quite amusing and, according to some, politically and socially valuable. The violation of conceptual and linguistic norms typically governing narratives takes several forms in *Onion* stories.

One common ploy of *The Onion* is to expose the postmodern gap between distinct dominant narratives by ridiculously mixing them together. For example, scientific and religious narratives have different standards for the justification of belief. Whereas religious beliefs are justified by faith, scientific beliefs are justified by research. *Onion* article, "Evangelical Scientists Refute Gravity With New 'Intelligent Falling' Theory" (8/17/05) mocks the idea that religious and scientific narratives compete with each other to explain the same range of phenomena. The mockery unfolds by generalizing to all of physics the view of biological science adopted by contemporary intelligent design theorists. "Evolutionists Flock To Darwin-Shaped Wall Stain" (9/5/08) plays with the fact that what counts for evidence of truth in some religious contexts would be absurd in scientific contexts. More subtly, "Astronomer Discovers The Center Of The Universe Is His Beautiful 9-Year Old Son" (5/27/98) ridiculously mixes the spiritual or emotional use of the term "center of the universe" with its scientific use.

Another subversive tactic employed by *The Onion* is to deliberately misapply widely overused narratives. "Miracle Of Birth Occurs For The 83 Billionth Time" (3/3/99) illustrates the contentlessness of the term "miracle" in common speech, and the popular media. The features in which *Onion* journalists explain the results of "scientific studies" often ridicule politically sensitive narratives. "Scientists Still Seeking Cure For Obesity" (7/14/04) reports that most cases of obesity are caused by poor diet and lack of exercise while at the same time excusing it as a disease. "Depression Hits Losers The Hardest" (3/5/97) explains a study that casts depression as a medical condition despite baffling evidence that the disease is especially common among people with no friends.

Truthfulness

Despite flagrant violations of Truth norms, *The Onion* does place a high degree of value on truthfulness in the sense of authenticity. *The Onion* regularly ridicules ordinary people for their lack of honesty and critical reflection. Take, for example, its portrait of former President George Bush in "Bush Says He Still Believes Iraq War Was the Fun Thing To Do" (6/18/08).

The Onion vividly represents postmodern thinkers in its call for authenticity without belief in truth. Postmodern thinkers demand that people endeavor to discover and assert what is true, yet doubt whether anything is objectively true.

This paradoxical stance is displayed week after week in *The Onion*'s "What Do You Think?" man-on-the-street opinion surveys. While implicitly criticizing people for holding shallow opinions, it simultaneously suggests that all opinion is ultimately laughable. For example, upon being asked about solutions to the political conflict between Palestinians and Israelis in the Middle East, "Paster Michael Weathers," said that "in these times of trouble, they should turn to The Bible" (10/18/00).

Since conventional journalism is the source of *The Onion*'s parody it is indirectly under attack in each *Onion* issue. *The Onion* satirizes the media's presentation of public people and events as much as the people and events themselves. *Onion* article, "No Jennifer Lopez News Today" (3/14/01) criticizes the media's obsession with mundane details about the lives of celebrities. "Abortion Issue 'Most Critical Of Our Time' Say Tobacco Industry Executives" (2/3/98) displays the fact that corporate ownership of the media dictates news coverage.

The Onion also attacks dishonest ideologies. "Transgendered Sea Anemone Denounced As 'Abomination' By Clergy" (1/20/99) exposes the nearly incoherent use of "natural" by many religious traditions. "Christ Kills Two, Injures Seven in Abortion-Clinic Attack" (11/25/98) challenges the tactics of some so-called Christian organizations.

The Onion displays the absurdity of each of our pathetic little lives in its "Area Man" articles. These articles should send an existential shiver down the spine of anyone who thinks human existence is full of meaning and purpose. Articles range from the utterly depressing "Loved Ones Recall Local Man's Cowardly Battle with Cancer" (2/24/99) to the blasé, "Area Man Holding Out Until Next Exit For Better Fast Food Options" (11/29/08).

The Onion may subject politicians to the harshest treatment of all. "White House Debuts Iraq War Infomercial" (2/8/06), "Thousands More Dead In Continuing Iraq Victory" (1/18/06), and "White House Denies Existence Of Karl Rove" (8/3/05) all question the Bush Administration. Appearing near the end of the Clinton sex scandal, *Onion* article "Nation's Legislators Resume Unfettered Whoring" (5/5/99) ridicules the hypocrisy of philandering Congressmen. "Palin Brushing Up On Foreign Policy At Epcot" (9/29/08) illustrates the fairy tale nature of the Alaska governor's run for Vice President.

Progress?

Al Gore says of *The Onion*: "This publication is tasteless and destructive to our shared values. Read it for yourself and you'll see what I mean. Seriously, what else could make me laugh—much less laugh uproariously—while being offended week after week after week."[4] Gore means this as a compliment, implying that *The Onion*'s efforts to destroy shared values is socially progressive.

But social progress is change from wrong to right. How is it possible for a newspaper that has abandoned the truth to be a vehicle of truth in this way?

The postmodern authors we have examined—Lyotard and Baudrillard—might go so far as to say that *The Onion* is achieving a truthfulness beyond truth. Fortunately, I don't have the space here to figure out whether this notion ultimately makes sense. I simply note that, in each of my analyses of *Onion* stories above, I did assume that the target of the parody was wrong, which in turn assumes that there is a right. I don't know how I could appreciate *Onion* stories without believing in Truth—somewhere out there.

So *The Onion,* like postmodernism itself, works in ways that are hard to understand rationally. But if this discovery causes you to stop reading *The Onion*, you ought to be the next pinpoint featured in *Our Dumb World*.

---

[4] *Dispatches from the Tenth Circle* (Three Rivers Press, 2001), Back Cover.

19

Candide's Legacy

DOUGLAS FICEK

In 1759, François-Marie Arouet—best known as Voltaire—published *Candide*, a novella that ridicules religious optimism.

In the story, old Dr. Pangloss teaches young Candide that God created our world as "the best of all possible worlds." But Candide soon has the opportunity to test his teacher's claim first hand. Exile, war, torture, rape, venereal disease, earthquakes, shipwrecks, burnings at the stake, and slavery—Candide encounters them all. Shaken to his core, Candide concludes that Dr. Pangloss's religious optimism is pretty much a load of crap.

Following the lead of Voltaire, *The Onion* is highly critical of "theodicy," the attempt to vindicate divine justice in spite of the glaring imperfection of the world. It has published several stories on the subject since its inception, and it is likely that they will keep coming. We do not suffer "Randomly Placed Swinging Blades" like Solid Snake and Lara Croft do ("Video-Game Characters Denounce Randomly Placed Swinging Blades," 8/9/00), but we do live in a deeply messed up world, and many of us want to understand how God could allow this. *The Onion* has expanded Voltaire's criticism of religious optimism, portraying theodicy as callous indifference to human suffering.

The Problem of Evil

If God exists, and if God is all-powerful (omnipotent) and all-good (omnibenevolent), then why is there evil in the world? This is what philosophers call the Problem of Evil, and it has challenged them for centuries, leading many to doubt or deny the existence of God.

The problem of evil predates Judaism, Christianity, and Islam, and it even appears in non-Western religious traditions. Recent research suggests that it arises in African religion and that African thinkers approach it in much the same way many Western thinkers do.[1] The problem of evil has been troubling a vast number of people for a very long time.

First and foremost, the problem of evil is a *logical* problem, a problem that arises for the theist because of an apparent contradiction in his worldview. The theist holds that God is omnipotent and omnibenevolent by definition. At the same time, however, the theist also lives in the world and thus has to admit that it can be an appalling place. It seems that a God who allows so much suffering cannot be omnipotent and omnibenevolent. Hence, God both is and is not what he is supposed to be by definition, which is impossible.

The Onion explores this contradiction in "Lord Under Investigation For Failure To Provide" (7/23/97), which informs us of a federal investigation into the alleged negligence of the "six-millennia-old sky-father deity Yahweh," whose all-powerful, all-good ways have finally been called into question. "On more than 70 trillion documented occasions," *The Onion* explains, "the Lord has failed to provide for dutiful worshippers, allowing them to go without Providence in times of great need." Offering more detail, *The Onion* continues:

> The list of Justice Department allegations ranges from the mundane, such as the Lord's reported September 1996 refusal to see to it that Terre Haute, IN, Presbyterian Joyce Halstrom receives a new set of drapes for her anniversary, to the catastrophic, such as last year's Mexico City earthquake, in which God allowed an estimated 150,000 devout Catholics to be crushed to death under tons of debris.

God is not being accused here of *causing* any of these things—it's not like He was angry at Joyce and Mexico City and just had to see them suffer. He is, however, being accused of negligence in that He *could have* and *should have* prevented these things from happening, but didn't. Put simply, God is on the hook for evil in the world, especially when it comes to his shocking failure to provide adequate education for fundamentalist Christians, who, according to

---

[1] Kwame Gyekye, *An Essay on African Philosophical Thought: The Akan Conceptual Scheme* (Temple University Press, 1995), pp. 123–28.

the story "remain, after thousands of years, among the least educated groups . . . ranking below pro-wrestling enthusiasts and carnival workers."

In addition to being a logical problem, the problem of evil is also an *existential* problem; it is a problem that is *lived*. Many theists—most of them, I would think—struggle with evil in their daily lives. They undergo hardships and adversities, and at times it is simply all too much. As a result, they experience a crisis of faith. They ask, "If God is all that we say He is, then why did *this* happen? Why did *that* happen?" They reason, "We are good people—we do not deserve so much disease, death, and despair."

Some people give up trying to understand why they have to suffer, accepting as a matter of faith that God has his reasons. As *The Onion* reports: "Despite the seriousness of the charges, many believers remain loyal to the embattled deity. 'I know it seems like the worst thing ever,' said Lynette Maddox, a Flatwoods, KY, manicurist and mother of nine, 'but we just have to trust that it's all part of God's plan'."

Leibniz's *Theodicy*

Many people, like Lynette, claim that there is purpose in worldly evil and imperfection, purpose that is beyond our understanding as human beings. This claim is so old and common that it has become a cliché. Seriously, how many times have you been told that "it's all part of God's plan"? Or that "everything happens for a reason"? For many of us, such comments are practically built-in—we often say them without thinking! Despite this, there is something philosophical happening in them, namely, theodicy.

The German philosopher Gottfried Wilhelm Leibniz (1646–1716) first used the term "theodicy" and was the model for Candide's naïve teacher, Dr. Pangloss. Leibniz argues that this world, our world, is the best world that God could have created, our complaints about it notwithstanding.

As human beings, we cannot see that this is the best of all possible worlds. God, however, as a being that is all-knowing (omniscient), *can* see this and *did* see this prior to creation. As Leibniz explains:

> The wisdom of God, not content with embracing all the possibles, penetrates them, compares them, weighs them one against the other,

to estimate their degrees of perfection and imperfection, the strong and the weak, the good and the evil. . . . By this means the divine Wisdom distributes all the possibles it had already contemplated separately, into so many universal systems, which it further compares the one and the other. The result of these comparisons and deliberations is the choice of the best from among these possible systems, which wisdom makes in order to satisfy goodness completely; and such is precisely the plan of the universe as it is.[2]

This is as good as it gets, in other words, and anything else would be worse – even if our imaginations tell us otherwise.

Leibniz thus "solves" the problem of evil by arguing that God, while unable to eliminate evil, minimized it for our mutual advantage. Unfortunately, this "solution" does not always speak to our experiences as human beings, which leads us back to Voltaire's dark satire, *Candide*.

Voltaire's *Candide*

Easily his most popular work, *Candide* is Voltaire's hilarious attempt to refute the religious optimism of Leibniz's *Theodicy*. It is not a *philosophical* work, technically speaking; it does not feature sophisticated arguments and counterarguments. It does, however, make a plausible philosophical point. In the text, Leibniz appears as the renowned Dr. Pangloss, a "professor of metaphysico-theologico-cosmolo-nigology."[3] (This exaggerated title is inspired by Leibniz's numerous interests.) Pangloss, like his non-fiction, flesh-and-blood counterpart, is an unwavering optimist: he argues that this is "the best of all possible worlds."

Dr. Pangloss tutors Candide at a castle belonging to Candide's uncle. Within its protected confines, it is easy enough for Candide to accept Dr. Pangloss's optimism. But then Candide is kicked out for kissing his uncle's daughter. Beyond the walls of the castle, Candide learns what life is really like, and it is not a pretty picture.

After a series of hair-raising adventures, Candide has to rescue his old teacher from slavery. A telling exchange occurs between them:

---

[2] G.W. Leibniz, *Theodicy: Essays on the Goodness of God, the Freedom of Man, and the Origin of Evil* (Routledge and Kegan Paul, 1951), quoted in William L. Rowe, ed., *God and the Problem of Evil* (Blackwell, 2001), pp. 7–8.

[3] Voltaire, *Candide* (Dover, 1991), p. 1.

"Well, my dear Pangloss," said Candide to him, "when you had been hanged, dissected, whipped, and were tugging at the oar, did you always think that everything happens for the best?"

"I am still of my first opinion," answered Pangloss, "for I am a philosopher and I cannot retract, especially as Leibnitz could never be wrong. . . ." (Candide, p. 81)

Pangloss is unmoved by his horrendous experiences. Nothing can convince him that the world should be better; nothing can convince him that God is even slightly to blame for evil in the world.

Is his tenacity admirable, coming from someone who has suffered disease and deformation? Or is it closed-minded and dogmatic? For Voltaire, it is definitely the latter, and this judgment is ultimately handed down by Candide himself, albeit subtly.

In the final chapter, Candide and his wretched companions meet an old Turk, who tells them that he does not fret about theoretical problems, preferring instead to focus on his garden and its fruits. The old Turk invites them to join him for a meal in his humble home.

Seeing the old Turk care for his family makes Candide realize that the religious optimism of his mentor is not only flawed but dangerous. "We must cultivate our garden" (p. 87), he later asserts, and the message is clear: instead of wasting time on the Problem of Evil, people should work hard to improve the world, to make it more bearable. Explaining or justifying evil in order to absolve God of any responsibility distracts us from concern for each other. What is imperative, Candide seems to suggest, is an investment in this life, here and now. And while Pangloss certainly does not agree, Candide is now sure of himself. "Let us cultivate our garden," he says once more, and that is the last line of the text.

The Onion on God

Like Voltaire's *Candide*, *The Onion* acknowledges the existence of unnecessary evil in the world; it recognizes that things *could be* and *should be* much better, not only in terms of the natural world, but also in terms of our moral imperfections as human beings. For all of these types of evil, *The Onion* has been more than willing to put God on the hook. We clearly saw this willingness in "Lord Under Investigation For Failure To Provide," but there are numerous other examples, some of which are especially disturbing.

Consider the story, "God Cites 'Moving In Mysterious Ways' As Motive In Killing Of 3,000 Papua New Guineans" (7/29/98), which describes God's willingness to take full responsibility for a deadly tsunami, among other things, from the Bubonic Plague to the Holocaust. It also portrays God as not caring too much for the sufferers of evil, as being kind of a jerk about the whole thing. *The Onion* reports:

> "Of course I hear their prayers," God said. "I see every sparrow that falls. But it is My will that these prayers not be answered, and that life continues to be nasty, brutish, and short for the majority of mankind. And My reasons are not yours to question."
>
> Added God: "Where were you when I created the Heavens and the Earth?"

This "official statement," inspired by the Old Testament Book of Job, is surprising—if not jaw-dropping—and for an obvious reason: it flies in the face of our image of God as an omnibenevolent being.

The Onion portrays God in an unflattering light here, and it is not, I think, doing so in jest only. *The Onion* wants to raise the logical and existential Problem of Evil for its faithful readers. And why would it want to raise this problem? Perhaps because it wants its readers to put God on the hook, too.

"God Cites" is not the only story in which *The Onion* lambastes God for the existence of evil in the world. In "Israelites Sue God For Breach Of Covenant" (2/23/00) God is blamed for the historical suffering of Jews; in "God Outdoes Terrorists Yet Again" (9/7/05), God is blamed for Hurricane Katrina and its aftermath; in "God Wondering Whatever Happened To That Planet Where He Made All Those Monkeys" (10/18/00) and "God Returns From 2-Millennium-Long Vacation" (11/8/08), God epitomizes absenteeism; and in "God Answers Prayers Of Paralyzed Little Boy" (12/9/98), God refuses to alleviate the excessive suffering of a young child.

The last of these stories is absolutely brutal, and it is easily one of the most infamous stories that *The Onion* has ever printed. Cringe-inducing and difficult to read, it is also utterly hilarious and brilliantly conceived. It informs us of an incredible event: God answering prayers—but not just any prayers. In the story, God goes out of His way to answer the prayers of Timmy Yu, a paralyzed (and parentless) 7-year-old boy. According to *The Onion*:

> God's response came at approximately 10 A.M. Monday, following a particularly fervent Sunday prayer session by little Timmy. Witnesses said that God issued His miraculous answer in the form of a towering column of clouds, from which poured forth great beams of Divine light and the music of the Heavenly Hosts. The miraculous event took place in the Children's Special Care Ward of St. Luke's Hospital, where Timmy goes three times a week for an excruciating two-hour procedure to drain excess fluid from his damaged spinal column.

The Onion continues:

> Said Angela Schlosser, a day nurse who witnessed the Divine Manifestation: "An incredible, booming voice said to Timmy, 'I am the Lord thy God, who created the rivers and the mountains, the heavens and the earth, the sun and the moon and the stars. Before Me sits My beloved child, whose faith is that of the mustard seed from which grows mighty and powerful things. My child, Timmy Yu, I say unto you thus: I have heard your prayers, and now I shall answer them. No, you cannot get out of your wheelchair. Not ever.'"

This response shocks and awes. It betrays the build-up both in terms of content and tone, which is to say that we do not expect God to refuse Timmy, nor do we expect Him to refuse him so callously.

The Onion portrays God as a villain here, plain and simple, even if nobody else in the story gets it, Timmy included. And Timmy *doesn't* get it. "I know that God loves me, because it says so in the Bible," he says. "So right now, I am just glad that God took the time to answer my prayer. If only I could walk, this would be the greatest day of my life."

Atheism?

Given these stories, it could easily be argued that *The Onion* advocates atheism, that it uses satire to encourage the wholesale rejection of the existence of God. This is probably true, and the evidence is definitely there to support such an argument. However, it is also true that *The Onion* has, on occasion, expressed some sympathy, however qualified, for organized religion.

Consider "Black Gospel Choir Makes Man Wish He Believed In All That God Bullshit" (1/16/02), for example, a story in which a white atheist named Doug Kamin describes his conflicted appreciation of the local Bethel African Methodist Episcopal Church. As *The Onion* reports:

> Kamin first discovered Bethel AME Church in May 2000, shortly after moving to the neighborhood. Long accustomed to dismissing all forms of Christian ceremony and worship as "hysterical" and "cult-like," Kamin overheard a rendition of "The Old Ship of Zion" that led him to amend his opinion.
> "I can't remember the words, but the soloist sang something like 'Join me on the old ship of Zion, and you'll find peace in the Lord,'" Kamin said. "The song probably went back to the slave days. Anyway, it stopped me dead in my tracks. I just stood in front of the church and let the music surround me. For that moment, I totally forgot what an artificial construct God is."

I suspect that some of the writers behind *The Onion* are a lot like Doug Kamin: critical of theism and organized religion, but nevertheless sympathetic to certain types of religious expression—the ones "born of struggle,"[4] especially.

I am not convinced that *The Onion* is one-hundred percent in the tank for atheism. On the other hand, I do think that *The Onion* is one-hundred percent opposed to theodicy.

Voltaire Lives

Two days after the events of 9/11, evangelical leader Jerry Falwell appeared on *The 700 Club* with televangelist and former presidential candidate Pat Robertson. They agreed that the terrorist attack was permitted by God, who "lifted the curtain and allowed the enemies of America to give us probably what we deserved."[5] Falwell blamed the ACLU first; then he blamed pretty much everybody else with whom he had ever disagreed. "I know," he continued,

> that I'll hear from them for this. But, throwing God out successfully with the help of the federal court system, throwing God out of the

---

[4] This phrase was coined in Leonard Harris, ed., *Philosophy Born of Struggle: Anthology of Afro-American Philosophy from 1917* (Kendall/Hunt, 1983).

[5] "You Helped This Happen." Retrieved 1 December 2008 from http://www.beliefnet.com/Faiths/Christianity/2001/09/You-Helped-This-Happen.aspx.

public square, out of the schools. The abortionists have got to bear some burden for this because God will not be mocked. And when we destroy forty million innocent babies, we make God mad. I really believe that the pagans, and the abortionists, and the feminists, and the gays and the lesbians who are actively trying to make that an alternative lifestyle, the ACLU, People for the American Way—all of them who have tried to secularize America—I point the finger in their face and say, "You helped this happen."

Falwell apologized the next day on CNN, explaining that he had intended to blame nobody but the terrorists themselves.

Falwell could not unsay what he had obviously said, however, and *The Onion* struck back hard twelve days later in its first post-9/11 issue. Inspired and remarkably affecting, this issue featured an image of Falwell with this unforgiving headline: "Jerry Falwell: Is That Guy A Dick Or What?" (9/26/01). *The Onion* did not add anything to this headline; there was no corresponding story, and there was no need for one. The message was clear: Falwell did something wrong in blaming secularists for 9/11, something *morally* wrong. Was his rant a cheap and opportunistic political attack? Of course it was—and his damage-controlling apology was thus entirely unsurprising.

The Onion, however, did not call Falwell "A Dick" because of the *political* content of his unfortunate rant; it called him "A Dick" because of its *theodicean* content, which was, in the end, far more troubling. After all, wasn't he basically blaming the victims of 9/11 in order to absolve God of any responsibility? Wasn't he basically arguing that God was punishing them, that they deserved to be killed in the attack?

This type of explanation-justification is familiar to us, and its rationale is simple: blame the victim. We see arguments like this in rape trials, in which women are blamed for being raped on account of their clothing choices, and we are rightly disgusted by such arguments. Well, theodicy, too, can employ this rationale; it can try to excuse God by blaming the victims and sufferers of evil, by claiming that theirs are not experiences of evil, but rather experiences of punishment—divine punishment. This is what Falwell argued in his terrible rant, and this, more than anything, is what *The Onion* found completely unacceptable about it. Thus, when it called him "A Dick," it was not rejecting God so much as the ardent believers who gladly throw humanity under the bus in order to defend him.

"Jerry Falwell" is uniquely pithy, but it is not the only piece in which *The Onion* has criticized theodicy as an endeavor that is both dangerous and dehumanizing. "God Cites," as we know, is a story in which God is blamed for a deadly tsunami. It is also, however, a story in which "religious leaders"—some, not all—are depicted as immediately willing to explain or justify the disaster, as immediately willing to blame the victims for their fates. As *The Onion* reports:

> Despite top religious leaders' reluctance to speculate on the Lord's motive in the killings, many contend it was an act of heathen-smiting.
> "I would never presume to understand God's plan, but it seems like more than a coincidence that these typhoons, tsunamis, and earthquakes always seem to hit non-Christian countries like India and Bangladesh," said Mathew Ellsworth, pastor for Holy Name Lutheran Church in Colorado Springs, CO. "When was the last time a tidal wave devastated France?"

Mathew Ellsworth definitely presumes here. More than that, he *wants* to accept this preposterous explanation-justification; he *needs* it to be true. And why?

Because the deaths of these Papa New Guineans have raised the logical and existential problem of evil for him. Deep down, he realizes that their deaths were gratuitous, but such a realization indicts God, which is unacceptable for him – *the perfection of God cannot be in question!* So, what does he do? Put simply, he does theodicy. He comes up with a way to affirm the omnipotence and omnibenevolence of God given the disaster at hand (and its philosophical implications). Mathew decides to blame *those people* for *their own* deaths—they did practice the wrong religion, after all— and this decision gives him comfort.

But is comfort appropriate under the circumstances? Is it an emotion that he should be shooting for, his faith having been challenged by the problem of evil? I do not think so, and neither does *The Onion*.

For one thing, such an endeavor encourages indifference— indifference to the sufferers of evil and imperfection, indifference to the children and women and men who are catching hell in the world. This is an indifference that is endangering: it makes the most vulnerable people even more vulnerable, their lives and interests having been discounted in the theodicean shuffle.

For another thing, theodicy is dehumanizing, which is to say that it turns people into mere things, things that do not register on the moral radar. While things do not necessarily deserve respect and equal consideration, people do. When Mathew blames the victims of the deadly tsunami, his disrespect renders them mere things that are morally invisible.

Dorothee Soelle, a twentieth-century German theologian, describes such indifference as a type of sadism. "When you look at human suffering concretely," she declares:

> you destroy innocence, all neutrality, every attempt to say, "It wasn't I; there was nothing I could do; I didn't know." In the face of suffering you are either with the victim or the executioner – there is no other option. Therefore that explanation of suffering that looks away from the victim and identifies itself with a righteousness that is supposed to stand behind the suffering has already taken a step in the direction of theological sadism, which wants to understand God *as the torturer*.[6]

In rejecting theodicy, *The Onion*—like Voltaire's *Candide* before it—rejects what Soelle refers to here as "theological sadism," an approach to theism in which one completely discounts the basic value of humanity.

For me, no *Onion* story makes this point better than "Poverty-Stricken Africans Receive Desperately Needed Bibles" (3/13/06). In this sad story, *The Onion* describes Christina Clarkson, "executive director of Living Light Ministries of Lubbock, TX," and the generous "Bible drop" she organized for the impoverished and starving residents of Maradi, Niger.

To her credit, Clarkson is not ignorant of their vast suffering. But because it does not register for her in a morally appropriate way, she completely misreads their reaction to her humanitarian effort: "When we opened up the back of the truck," she explains, "and they saw that it was full of Bibles . . . Grown men and women wept in front of their children. That's how moved they were by the Holy Spirit. That's how I know it's all been worth it." Clarkson is so morally oblivious to the Nigeriens that she doesn't realize they wanted and needed food and medicine instead. A modern-day Dr. Pangloss, she stands as *The Onion*'s poster-child for the idiocy of theodicy.

---

[6] Dorothee Soelle, *Suffering* (Fortress, 1975), p. 32.

Entertainment

20

Fake News Story Not True

ANDREW TERJESEN

"Child Bankrupts Make A Wish Foundation With Wish For Unlimited Wishes." That was the headline of an *Onion* story about "Chad Carter," a nine-year-old leukemia patient, who took advantage of a "bureaucratic loophole" in the well-known charity organization (1/16/08). People encountering the video on blogs and other sites posted nasty comments about young Mr. Carter and wished him dead. Enough people thought that the story was true that snopes.com was prompted to run a piece explaining that it was "all just a bit of whimsical fun."

The "Make A Wish" story is an example of fake news that generated real-world responses. Other *Onion* stories have had more serious repercussions.

In 2002, upon seeing the *Onion* story "Report: Al-Qaida Allegedly Engaging In Telemarketing" (9/18/02), a sheriff in Coldwater, Michigan, released the following "urgent" press release:

> In the course of this investigation, it was learned that this is going on throughout the United States, and some of these telemarketing programs are believed to be operated by al-Qaida. The CIA has announced that they acquired a videotape showing al-Qaida members making phone solicitations for vacation home rentals, long-distance telephone service, magazine subscriptions, and other products.[1]

The sheriff had been investigating telemarketing scams that targeted the elderly and came upon the *Onion* story through an

---

[1] "Onion Taken Seriously, Film at 11," <www.wired.com/culture/lifestyle/news/2004/04/63048>.

Internet search. The mistake was caught only after a local newspaper reported on this alleged terrorist scheme and that story was picked up nationally. In the end, the story was debunked, but not before fanning the flames of hysteria.

One would think someone would have been suspicious of some of the details of the original story, such as US troops finding in a cave on the Afghan-Pakistan border "a bank of empty cubicles with individual phone lines, a bullhorn, and 10 desktop bells, commonly rung in the event of a 'sale'."

These are just two examples of *The Onion* being taken too seriously. Carol Kolb, head writer at ONN, told *Wired* that the goal of *The Onion* is to do "a really straight, AP style." Given that goal, it's a wonder that this kind of thing doesn't happen more often. Straight-faced satire is a pretty difficult thing to achieve. You have to present the topic in a manner that has the trappings of being serious and yet at the same time provide clues for the audience that it is not meant to be taken seriously. Writers at *The Onion* need to find a way to say something so that you know they're "just kidding."

The Dangers of Relying on "Man's Intuition"

How can we know when a person is just kidding? It's not always easy to figure out what someone is thinking even if you know them really well. Just think back to the first time you had this conversation:

TERRY: Just apologize, and then we can let the whole matter drop.

SAM: Apologize for what?

TERRY: For what you did!

SAM: I didn't . . . what did I do?

TERRY: You know what you did. Just say you're sorry.

SAM: I don't know what you're talking about.

TERRY: Yes, you do.

SAM: What do you think I know? . . . Wait—is this about what I did last week?

TERRY: I'm not talking about last week. What did you do last week?

SAM: Oh, you know what I did last week.

This particular exchange exemplifies what philosophers call The Problem of Other Minds.

The Problem of Other Minds can be seen at least as far back as the work of philosopher René Descartes (1596–1650). In his *Meditations*, Descartes muses about the people outside his window wondering, "What do I see from the window beyond hats and cloaks that might cover artificial machines, whose motions might be determined by springs? But I judge that there are human beings from these appearances . . ." Although Descartes's example may at first seem a bit silly, his basic point remains. When I meet someone, how can I be sure they are thinking as opposed to acting out a set of fixed behaviors? How do I know they have a mind like mine?

The reason we can't be certain that someone else has a mind is that we can't see their thoughts. Since we can't see anyone's thoughts, it stands to reason that we can't be sure what thoughts they are having, if any. This is the Problem of What Other Minds Are Thinking. Denying the Problem leads to frustrating conversations like Sam and Terry's. On the other hand, sometimes we really do know what we did and we're exploiting the Problem to cover our asses.

The problem comes up often in romantic situations. Consider the *Onion* opinion piece "My Man's Intuition Tells Me That My Neighbor Wants To Sleep With Me" (8/1/07). Ed Jonas is convinced his neighbor wants it bad because she waves and says "Hi, Ed." Even more significantly, she walks in front of the dining room window every night.

Ed accuses his friend Deborah of jealousy when she claims that a happily married woman would never want to get with a guy like Ed. He's convinced he has "man's intuition" that picks up on the subtle signs of his neighbor's sexual interest. However, he has no real proof that his "man's intuition" works, especially given the intangible things that set it off.

No philosopher has ever claimed there is a Problem of My Mind precisely because we are intimately aware of our own thoughts. The Problem concerns *other* minds. It doesn't help matters that people do not outwardly express everything they're thinking. There are a number of reasons why we can't express everything we're thinking, even though it would be a much simpler world if we could. Then we would avoid awkward misunderstandings like the one described in the *Onion* article "Tell Me Now If You Don't Want To See My Penis" (5/7/97).

Trying to figure out if someone is "just kidding" is a classic case of trying to solve the Problem of Other Minds. The solution hinges on a form of intuition somewhat like Ed Jonas's "man's intuition." Let's call this form of intuition "sense of humor."

We don't need to prove that our sense of humor is always right. We just need to give a reason why it's okay to rely on it in certain situations. Although our vision is not one hundred percent accurate, we have good reason to believe that what we see is real. Similarly, we have good reason to believe that our sense of humor can reliably tell us when someone is "just kidding."

In the case of eyesight, major mistakes are unusual. Normal people don't see pink elephants without the help of some good drugs. However, normal people can fail to appreciate a gem like the article "Terror Experts Warn Next 9/11 Could Fall On Different Date" (1/6/09). We'll need an argument then for attributing to them a major mistake. What basis is there for defending the form of intuition known as "sense of humor"?

Live from Congress

The *Beijing Evening News* ran a story about how Congress would relocate to Memphis (or Charlotte, but, having lived in both areas, I can't imagine Charlotte was ever a serious alternative), if they didn't get a new state-of-the-art Capitol building. The story was plagiarized almost word for word from *The Onion* ("Congress Threatens To Leave D.C. Unless New Capitol Is Built, " 5/29/02). Nor is this the only time a foreign news source fell prey to *The Onion's* straight-faced satire. Aside from the fact that foreigners are less likely to be familiar with *The Onion*, someone from a different culture is not going to have the same points of reference for detecting that the *Onion* is "just kidding."

This may give us a clue for solving the Problem of Other Minds. According to the philosopher Bertrand Russell (1872–1970), we rely upon similarities between ourselves and other people in order to know what they are thinking.[2] If I see someone screaming "That hurts!" while clutching their arm, it reminds me of the time I did something like that after I hurt my foot. Using the analogy between their current behavior and my past behavior, I conclude that they have pain in their arm like the pain I had in my foot.

Perhaps the same principle could explain how we know when someone is kidding. When the *Beijing Evening News* got called out, their first response was to stand by the story and to demand proof that the story was false. Eventually they admitted that the story was fake, but then tried to excuse their behavior by stating that "Some small American newspapers frequently fabricate off-beat news to trick people into noticing them with the aim of making money."

Their behavior—printing a plagiarized story that wasn't true, denying that it wasn't true, and finally blaming the source they plagiarized for their mistake—is very similar to one time when I said something really uncalled for to my wife in the heat of argument, denied that I had said it and later conceded I said it but blamed her for "misconstruing" the meaning of what I said. At that time I knew that I was in trouble and I was doing anything I could to get out of it. From the analogy between the *Evening News*'s behavior and my behavior, I can infer that the editors of the *Evening News* were thinking the same things I was thinking when they did the same thing I was doing.

Analogies are tricky, though, and this may explain why the *Beijing Evening News* plagiarist failed to realize that the story was fake. Anyone reading the original *Onion* story would probably have recognized that Dennis Hastert's complaints about the capitol building ("It's no longer suitable for a world-class legislative branch. The sight lines are bad, there aren't enough concession stands or bathrooms, and the parking is miserable") sound a lot like the complaints that sports team owners were using to convince their cities to construct brand new stadiums for them. As does the quote attributed to Dick Gephardt: "If we want to stay competitive, we need to upgrade. Look at British Parliament. Look at the Vatican. Respected institutions in their markets. But without modern facilities, they've been having big problems attracting top talent."

---

[2] *Human Knowledge: Its Scope and Limits* (Allen and Unwin, 1948), Part VI, Chapter 8.

In a further parallel to the calls for new stadiums there was the report that San Francisco was considering a county sales tax and local cigarette tax as part of their bid to win the Capitol. The *Beijing Evening News* even reproduced the biggest giveaway to the story—a picture of the Capitol building that Congress wanted to build, complete with retractable dome.

Most Americans would have been quick to pick up on the allusion to the behavior of sports team franchises. This is something that would not have been apparent to someone from another country who isn't constantly bombarded by news about American sports franchises and their stadium arms races. So, while an American might think, "This outrageous-sounding news report that sounds just like another sports team trying to negotiate a new stadium reminds me of the outrageous sounding story I told my friends as a joke to highlight a certain political problem" someone from another country could think, "This story sounds outrageous, but it would not have been published if it weren't true." Differences in cultural context can interfere with analogies so that it is not always clear that someone is "just kidding."

New Study Finds TV Journalists Don't Exercise Critical Thinking Skills

So cultural differences explain why someone from the *Beijing Evening News* missed the satire of *The Onion*, but how did it slip by Deborah Norville? On March 12th, 2004, she ended a broadcast with the following statement:

> . . . if you were watching the show earlier this week, you heard Health and Human Services Tommy Thompson encourage Americans to work out and watch what they eat.
>
> Good advice, because it turns out most Americans are watching their workouts. Yes, according to a new study by Thompson's department, fifty-eight percent of all the exercise done in America is broadcast on television. For instance, of the 3.5 billion sit-ups done during 2003, two million thirty thousand of them were on exercise shows on Lifetime or one of the ESPN channels. Put it another way, according to the study, ninety-nine percent of the time that someone is using one of those Soloflex machines, it's when it's being broadcast on one of those late-night commercials.
>
> I guess the secretary knew what he was talking about when he recommended most of us begin an exercise program by walking. It might be all most of us are able to do.

Much to her embarrassment, Norville later learned that the source for her story was an *Onion* satire ("Study: 58 Percent Of U.S. Exercise Televised," 3/10/04).

Norville and her show were taken to task for failing to fact-check their story—after all, it would only take a quick call to the DHHS to confirm whether such a study existed. There's no denying that the lack of consistent fact-checking is a problem in today's rushed twenty-four-hour news cycle; but we should also consider why they didn't feel the need to check their facts.

In an ideal world, every alleged fact would be carefully checked. However, the demands of competitive news and the cost of employing someone to do this make it impossible. Instead, people tend to check those facts that seem controversial or unlikely to be true. They rely on Russell's principle of analogy, just like I did when I determined that someone's arm hurt. When dealing with alleged facts, the analogy being used is: if someone says something straight-faced and cites evidence, then they are like me when I intend to be taken seriously.

Russell's principle of analogy was at work in the Michigan sheriff who got burned on the terrorist telemarketing piece. After learning of his mistake, he said: "I hadn't heard of *The Onion*. It appeared to me to be a legitimate news story, so I passed [it] along." Although the sheriff was attuned to the cues for kidding, he did not find them in that story. Since he hadn't heard of *The Onion* by 2002, we can safely assume he wasn't the kind of person who's interested in straight-faced satire. He had no straight-faced satire experiences of his own to compare to *The Onion's* behavior. Consequently, he was not able to analogize accurately.

The exercise survey does not signal anything fishy. It is a strange topic for a scientific study, but it is not out of the realm of possibility or believability—at least, not to someone who has no commonsense intuition for the number of people who exercise every day. Nor is it something that someone would make up in order to further an agenda. And presented out of context, it's not that funny. It is making fun of all the inane studies that the news stations report every week with little or no context to the study (or discussion of the quality of the study). Hence, when presented as real news on MSNBC, the humor is lost.

What happened to Deborah Norville and the Michigan sheriff highlights one of the main problems with relying on analogies to solve the Problem of Other Minds. The analogy solution is based upon the experiences of a single individual (you, because there is no reason you should trust anyone else's analogies). But our experiences can be very different and we have no way of determining whether we are a good bellwether for the behaviors of others.

Studies Show People Believe What They Want To Be True

The Deborah Norville snafu highlights more than the collapse of journalistic standards: it also reminds us that people tend to think something is true because it fits the way they look at the world. The exercise study fed into the perception that there is a growing obesity crisis in America. Similarly, the *Beijing Evening News* thought the Congress story was correct because it fit into their view that Americans are arrogant and self-centered (especially American politicians).

Ultimately, people believe what they want to be true, and this is a problem for the analogy solution. The analogy solution says that we know other people have minds because we know that we have a mind, and other people say and do the same things we do. But what if this is just something we want to believe? What if it is an unjustified prejudice?

We can see the problem with prejudice when we look at what happened when the *Onion* published a piece that proclaimed "'98 Homosexual Recruitment Drive Nearing Goal" (7/29/98). Anti-gay activist Fred Phelps jumped on this piece as proof of a gay conspiracy and linked to it on his website. Presumably Phelps found this piece on the web and did not bother to check out its veracity. In his mind there was already ample evidence of a gay conspiracy and this only put the icing on the cake. His worldview was so rigid that even the more outrageous aspects of the story failed to tip him off that it was a joke. (Or maybe he has no sense of humor and therefore can't analogize from instances where he makes a joke to where others are joking).

Even the aspects of the story that seem to scream out satire—that there is something called the National Gay and Lesbian Recruitment Task Force that has the goal of "ensnaring" over three hundred thousand straights a year or that their success was attributed to targeting children as young as five—fit the paranoid fantasies of those who fear a gay conspiracy. Nor did Phelps seem to recognize that there was something fishy about the co-director of the NGLRTF talking about the group's "message of sexual promiscuity and deviance," or that it is unbelievable that someone would leave their family and move across the country in order to pursue a career in bath-house management and have "non-stop, mind-blowing anal sex."

To normal, decent people, such negative descriptions of homosexual people would make sense only as a joke. To homophobic people, however, they make sense as facts. Obviously homophobic people are just prejudiced. But who knows whether prejudices may be lurking around in *our* minds as well? The very possibility indicates that it is dangerous to use our own beliefs to infer things by analogy about others' beliefs.

Gullible People Will Really Believe Anything

Don't be tempted into thinking prejudice is an isolated phenomenon limited to racism and homophobia. The reaction to the *Onion* story "*Harry Potter* Books Spark Rise In Satanism Among Children" (7/25/00) would suggest otherwise. A number of Christian groups got quite upset about this story after it started to make the email rounds. You'd think that they would have realized something was up when *The Onion* went so far as to attribute flaming Satanism to J.K. Rowling, the middle-aged English lady who wrote the books:

> "I think it's absolute rubbish to protest children's books on the grounds that they are luring children to Satan," Rowling was said to have told a London *Times* reporter. "People should be praising them for that! These books guide children to an understanding that the weak, idiotic Son of God is a living hoax who will be humiliated when the rain of fire comes, and will suck the greasy cock of the Dark Lord while we, his faithful servants, laugh and cavort in victory."

Would anyone who knows anything about J.K. Rowling think those words could come out of her mouth? Or, to put it a different way, could she have said something like that in the year 2000 without it creating an international news story that was on all the channels and in all the papers?

The reaction of these anti-Potter people is less justified than the bigotry and paranoia of someone like Phelps. Phelps dehumanizes a group of people that he presumably has no social contact with (at least none that is not a confrontation). As a result he cannot get the kind of experiences necessary to form good analogies. For the Potter scenario, anyone who has ever made something up has good analogies to draw on. If those anti-Potter people took a moment to think about it, they'd have lots of reasons to doubt the story.

What the Potter example shows us is that, under the right conditions, almost any bit of straight-faced satire could be mistaken for something serious—no matter how much the satirist might think it is obviously not true. After all, how could any reasonable person have thought for a moment that the Make-A-Wish story was true after they watched the whole video?

Given that there are people who seem willing to believe anything, especially if it is taken out of context, more could probably be done to drive home the fact that the *Onion*'s stories are satire. And sometimes the staff of *The Onion* feels compelled to do just that. When Phelps linked to the Homosexual Recruitment story, the *Onion* webmaster changed the link so that every one of Phelps' "groupies" would be taken to the main page of *The Onion* where they could figure out it was satire ("he hoped"). The fact that he could only hope that they would figure it out is not necessarily a comment on the intelligence of Phelps's groupies. Sure, if they see a headline like "Queen Elizabeth II Announces She Is Pregnant Again" (7/23/08) or "Al Gore Places Infant Son In Rocket To Escape Dying Planet" (7/30/08) they should realize something is up. But many *Onion* headlines are more subtle.

People might be justified in concluding that the *Onion* is a legitimate small-town paper when they see headlines like "Local Woman Devotes Life To Doing God's Busy Work" (10/4/08), "God Help Him, Area Man Loves That Crazy Bitch" (11/22/08), or "Area Woman Wouldn't Mind Feeding Your Cats" (12/6/08). Even if they read the full story, they may never figure out it is a satire. Maybe if they scroll to the bottom of the webpage and notice the disclaimer, "*The Onion* is not intended for readers under 18 years of age" they would realize that this is not your average news source. Maybe not—especially if they think that there might be such a thing as "adult news."

Satirical Website Announces It Is Satirizing Shit

Part of the reason why *The Onion* is sometimes taken seriously is because people link its articles in blogs and circulated them in emails (and not always with a credit to *The Onion*). As *The Onion* has become better known, the number of people who take it seriously has decreased, but even today I will see blog postings that refer to "the satirical *Onion*" or that include the sentence "*The Onion* is satire." And throughout the comments on the blogs you can see people repeatedly saying things like "this is fake" or "I hope that the original poster realizes that this is satire" and so on.

Certainly, *The Onion* could brand all of its articles with "*The Onion* is a satire" or it could stick to outrageous stories that would really limit the situations where it is taken seriously by mistake. But doing so would also undermine its mission. *The Onion* hit big precisely because it gave up such heavy-handed humor and followed

Scott Dikkers's plan to use "deadpan journalese to assault the banality of everyday life and to spoof major news events."[3]

If *The Onion* started reminding us that it was satire, it would lose a lot of its comedic value. The fact that it is not too far removed from the style of journalism that it satirizes is what makes it funny. In fact, the humor works by analogy, but an analogy different from the one proposed by Russell to explain our knowledge of other minds. We laugh because we realize that *Onion* stories, while absurdly false, are very similar to "real" news stories.

Although "Area Man Holds Out Until Next Exit For Better Fast Food Options" (11/29/08) seems a pretty inane story, it is not that far from many of the other quotidian events that make the news. (And it's also funny because it reminds us of our own silly behavior in such situations.) "GM Introduces New Line Of Layoffs" (2/8/08) tells the truth about trouble in the auto industry while at the same time accusing it of manipulative marketing tactics.

The Onion is a lot like another masterpiece of straight-faced satire, *The Colbert Report*. On the show, "Stephen Colbert" says things that are sometimes paraphrases of conservative pundits and other times are clear exaggerations. The joke is that he segues seamlessly from the one to the other as though there were no difference. This is meant to show just how ridiculous conservative pundits actually are. We're not alarmed by such statements because we know that the man playing "Stephen Colbert" doesn't really believe those things; he just plays a character who believes them and uses that character to make fun of the real conservative pundits.

But why are we so sure of that? After all, the actor's real name is Stephen Colbert. Throughout the course of his nightly broadcasts he stays in character. He even does appearances as "Stephen Colbert" including the infamous White House Correspondents Dinner routine in 2006. Praising Bush for being "steady" he said, "Events can change; this man's beliefs never will. He believes the same thing Wednesday as he did Monday. No matter what happened Tuesday." According to reports, very few people in attendance found the routine funny. Was this because they didn't know he was playing a character?

Perhaps we know "Stephen Colbert" is not the real Stephen Colbert because he started his career with the Second City comedy

---

[3] "Award-Winning Local Journalists Reflect Own Self-Hatred Back on Nightmare World," *Wired* (July, 2003).

troupe and then worked as a comedian on *The Daily Show*. This suggests that his current show is a farce.

It's not entirely out of the realm of possibility, however, that he is a conservative sleeper agent trying to make conservative views palatable to an entire generation of young people who might otherwise be swayed by a leftist agenda.

Now I sound like a Phelps groupie or an anti-Potter crusader.

Still, if this were true, it would completely change people's reactions to the show: conservatives would now find it a hilarious hoodwinking of the left and probably no one else would find it funny anymore.

Point-Counterpoint: Funny versus Really, Really Funny

Stephen Colbert would not be as funny if every show (or everything he said) were preceded with a disclaimer such as "The Following Is an Exaggeration of Things Said by Conservative Pundits in Order to Expose Some Hypocrisy on Their Part. No One Should Take Anything that Stephen Colbert Says Seriously." Nor would the *Onion* be as enjoyable if it contained the disclaimer "This is An Exaggeration of Current Journalistic Practices in Order to Show How Degenerate They Have Become. Nothing that *The Onion* Reports Is True."

It also would be an inaccurate disclaimer. To say that "Nothing that *The Onion* Reports is True" would be to deny the humor in some of its pieces. What is funny about "Study: Iraqis May Experience Sadness When Friends, Relatives Die" (7/25/07) is not that it is a study reporting something untrue. Quite the opposite— and this is what makes it biting satire. An accurate disclaimer for *The Onion* would need to be as nuanced as *The Onion's* satire. In that case, anyone who could understand all the nuances of the disclaimer about reading *The Onion* is someone who wouldn't need it.

We have to think in order to separate the truth from the falsehoods in *The Onion*, and this is precisely what is so appealing about it. *The Onion* stories are rarely simple jokes. And once we've figured out the joke we are rewarded with a feeling of satisfaction that we had the skills needed to solve the latest instance of the Problem of Other Minds on the pages of *The Onion*.

The essence of humor is misunderstanding. The fact that *Three's Company* overdid it, doesn't change the fact that humor comes from expecting one thing and then getting something entirely different. Being funny means getting people to have one set of expectations, with a second set lurking in the background so that the punch line does not seem totally disconnected. In this way, jokes deliberately try to trip up our ability to analogize. Hence all humor carries the possibility of being taken seriously.

No matter how obviously we might think we have raised the "just kidding" flag, someone will miss it. A non-*Onion* fake news story about the connection between beer pong and herpes had an incredible run on national news shows like *Fox and Friends*.[4] It is amazing that the story ran as widely as it did when you consider that it included a quote from CDC spokesman Dr. Cole Desorio. (Say his name fast and out loud. Even someone who is only qualified to host a morning show should be able to pick up on that clue.)

We feel good knowing a joke will make some people trip and fall. The very thing that makes *The Onion* enjoyable to us is what will make it misunderstood by others. But I don't think we'd have it any other way. *The Onion* amuses us in ways no obvious satire could and as a result it adds a new dimension to the kinds of things we find funny.

---

[4] For the original story, see <www.bannedinhollywood.com/popularity-of-beer-pong-leads-to-rise-in-cold-sores>.

21

A Philosophical Joke Book?

THOMAS J. BROMMAGE

In a recent poll, Ludwig Wittgenstein was ranked the most important philosopher of the last two hundred years.[1] But despite Wittgenstein's importance as a philosopher, he was never much fun to be around (as surprising as that might seem!). In fact, he was a miserable man, who was always moping about and contemplating suicide. Nearly all biographical accounts of him agree that he was always very serious, and disliked small talk.

Perhaps at least Wittgenstein had a theory of humor? Not really. A search for the word "humor" among his published writings and aphorisms garners only a handful of passages. Nevertheless, Norman Malcolm, a student and friend of Wittgenstein's, recalls in his *Memoir* an odd remark that Wittgenstein once made: "A serious and good philosophical work could be written that would consist entirely of jokes."[2]

How Wittgenstein's philosophy joke book might be "*good*" is not so troubling; but how it might at the same time be "*serious*" raises a number of questions. After all: isn't seriousness the opposite—if not the enemy—of levity?

Not so. And *The Onion* proves it.

---

[1] <http://leiterreports.typepad.com/blog/2009/03/so-who-is-the-most-important-philosopher-of-the-past-200-years.html>.

[2] Norman Malcolm, *Ludwig Wittgenstein: A Memoir* (Oxford University Press, 1984), pp. 27–28.

Wittgenstein's Method

Ludwig Wittgenstein was born in 1889 in Vienna to a wealthy aris-
tocratic family. After completing school, he initially went to
England to study engineering, but soon afterwards shifted his focus
to philosophy as he became interested in a series of problems in
the philosophy of mathematics. In 1911, he went to Cambridge
University to study with Bertrand Russell, a famous philosopher
who was then working on issues in the philosophy of mathematics
and logic.

Britain was at the time the seat of the movement that would
come to be known as "analytic philosophy." Analytic philosophy
focuses primarily on language. According to the early analytic
philosophers, the goal of philosophy should not be to expound on
the nature of the world or the mind, but rather on the medium of
language itself.

Second, analytic philosophy attacks the gigantic and incomprehensible metaphysical systems of the past. Analytic philosophers
contend that metaphysics causes madness. This is evident in the
program advocated by Charles West, who, according to *The Onion*,
argued that children must "return to the fundamentals taught in the
Pnakotic Manuscripts and the Necronomicon in order to develop
the skills they need to be driven to the very edge of sanity."
According to West, students must learn to "perform the tuneless
flute songs of the blind idiot god Azathoth." He also advocates
"offering art students instruction in the carving of morbid and
obscene fetishes from otherworldly media" ("Lovecraftian School
Board Member Wants Madness Added To Curriculum," 3/2/09.)

Wittgenstein's study of logic led to his first philosophical
work—the only one published during his lifetime—*Tractatus
Logico-Philosophicus*. Following its publication in 1921, he spent
some years away from academic life, but returned to Cambridge in
1929. From that point onwards, he changed his views significantly.
Most commentators understand Wittgenstein's philosophy as having two distinct stages—the "early" work characterized by the philosophy of the *Tractatus*, and the "later" work exemplified by the
posthumously published *Philosophical Investigations*.

Although the early and later philosophies are often thought to
be inconsistent with one another, Wittgenstein's views on the function of philosophy never changed. He thought that philosophy was
valuable not for the *answers* it might provide, but rather because

of the activity of thinking involved with the questions it asks. In the *Tractatus*, for example, Wittgenstein tells us that "philosophy is not a theory but an activity."[3] He also tells us in the *Philosophical Investigations*: "If one tried to advance theses in philosophy, it would never be possible to debate them, because everyone would agree to them."[4] The goal of philosophy for Wittgenstein is not to *solve* philosophical problems, but to dis-solve them. That is, to show the pointlessness of certain philosophical questions, and how the supposed answers that philosophy provides often create more problems than they solve. "Most of the propositions and questions to be found in philosophical works are not false but nonsensical," he tells us in the *Tractatus*. "Consequently we cannot give any answer to questions of this kind, but can only point out that they are nonsensical."

Wittgenstein describes his later philosophy as "therapeutic." In the *Philosophical Investigations*, he likens philosophical problems to a "disease," which requires "treatment" or "therapy." But he is also careful to point out that there is no single therapy for all philosophical ailments; rather there are many philosophical methods, "like different therapies." The point he is trying to make is that, for whatever ails you philosophically—each specific trouble will require a different course of treatment, targeted to the character of the disease itself.

The goal of philosophy for Wittgenstein is, in a way, to *do away with philosophy*, and to resist the urge to feed the philosophical disease. "The real discovery," he tells us, "is the one that makes me capable of stopping doing philosophy when I want to—The one that gives philosophy peace, so it is no longer tormented by questions which bring itself in question." (§133). In this way, Darrin Floen, the Dartmouth philosophy student who "seriously needs to shut the fuck up," could stand to read some Wittgenstein ("Guy In Philosophy Class Needs To Shut The Fuck Up," (9/28/05.)

Instead of providing answers, or devising elaborate theories about what lies beneath our linguistic practices, the positive function of philosophy for Wittgenstein is instead to lay open these practices to investigation. In the *Philosophical Investigations*, he tells us:

---

[3] Ludwig Wittgenstein, *Tractatus Logico-Philosophicus* (Routledge, 1961), section 4.112.

[4] Ludwig Wittgenstein, *Philosophical Investigations* (Blackwell, 2001), §128.

Philosophy simply puts everything before us, and neither explains nor deduces anything—Since everything lies open to view there is nothing to explain. For what is hidden, for example, is of no interest to us. One might also give the name philosophy to what is possible *before* all new discoveries and inventions. (§126)

The problem with 'theories' of language, he thinks, is that they focus on finding a kind of forced unity in our linguistic practices, rather than attempting to let them be seen in their inherent diversity. Early on in the *Investigations,* he often compares words to tools:

Think of the tools in a tool-box: there is a hammer, pliers, a saw, a screw-driver, a rule, a glue-pot, glue, nails and screws.—The functions of words are as diverse as the functions of these objects. (And in both cases there are similarities.)

Of course, what confuses us is the uniform appearance of words when we hear them spoken or meet them in script and print. For their *application* is not presented to us so clearly. Especially when we are doing philosophy! (*Philosophical Investigations*, §11)

Imagine someone's saying: "*All* tools serve to modify something. Thus the hammer modifies the position of the nail, the saw the shape of the board, and so on."—And what is modified by the rule, the glue-pot, the nails? (§14)

Just as there is no single function for all tools, so too there is no single function for all words. Telling a joke is itself a function of language that is different from describing the world, giving orders, telling stories, or asking questions, and it can only be analyzed in its own way. But unfortunately, this means that we cannot look to Wittgenstein for a single reason why a joke is funny.

What is unique about Wittgenstein's view of philosophy is that it shows us the errors with our philosophizing. The goal of philosophy is not to provide *solutions*, but rather to question the questions themselves.

Humor and Forms of Life

Although linguistic expressions vary widely in their function, they share certain necessary features without which language would mean nothing at all to us. What Wittgenstein thinks underlies our linguistic practices are certain basic shared background conventions, which he calls "forms of life." The phrase serves a very important role in his analysis of language. Here are two key passages:

> It is easy to imagine a language consisting only of orders and reports in battle.—Or a language consisting only of questions and expressions for answering yes and no. And innumerable others.—And to imagine a language means to imagine a form of life. (§19)

> . . . the speaking of language is part of an activity, or of a form of life. (§23)

It's tempting to think that one of the "innumerable others" is jokes.

Consider one of my favorite *Onion* articles, "Bill Gates Grants Self 18 Dexterity, 20 Charisma" (6/18/97). The joke relies upon quite a bit of background knowledge. First, you have to know who Bill Gates is. Second, you have to know that "dexterity" and "charisma" are two attributes of characters in the role-playing game *Dungeons and Dragons*. But even if you know these two things, you still might not get the joke. To get the joke, you have to see how those in the information technology field resemble those who play role-playing games in terms of their geekiness. Without all of this background knowledge, the article isn't funny.

According to Wittgenstein, we acquire background knowledge from a shared form of life. In one of the few places where he explicitly addresses humor, he writes,

> Two people are laughing together, say at a joke. One of them has used certain somewhat unusual words and now they both break out into a sort of bleating. That might appear very extraordinary to a visitor coming from a quite different environment. Whereas we find it completely reasonable. (*Culture and Value,* University of Chicago Press, p. 78)

Likewise he asks us: "What is it like for people not to have the same sense of humor? They do not react properly to each other. It's as though there were a custom amongst certain people for one person to throw another a ball which he is supposed to catch and throw back; but some people, instead of throwing it back, put it in their pocket" (p. 83).

As an example of this, consider the recurring "Ask" advice columns that are featured in *The Onion*. One of these, called "Ask Someone Who Writes Into Advice Columns" (4/4/99), answers questions with other questions asking for advice. Another, "Ask Sir Mix-A-Lot" (12/9/97), responds to queries with song lyrics. Lastly, in "Ask a Salmon" (2/26/97), we can get insight into some of our problems—only if they involve grizzly bears, and swimming upstream to spawn. "Will spawn with females!" answers the salmon. "Must swim! Must spawn! Upstream! Must throw self up and over waterfalls! No stop! No stop to eat! No rest! Must spawn!"

What is funny about these, in each case, is that the answers don't seem to answer the questions in any way. Within our form of life, one expects "answers" to address the questions themselves. Nonsense answers which have no relevance to the questions—or, worse, questions asked back to questions—mess with our expectations.

The Familiar and the Uncanny

As many investigators into the philosophy of humor have noted, something is often funny due to an incongruity between the joke and our forms of life. Wittgenstein once said "Humor is not a mood but a way of looking at the world." And as William James—a philosopher who Wittgenstein greatly admired—once noted, "Philosophy . . . is able to fancy everything different from what it is. It sees the familiar as if it were strange, and the strange as if it were familiar."[5] I think this would apply equally to humor: it allows us to focus in on our practices and see these familiar occurrences as strange.

What is important about our forms of life is that they are central to the way that we understand the world around us. We tend to think of our own practices as having a certain necessity, even though our background practices are constantly in flux. This becomes clear when we reflect on the past—how different our lives would have been without cell phones and the Internet, or even cars and air conditioning.

We tend to think that our own way of being is the only game in town and struggle to understand forms of life different from our own. Part of what makes *The Onion* particularly relevant to many of us is the aspect of social criticism that underlies its jokes. The

---

    [5] William James, *Some Problems of Philosophy* (Harvard University Press, 1979), p. 11.

brand of social criticism that *The Onion* provides disrupts that feeling of necessity, showing how contingent our own way of life is.

Consider the article "More U.S. Children Being Diagnosed With Youthful Tendency Disorder" (9/27/00). The article discusses an ailment called "Youthful Tendency Disorder" (or YTD), with which an increasing number of children are being diagnosed. It is characterized by "a variety of senseless, unproductive physical and mental exercises, often lasting hours at a time. In the thrall of YTD, sufferers run, jump, climb, twirl, shout, dance, do cartwheels, and enter unreal, unexplainable states of 'make-believe'."

The joke is really on our society itself, and the increasingly diagnosed number of childhood cases of ADHD—which are symptomatically identical with just being a child. Further, it parodies the practice of the large pharmaceutical companies, who seem to concoct certain disorders in order to market their drugs. What makes this funny is its parody of our social practices. It takes the ordinary, and—holding it at a distance—turns it into the strange.

Often *The Onion* is much more explicit, and uses the banality of everyday life as part of its framework for humor. Consider the short item "Man In Bar Makes General Inquiry About The Ladies" (6/11/03). It reports about a local tavern-goer named Barry Todd who dares to ask: "'So, what's the deal with the ladies tonight? . . . Are they alone, or are they here with somebody?" The article continues: "After receiving no definitive answer, Todd spent the remainder of the evening flipping through the CDs on the jukebox and nursing his warm Michelob Light." Part of what makes this funny is its targeting certain social practices of which many of us are aware. We all know 'that guy' in the bar.

Last, but not least, consider the ONN video "Prague's Franz Kafka International Named World's Most Alienating Airport." Overtly, we see that the humor results from the connection between the 'life is absurd' message of existential philosophy and a fictitious airport named after Franz Kafka. Rarely, of course, does the name of the airport determine service received from it. But in this absurdist depiction, the average flight delay is over thirty-one hours. Airlines on which certain passengers have flights suddenly cease to exist. Gate B14 is in the F terminal. "If there is a problem," says one airport official, "fill out a complaint form and place it in an envelope addressed to the hospital in which you were born." While on one level this is funny due to the odd juxtaposition of existentialist angst and our common practices, on another level it plays on our common frustrations with airline travel. Long delays, lack of organization, and weird, unhelpful officials are common. Although Franz Kafka International is clearly an exaggeration, we can understand it as a subtle criticism of the things we put up with during air travel.

Philosophy and Humor

So far, I've explained what Wittgenstein might have thought about humor through an elucidation of his philosophical methodology. What remains is for me to illustrate what he meant by his claim that "a serious and good philosophical work could be written that would consist entirely of jokes."

Wittgenstein's philosophical style is idiosyncratic. He often argues by analogy to either confirm or disconfirm the general point he was trying to make. Often, he dismisses a point by showing the absurdity of a parallel case. Malcolm also recalls:

> A curious thing, which I observed innumerable times, was that when Wittgenstein invented an example during his lectures in order to illustrate a point, he himself would grin at the absurdity of what he had imagined. But if any member of the class would chuckle, his expression would change to severity and he would exclaim in reproof, "No, no; I'm serious." (*Memoir*, p. 37)

Malcolm explains that for Wittgenstein, "the imagined events and circumstances were so odd and so far beyond the reach of natural possibility that he himself could not help being amused; yet the intention of his example, of course, was serious."

By using examples to illustrate his point, Wittgenstein shows us how to approach the discontinuity with our ordinary ways of thinking. For Wittgenstein, providing a good example is in a certain sense providing an argument. Honing in on these concrete cases helps us understand the conceptual muddles in which we find ourselves when we think philosophically.

Given the similarity between philosophy as Wittgenstein sees it and the humor of *The Onion* as I see it—where both are attempts to show the strangeness of our familiar practices—it follows that they ultimately might be seen as serving the same function. That is, we could have a "serious" work of philosophy consisting only of jokes, since jokes can be serious philosophy. As he points out in the *Philosophical Investigations*:

> The problems arising through a misinterpretation of our forms of language have the character of depth. They are deep disquietudes; their roots are as deep in us as the forms of our language and their significance is as great as the importance of our language.—Let us ask ourselves: why do we feel a grammatical joke to be deep? (And that is what the depth of philosophy is.) (§111)

We can't help but find certain conceptual confusions funny. This is the basic grip of puns and double entendres. Thus, in clarifying these confusions, humor can be used as a type of argument. I believe this is a partial explanation for what is philosophical about *The Onion*—that *it presents arguments*. Arguments that not only parody our own social practices, but also make us think about the common in a different way—as anything but. Thus a philosophy book consisting of jokes could be funny for the same reason that it would be good philosophy: it allows us to think about everyday things differently.

22

Liar! Liar!

CYNTHIA McWILLIAMS

Your zealous neighbor Jenny is obsessed with making sure evil pedophiles don't live near her house or her son's elementary school. She was googling for "pedophile," "elementary," and "Seattle" when she found the *Onion* article "Pedophile Nervous For First Day Of School" (8/31/08). Certain that the nondescript-looking guy in the accompanying photo was her weird neighbor George, an enraged Jenny went to George's apartment and beat him senseless with a baseball bat, as that's what pedophiles deserve. Is *The Onion* responsible?

Now, we should all know that the stories in *The Onion* aren't the truth (well, not mostly, at least!) but clearly Jenny doesn't. She had never seen *The Onion* before and it really looked like a regular news site. So is it okay to print articles containing falsehoods, for the purpose of entertainment, knowing full well that some less-than-optimally-clever people like Jenny may read *The Onion* and believe and act upon what they read?

We might also wonder whether the stories in *The Onion* count as lying and whether this is morally permissible. If such instances of "lying" are permissible, are there any limits on what can be published and, if so, how do we delineate between instances that are morally permissible and those that are not? Can we show there is a clear difference between, for example, an article discussing the complete absence of oral sex in President Bush's White House— "White House Celebrates Fifth Straight Year Without Oral Sex" (12/28/05)—and an article discussing a pedophile in Seattle who hangs out near an elementary school, anxious for the first day of school?

. . . Pants on Fire!

The typical reasons that people, ethicists included, offer for being against lying come mainly in two forms.

The first type of argument against lying says it's just wrong to lie and we have a duty to tell the truth. Immanuel Kant, an eighteenth-century philosopher whose ethical theory has been amazingly influential, offers a classic duty-based, "it's just wrong to lie" argument by applying a formulation of his "Categorical Imperative." Basically, this formulation of the Categorical Imperative is a rule that says that we shouldn't use people just to get something we want. Lying is always wrong, Kant argues, because it treats the person to whom I lie as a means only, rather than as an end in herself. It is always wrong to treat another rational individual as merely a means to my own ends.

We use people each day. Sometimes we even use ourselves. For example, *The Onion* reports that Tina Turner burned down her own legs for the insurance money (1/23/09). Such usage violates the Categorical Imperative only when we don't respect the person we are using as rational, autonomous being.

Suppose I really want to buy a nice bottle of red wine, but I'm broke, I could ask my friend Caroline to loan me money. I know she'll give me the money if I tell her I need it to buy medicine for my daughter, but I don't know if she'll give me the money if I tell her the truth. Using Caroline to get money for my wine is using her, regardless of whether I tell her the truth, but it's only morally problematic, says Kant, if I use her *merely* as a means to my end of getting wine. If I tell her the truth, I allow her to make her own decision and thereby respect her as a rational, autonomous individual. If I lie to her, I disrespect her by depriving her of her rational decision-making autonomy and thereby use her *merely* as a means to my wine.

The second type of moral reason often given against lying concerns the problematic consequences of lying. Another famous ethicist, John Stuart Mill (born two years after Kant's death), argued that lying is usually wrong because it leads to bad consequences. Mill was a proponent of the ethical theory known as utilitarianism which states that we should act in a way that will maximize benefit and avoid harm for all those affected by our action. An action like lying is not morally acceptable if it leads to less beneficial consequences for those involved (everyone involved, not just the liar) when compared to other alternatives.

Lying to Caroline would be wrong, according to Mill, if the consequences for all those involved are worse than if I had told her the truth. Notice that according to utilitarianism, lying isn't always wrong. In fact lying is justified if it maximizes benefit while avoiding harm, which it sometimes happens to do. Consider *The Onion*'s surprising report: "Presidents Washington Through Bush May Have Lied About Key Matters" (12/04/02). No doubt those were all justified instances of lying.

So what about Jenny? Was she lied to and, if so, was it okay to do so? We need to decide what lying is to answer this.

Just a Little White Lie

What counts as a lie? It would seem that any false statement would count. However, this is not always the case. If, for example, I correctly tell you that Austin is the capital of Texas when I really believe incorrectly that Dallas is the capital, I have still lied to you, even though my statement is true. For my statement to be a lie I must *believe* that the statement is false. If I tell you that Dallas is the capital of Texas, and I really believe this to be the case, I haven't lied to you even though my statement ("Dallas is the capital of Texas") is false. Conversely, if I tell you that Dallas is the capital of Texas, and I correctly believe this to be false, I have lied to you. So a lie is—at least—a statement that is believed by the speaker or writer to be false. Many articles in *The Onion* surely fit this criterion. "Asian Teen Has Sweaty Middle-Aged-Man Fetish" (1/30/09) is a great example—it couldn't possibly be true!

But some would say that another essential component of a lie is the intent to deceive. If I say, "There once was a man from Nantucket . . ." (fill in the blank as you see fit) you probably wouldn't try to claim that I lied to you as you would know instantly that my statement wasn't true and that I wasn't trying to convince you that it was true. But again this is not an essential component of lying. If someone forces me at gunpoint to tell you that Dallas is the capital of Texas, which I know to be false, I may hope that you don't believe it and I may not intend to deceive you, but I have still lied. A lie with the intent to deceive may be morally worse than one without the intent to deceive, but they are both, by this definition, lies.

Let's return to Kant's duties and Mill's consequences for a moment. Lies told with the intent to deceive surely seem to be worse, morally speaking, than lies told without the intent to deceive. If I lie to you without the intent to deceive then I do not seem to be using you merely as a means to my own ends, so Kant would say that it wasn't wrong. Mill would tell a different story, however. If my lie has problematic consequences that I could have foreseen, whether or not I intend to deceive you, then it may be wrong on utilitarian grounds, according to Mill. So the lack of intent to deceive might exculpate *The Onion* from wrongly lying to Jenny on Kantian grounds, but not on utilitarian grounds. And yet still it seems that if harm was caused, someone should be responsible.

But I Was Only Kidding . . .

Lots of movies, cartoons, and websites make stuff up or exaggerate for the sake of humor. Why would *The Onion* be any different? After all, *The Onion: America's Finest News Source* really *looks* like a regular news source in many ways, even including links to CNN.com. And some things printed in *The Onion* are true.

The Onion's "American Voices" is a fake opinion poll, but it concerns true current events, such as the death of Chief Justice William Rehnquist (11/06/05). "The chief justice of the U.S. Supreme Court, died Saturday at age 80. What do you think?" American "Richard Spears, Respiratory Therapist" responded, "My heart would go out to his family and friends if it weren't already out to 100,000 Southerners."

Yet many *Onion* articles couldn't possibly be taken as true by a reasonable person. According to the article "We Must Deploy Troops To Jessica Linden's Uterus Immediately" (9/22/99), General William Patterson recommended that Congress establish a new Military Medal of Valor, to be called "The Distinguished Cervix Cross For Courage In The Uterine Theater." You'd really have to wonder about someone who believed that.

However, many *Onion* articles could easily be taken as true:

Obama Inauguration Speech Ruined By Incessant Jackhammering (1/21/09)

Project Manager Leaves Suicide PowerPoint Presentation (2/09/05)

Chinese Woman Gives Birth To Septuplets, Has One Week To Choose (1/15/98)

ACLU Defends Nazis' Right To Burn Down ACLU Headquarters (10/14/03)

Sean Penn Demands To Know What Asshole Took SeanPenn@gmail.com (1/17/06)

And *The Onion* is *not* relevantly similar in this respect to many other popular satires. No one in their right mind would believe *South Park* is real.

Perhaps we have a first stab at a standard here: entertainment making false claims or telling lies isn't morally problematic if no one in their right mind would take it to be true.

On the one end of the believability spectrum we have shows like *South Park* or *Onion* stories like "Supreme Court Rules Death Penalty Is 'Totally Badass'" (6/23/08), or "Report: Many U.S. Parents Outsourcing Child Care Overseas" (7/2/07), or "Supreme Court Upholds Stopping In The Name of Love in 2-1 Decision" (7/31/08). No sane person would take these to be the truth.

On the other end of the believability spectrum we have stories or productions which seem completely real. An infamous example of entertainment that seemed real to most listeners and could have led to harm is *The War of the Worlds*. While not illegal, the 1938 radio-broadcast production of *The War of the Worlds* was considered in its day to have pushed the limits of morally acceptable free speech for entertainment purposes.

Orson Welles adapted the H.G. Wells novel *The War of the Worlds* into a one-hour radio production in which Martians were reported to have landed and invaded the US. This production was one of the first, and surely the most famous, to employ simulated news reports for entertainment purposes. To the casual listener, the show resembled a regular news report in all discernible respects (although it had been listed unambiguously in the programming schedule). To add to the drama, it was only announced once during the production, and once before and after the production, that the events described were not real.

Although it seems that no one was seriously physically injured by this production, many people reported significant emotional distress as a result, especially those living near Grover's Mill, N.J.—ground zero for the fictional invasion.

The War of the Worlds was translated and adapted for a 1949 performance in Quito, Ecuador, with far more tragic results. In order to increase the illusion of an invasion, the producers of the Ecuadorian show did not schedule the broadcast through the station, nor did they list it anywhere in advance. Many people in the area listening to the show seem to have been genuinely frightened and convinced that someone was attacking the area. The radio station broadcasting the show was attacked and burned by an angry mob after locals discovered the broadcasted invasion wasn't real. At least six people were killed in the riot <www.war-ofthe-worlds.co.uk/war_worlds_quito.htm>.

Let's pretend, for the sake of argument (I'm using a lie here for illustration, although I don't intend to deceive with it!), that the producers of both of these science-fiction radio shows *intended* to incite a riot and *knew* that what they were doing could lead to real harm. This would clearly put these productions past a line of acceptability in both believability and intent to deceive.

Where does "Pedophile Nervous For First Day of School" fall in relation to this line? It seems highly unlikely that the writers intended harm (so again they're safe on Kantian grounds), but the more interesting question is, could they reasonably have expected someone like Jenny would believe the story and act upon the false information it contained? We can apply utilitarian standards to aid in answering this question.

Surely *The Onion* recognizes the prevalence of dumb people. If you doubt this, just have a glance at its atlas, *Our Dumb World* ("Russia: Where Russians Are Sent To Die" and "India: Please Hold While We Die Of Malaria" and "United States: The Land Of Opportunism"). So it may be argued that they recognize that some people will believe what they print. But could they expect that someone like Jenny exists who *both* isn't clever enough to recognize a joke when she sees one *and* is zealous enough to act on what she mistakenly assumed to be real?

If harm could reasonably be expected from printing the article, then the article may be problematic on utilitarian grounds. And so believability alone isn't enough for our criterion—we also need to examine whether harmful consequences can reasonably be expected from the entertainment.

Let's return to "White House Celebrates Fifth Straight Year Without Oral Sex" for comparison. If someone believes, based on *The Onion* story, that President Bush doesn't have oral sex, it would be difficult to imagine any tangible harm that could come of it. It is also important to note that, on utilitarian grounds, the happiness achieved from entertainment is a tangible consequence that needs to be considered. If no harm is caused and people are entertained, it's a morally acceptable act, on utilitarian grounds. Conversely, the harm caused by the Ecuadorian broadcast of *The War of the Worlds* would lead a utilitarian to conclude that this broadcast was not morally permissible, especially if we say that the panic from the local citizens was a predictable outcome of the broadcast—unless the amount of joy provided by the entertainment exceeded the amount of suffering resulting from the panic.

But back to Jenny and George. The fake story's beneficial consequences of entertainment and humor would matter on a utilitarian account of moral permissibility, assuming of course that it was funny (and I thought it was!). I would argue, on utilitarian grounds, that the harm caused to George was not reasonably predictable and that the expected entertainment factor matters. And since it's unlikely *Onion* writers intended to provoke someone like Jenny to harm George, it's probably morally permissible on Kantian grounds as well.

So it seems we have arrived at a two-fold criterion for judging entertainment making false claims: it isn't morally problematic if no one in their right mind would take it to be true or if we couldn't reasonably expect any harmful consequences that would outweigh the benefit of the entertainment value.

Yelling "Fire!" in a Crowded Theater

You may rightly question whether the moral restriction against lying is the appropriate topic here rather than the legal restriction on freedom of speech. I'd say both are relevant. The First Amendment protects freedom of speech, although within limits, as set forth in *Schenk v. United States* (1919) in which the Supreme Court ruled that free speech rights did not protect the wartime distribution of flyers to encourage those who had been drafted to oppose the draft. The Court argued that such an act posed a "clear and present danger" of causing evils that the government is allowed to prevent. This ruling is also the source of Justice Oliver Wendell Holmes's oft-quoted remark: "The most stringent protection of free speech would not protect a man in falsely shouting fire in a theater and causing a panic."

The "clear and present danger" constraint, however, was amended to the threat of "imminent lawless action" in

Brandenburg v. Ohio (1969). This case involved the public speech of a Ku Klux Klan member who was convicted under an Ohio law that was later found by the Supreme Court to be unconstitutional since it violated the First Amendment right to freedom of speech. The Court held that Brandenburg did not threaten imminent lawless action by what he said (even if it was a morally repugnant speech) and so his First Amendment rights were violated when he was convicted under the Ohio law in question.

Surely *The Onion* doesn't come close to violating the "imminent lawless action" standard, so it would be strange to argue that "Pedophile Nervous for First Day of School" is illegal on these grounds. Freedom of speech is a protected right. So the legal question is separate from the question as to whether it is morally acceptable to publish such stories, knowing that some people may believe them. After all, the First Amendment rights of Klan member Brandenburg were protected, but what he said (which included racist comments and the threat of vengeance if the government continued to oppress Caucasians) wasn't morally acceptable. Of course there's a huge difference between the two, as Brandenburg, unfortunately, wasn't kidding.

Kind of, Sort of a Lie, But neither Immoral nor Illegal

And so we can see that *The Onion* isn't responsible for George's beating, as it was an unforeseen consequence and it didn't violate the "imminent lawless action" constraint on free speech. And we see that even though printing something known to be false counts as lying, it doesn't fall under the category of lies forbidden by Kantian ethics. Utilitarian ethics would also give it a pass as the expected beneficial consequences outweighed the expected harm. But we also see that there are definitely lines to be drawn, somewhere in the gray areas, as the Ecuadorian *The War of the Worlds* clearly crossed the line.

Are there any *Onion* articles that cross this line? I'd say articles like "Diet Book Author Advocates New 'No Food Diet'" (5/19/08) and "Bush Dies Peacefully In His Sleep" (1/20/09) are candidates, mostly because they are more disturbing than funny. Maybe making fun of racism, as in "Black Man Given Nation's Worst Job" (11/5/08) and "Hurricane Bound For Texas Slowed By Large Land Mass To The South" (8/25/08), or sexism, as in "Report:

Economically Disadvantaged Men More Skilled At Communicating Attraction To Women" (11/28/01), which most individuals take to be morally problematic in the first place, is much more entertaining than poking fun at anorexia or dieting or death, to which most of us can relate.

But even these "borderline" articles couldn't be expected to cause harmful consequences, other than annoying some people. One may ask whether an *Onion* story which is generally perceived by readers or listeners to be unfunny (hence, no real beneficial consequences) would be wrong on utilitarian grounds. But surely we can expect that not every article will be equally amusing and that even *The Onion* will write unfunny or even offensive articles once in a while.

Perhaps a good rule of thumb would be to adopt the aforementioned two-fold measure: entertainment making false claims isn't morally problematic if no one in their right mind would take it to be true or if we couldn't reasonably expect any harmful consequences that would outweigh the benefit of the expected entertainment value.

So *The Onion* is off the hook. Sorry, George. And by the way, just in case there are any Jennys reading this, I should say that I made up the Jenny and George story.

America's Finest Philosophers

MATTHEW C. ALTMAN is an assistant professor of philosophy and director of the William O. Douglas Honors College at Central Washington University. He has published several articles in applied ethics, ethical theory, and the history of philosophy, as well as a book titled *A Companion to Kant's "Critique of Pure Reason"* (2008), which is surprisingly good summer beach reading. One day he hopes to write a weekly syndicated advice column called "Ask a Guy Who Thinks Schopenhauer Was Right About Everything."

ROBERT ARP is employed as a contractor for the government working on various projects having to do with... On second thought, he can't tell you about his work because if he did, he'd have to kill you.

RANDALL E. AUXIER teaches at Southern Illinois University Carbondale, but actually, his long-term plan is slightly more complicated, involving, at the right time, becoming Catholic and then dying. So far, they seem to have the best afterlife offer, and for almost nothing down and no interest. He asks that you pray for him, eventually, when it seems like he's probably got to be dead by now. He has contributed thirty-three chapters to Open Court's Popular Culture and Philosophy series, and needs to shut the fuck up.

RICK BAYAN is the author of *The Cynic's Dictionary* and webmaster of The Cynic's Sanctuary (www.i-cynic.com). He has been an editor, a staff writer for Time-Life Books, and, for more years than he'd like to admit, an advertising copywriter and copy chief. In fact, he's also the author of the copywriting classic *Words That Sell*. Currently he's attempting to survive as a freelance writer, a pursuit that will inevitably deepen his cynicism. Bayan is a virtue-loving cynic in the ancient tradition, though he hasn't yet made a habit of hanging out on the street to mock his fellow pedestrians. He lives in Philadelphia with his five-year-old son.

DAVID BENATAR is a Professor of Philosophy at the University of Cape Town, South Africa. He first encountered the *Onion* during a sojourn in Madison, Wisconsin, birthplace of America's finest news source, and has since had difficulty reading other newspapers. His anti-natalist book, *Better Never to Have Been: The Harm of Coming into Existence* (2006) pissed off Area Procreators but has been widely praised by Area Condom Manufacturers.

THOMAS BROMMAGE studied philosophy at the University of South Florida, where the faculty figured out that the best way to get rid of him is to award him the PhD. He has taught in the Department of Philosophy and the Honors College at USF, as well as the University of Tampa and Denison University. His primary research focus is in the philosophy of language and logic. He is currently looking for a permanent job teaching philosophy, and reminds potential employers that he will teach for beer.

352 PEOPLE ALMOST KILLED IN NARROWLY AVOIDED TRAIN COLLISION

Having survived as a baby a train wreck that had it happened would have been really annoying, **DEBORAH BROWN** was taken and raised by dingoes, who quickly thereafter returned their newest howler. Her earliest memories were of her mother crying in the dark 'Aw shit, Trev', the dingo's brought my baby back!' Recruited to the set of the canine thriller, "A Cry in the Dark," for her ability to discourse with dingoes on the morality of baby-snatching, Brown became a favorite of Meryl Streep and was whisked off to America to become, unbeknownst to her, one of America's finest philosophers. Storming the philosophical world with the pace of a one-legged man with rickets, she returned to The University of Queensland, Australia, where she has since become renowned for engaging in philosophical research "a mile wide and an inch deep," to quote one generous reviewer. She became acquainted with the *The Onion* when it was used to line the bottom of her cage and instantly saw in it a means to navigate the rugged cultural terrain of modernity.

LUKE CUDDY is the editor of *The Legend of Zelda and Philosophy* (2008), co-editor of *World of Warcraft and Philosophy* (2009), and editor of *Halo and Philosophy* (2011). He finds all insights about the rules of professional sports to be interesting and true (except for the infield fly rule). He teaches philosophy in Southern California.

A proud North Dakotan, **DOUGLAS FICEK** teaches philosophy at John Jay College of Criminal Justice, CUNY, which is ironic given his predilection for stealing precious jewels. He is also a doctoral candidate at Temple University, where he does work in Africana philosophy, critical race theory, and sociopolitical philosophy. When he's not casing museums, he's publishing articles in *Free Inquiry*, *Radical Philosophy Review*, and *Philosophy and Social Criticism*.

GREGORY D. GILSON is an Assistant Professor of Philosophy at the University of Texas-Pan American. His research interests include the philosophy of mind, the philosophy of language and Latin American philosophy. He wrote his contribution to this collection primarily to justify all the time he wasted reading *The Onion* as a graduate student at the University of Wisconsin.

CHRIS HALLQUIST is an undergraduate at the University of Wisconsin-Madison. Lacking a distinguished publication record, he will proudly list this book in future back-of-book-bios. Not really an asshole, sources say.

DAVID KYLE JOHNSON is currently an assistant professor of philosophy at King's College in Wilkes-Barre. His philosophical specializations include philosophy of religion, logic, and metaphysics. He has also written chapters for volumes on *South Park*, *Family Guy*, *The Office*, *Battlestar Galactica*, *Quentin Tarantino*, *Johnny Cash*, *Batman*, and *The Colbert Report*, and has edited a book on *Heroes*. Kyle's favorite thing is when people mistake *Onion* articles for real news. "It's like a window into their psyche," he says.

SHARON M. KAYE was born, raised, and undergraduated in Madison, Wisconsin. She is now a Professor of Philosophy at John Carroll University in Cleveland. She has published a number of books including *Medieval Philosophy* (2008), *Black Market Truth* (2008), which is the first volume of a philosophical thriller series called The Aristotle Quest, and *Critical Thinking* (2009). Publications notwithstanding, she has been growing steadily dumber since the day she finished graduate school.

MATT LAUBENTHAL is an undergraduate at Cleveland State University who loves made up stuff; namely, the stories of superheroes, science-fiction and Neil Gaiman's *The Sandman*. His philosophical interests are in metaphysics and causality. If the sight of a grown man jazzercizing weirds you out, then you should probably call before you come over.

Damien Ledwich was born in Melbourne, Australia, which was handy as his mother happened to be there also at the time cutting down on the commuting. He moved to Brisbane in the sub-tropical north at a young age and was raised by cane toads, who quickly put him down again due to their relatively low load-bearing capacity.

He set out to accumulate a list of odd jobs suitable for a pulp writer's bio (the gold standard for bios). He has worked as a cleaner, taxation officer, cartoonist, theater designer, animator, video editor, and co-editor of the now-extinct Australian humour magazine *The Cane Toad Times*. He now creates logos, political campaign material, and museum installations and does not have an excessive interest in bird-related artwork.

Noah Levin is a graduate student at Bowling Green State University. When he's not enjoying spicy food or making bad puns (at which he has a five-percent success rate of obtaining laughs), he's using his mad philosophical skills to win arguments with his students. Some day he hopes to get a "real job" and continue to publish quality philosophical essays.

Greg Littmann is an Assistant Professor of Philosophy at Southern Illinois University Edwardsville. His primary philosophical interests are metaphysics, philosophy of logic and moral philosophy. Greg Littmann is a subsidiary of the Microsoft Corporation.

Paul Loader, contributor to *The Onion and Philosophy* today failed to think of anything funny to say about himself in the biographical sketch at the back of the volume. Said Loader, "I tried being self-referential but it just came across as kind of lame." (*This still isn't funny—Editor*)

Mimi Marinucci is an Associate Professor of Philosophy and Women's and Gender Studies at Eastern Washington University. When she is not busy recruiting lesbians, she teaches classes and publishes articles on a range of topics, particularly those at the intersection of knowledge, culture, and identity.

Cynthia McWilliams works in sunny southern Texas at the University of Texas—Pan American where she is an assistant professor of philosophy and a co-director of the ethics center. She has distinguished herself by identifying the large land mass to the south of Texas ("Hurricane Bound For Texas Slowed By Large Land Mass To The South," 8/25/08).

Dan Miori is a physician assistant, father to three girls and grandfather to two. Upon realizing that a career in medicine had ruined him for honest labor, he went into palliative care and joined his hospital ethics committee. Finding a refuge there, he moved on to the, somewhat oxymoronic, corporate ethics committee. His Italian heritage and status as a recovering Catholic prepared him well for the moral ambiguity and twisted logic at the corporate level; and convinced him that his talents truly lay in misanthropic obfuscation, with scholarly authorship being the next logical step. He realized that even with his dubious experience, larcenous nature and viscous and intemperate disposition, he wasn't quite ready for the world of academia, and so for the moment has contented himself with this project and a textbook chapter discussing the ethics of supply chain inventory systems in healthcare. His ultimate ambition is to be one hundred percent disabled by a work related low back injury.

ROBERTO RUIZ is lecturer in philosophy and ethics at Bergen and LaGuardia community colleges. He received his MA from Binghamton University. He runs the philosophy and science blog Philosophy Monkey (http://berto-meister.blogspot.com). His academic interests include the philosophy of mind, evolutionary psychology, the metaphysics of personal identity, the history and philosophy of science, and female anatomy. He is fascinated by, and keenly suspicious of, dialetheic logic. Professor Ruiz was the focus of *The Onion*'s story "Absent-Minded Professor Says Cure for Cancer 'Around Here Somewhere'."

ANDREW TERJESEN is a visiting Assistant Professor at Rhodes College in Memphis, Tennessee. Previously he had taught at Washington and Lee University, Austin College (in Texas, but NOT Austin, TX) and Duke University. He has published articles on empathy and morality, as well as several pieces on the philosophical aspects of popular culture and everyday life, including contributions to *What Philosophy Can Tell You About Your Dog* (2008) and *Supervillains and Philosophy* (2009). He hopes to one day write a searing expose of the Philosophy industry and its unrepentant support of Michael Bay's career.

ROBERT WHYTE is an Australian writer. His published works include *Negative Thinking, Life and Works of Robot Wireless, From Inside the Asylum, A 3-D Glimpse of the Hearing Process*, and *Manacles*. Reading *The Onion* makes him cry.

Index of *Onion* Articles Referred to in This Book

Inside *The Onion and Philosophy*